AGATHOCLES

T0371502

AGATHOCLES

by

H. J. W. TILLYARD, B.A.

ASSISTANT AND LECTURER IN GREEK AT EDINBURGH UNIVERSITY;
SOMETIME RESEARCH STUDENT OF GONVILLE AND CAIUS COLLEGE

THE PRINCE CONSORT PRIZE, 1908

Cambridge
at the University Press
1908

CAMBRIDGE
UNIVERSITY PRESS

University Printing House, Cambridge CB2 8BS, United Kingdom

Cambridge University Press is part of the University of Cambridge.

It furthers the University's mission by disseminating knowledge in the pursuit of
education, learning and research at the highest international levels of excellence.

www.cambridge.org
Information on this title: www.cambridge.org/9781107585829

First published 1908
First paperback edition 2015

A catalogue record for this publication is available from the British Library

ISBN 978-1-107-58582-9 Paperback

PREFACE

THE subject of the present book, which was awarded the Prince Consort Prize in January 1908, was chosen by myself, and approved by the Electors. I have written throughout from the original authorities, but I have tried to make full use of modern writers, and to weigh the merits of their theories. On the critical side, Schubert's *Geschichte des Agathokles* has been most useful, as will be evident to anyone reading my first chapter. Among other writers, I have found Freeman and Holm, and, for Geography, Tissot, of great value. I saw most of the historical sites in Africa and Sicily in 1906. My views as to the battle of the Himeras were formed on the spot. All the illustrations but two are from my own photographs.

I gladly express my gratitude to the Master and Fellows of Gonville and Caius College for the award of a Research Studentship and for other aid to my travels: to Professor J. S. Reid for several references and much valuable counsel: to Dr T. Ashby, Director of the British School at Rome, for his company and advice in Sicily, and for two illustrations: to Mr R. H. Churchill, H.B.M. Consul at Palermo, whose good offices facilitated our journey: to Cavaliere Angelo Verderame, H.B.M. Vice-Consul at Licata: to Monsieur A. Merlin, Head of the Department of Archaeology in Tunisia for much kind and ready help to me in travelling in that country: and to Professor T. McKenny Hughes for a 17th century history of Agathocles.

H. J. W. T.

CAMBRIDGE.
    20th August 1908.

LIST OF CHIEF BOOKS REFERRED TO

(The following volumes will be quoted, as a rule, by the author's name and the page merely. Other volumes will be quoted fully, as is required.)

Diodorus Siculus. (=D.)

Justinus. (=J.)

Marmor Parium. (= Parian Chronicle: new fragment in *Athenische Mitteilungen* XXII. 187.)

Müller. *Fragmenta Historicorum Graecorum.* (=*F.H.G.*)

MODERN HISTORICAL WORKS.

Beloch, J. *Griechische Geschichte* III. 1.

De Sanctis. in *Rivista di Filologia* XXIII.

Droysen. *Geschichte des Hellenismus* II. 2.

Freeman. *History of Sicily*, with notes by Dr Evans, IV.

Grote. *History of Greece* XII.

Holm. *Geschichte Siziliens* II.

Meltzer. *Geschichte der Karthager* I.

Niese. *Geschichte der griechischen und makedonischen Staaten* I.

Pais, E. *Ancient Italy* (trans. E. D. Curtis) XIV.

Perrinchiefe. *The Sicilian Tyrant* (London 1676).

Plass. *Die Tyrannis in ihren beiden Perioden bei den alten Griechen.* 2te Abteilung.

Roesiger. *De Duride Samio, Diodori Siculi et Plutarchi auctore.*

Schubert, R. *Geschichte des Agathokles.*

Wiese. *De Agathocle Syracusanorum Tyranno.*

GEOGRAPHICAL WORKS.

Craven. *Tour through the Southern Provinces of the Kingdom of Naples.*

Davis, N. *Ruined Cities within Numidian and Carthaginian Territories.*

Lenormant. *La Grande Grèce.*

Lupus. *Die Stadt Syrakus im Altertum.*

Maltzan. *Reise in den Regentschaften Tunis u. Tripolis.*

Schubring. *Historische-geographische Studien über Alt-Sizilien* in *Rheinisches Museum* xxviii. 1873, 66 ff.

Smyth, W. H. *Memoir descriptive of the Resources, Inhabitants, and Hydrography of Sicily and its Islands.*

Tissot. *Géographie Comparée de la Province Romaine de l'Afrique* (quoted by the author's name, Vol. i. being meant, unless otherwise noted).

The staff-maps of Tunis, made by the French Government, and of Sicily, made by the Italian military survey, have also been found useful.

CONTENTS

CHAPTER IV. AGATHOCLES' WARFARE IN AFRICA.

CHAPTER V. AGATHOCLES' LAST WAR AGAINST THE SICILIANS.

CHAPTER VI. AGATHOCLES AS KING.

CHAPTER I.

ANCIENT AUTHORITIES FOR THE HISTORY OF AGATHOCLES.

HISTORICAL authority is of two kinds, literary and material. For the life of Agathocles the chief extant writers are Diodorus Siculus, Justin, and Polyaenus; and it will make easier a true understanding of the history about to be narrated, if a short account of these writers be presented, with such facts as can be discovered as to the original sources from which they drew.

Considering the importance of Agathocles' reign, there is a remarkable dearth of material remains. No building, graven stone, or bust is left to commemorate him. Of his coins indeed a long and valuable series has come down. These have been ably discussed by expert writers[1], and the subject forms no part of the plan of the present work.

One important, but, as it happens, rather puzzling document remains to be mentioned. This is the new fragment of the so-called Parian Marble, lately found on the island, and published in 1897[2]. This inscription gives a system of Greek chronology from the death of Philip II to the year 299. The system itself reached down to 264.

[1] Cf. Head, *Hist. Num.* 158 ff. and *Coinage of Syracuse*, 42 ff. Evans, note in Freeman, *Hist. of Sicily*, IV. Suppl. v. (with plate). P. Gardner, *Types of Greek Coins*, 184 and pl. XI. 21.

[2] *Ath. Mitt.* XXII. 183 ff.

Although this example of early dating is naturally of very great value, it has not by any means the authority of an official document, and its evidence does not necessarily outweigh the literary account in case of disagreement.

1.   EXTANT AUTHORITIES : DIODORUS.

Diodorus Siculus was born at Agyrium and lived in the time of Julius Caesar and Augustus.   His great World's History claimed to be a record embracing all noteworthy events from the earliest legendary days down to the beginning of Caesar's wars in Gaul.   Diodorus says that he took thirty years to gather facts and ideas for his work; and that in this time he visited many of the fields where his history was enacted.   The compiler of so huge a work must inevitably have followed received accounts without much discrimination.   As a Sicilian he seems to have followed with some zeal the career of Agathocles, so that the portions of his work bearing on the subject in hand are very good specimens of his manner and arrangement.   As a rule he is clear and reasonable, but sometimes he seems to be giving a patchwork of state-ments from different authorities regardless of order[1].

The general plan of Diodorus' work is annalistic.   Each year is opened with the Roman consuls and the Athenian archon; and the events of each part of Europe are given in order.   The drawbacks of such an arrangement are clear ; for sometimes a series of acts had to be broken because it overlapped the end of the year; and the

[1] Examples in the Agathoclean books. xix. 3, Agathocles' warlike deeds told twice, §§ 2 and 4. xix. 107, in § 2 Diodorus begins an account of Agathocles' treatment of Gela: he breaks off to tell an altogether separate story, coming back to Gela in § 3.   Other examples might be given, but they will be noticed as they occur.

system made it very easy both for writer and reader to lose all continuity in tracing the history of any particular country.

To obviate this unpleasantness Diodorus had two devices: either he could overleap the end of the year and follow his topic without a break; or else he could hold over a portion of his facts until the person concerned did something noteworthy, and then the overdue part could be tacked on as a special digression. Of the former course examples will be found in Agathoclean history[1], and of the latter there are several striking cases. The life of Agathocles, up to his rise to the tyranny, is all given under the year 317: the early life of Acrotatus, and the start of Ophellas[2], are treated in the same way. By these means the reading becomes pleasanter, but the exact dating is lost, so that in some cases the chronology is uncertain.

Besides this strictly historical part of his work Diodorus sometimes brings in passages of another kind. Speeches were not much to his taste; indeed he specially deplores their too common use[3]. The speeches of Agathocles when he was chosen general in the Syracusan assembly, and on the African coast when he burnt his ships, as also the invitation carried by Orthon to Ophellas, are all reported in a summary fashion. Reflexions and diatribes of the historian himself are, on the other hand, fairly common. They usually relate to the wickedness of Agathocles, or to the fickleness of fortune, or else to the wrath of heaven as smiting evildoers. Thus for example the slaughter of the Syracusan nobles in the Timoleonteum, the fall of Messena, the fate of Ophellas and the

[1] D. xix. 70—72, and elsewhere.
[2] Now often spelt Ophelas.
[3] D. xx. 1.

1—2

failure of Bomilcar, the treachery of Agathocles after Gorgium, are commented upon with correct sentiment. Examples of the judgment of heaven will be given when Timaeus' share of Agathoclean history is reviewed.

There is furthermore an anecdotal element in Diodorus' work, for which the historian must be on the watch. The taste for stories, ruses and sayings of well-known men grew to a great extent in the later Hellenistic age, and fairly ran riot under the Roman Empire. To satisfy this craving for learned tittle-tattle the fashion arose to make collections of "stratagems," "apophthegms," and the like, such as are known in the works of Plutarch, Valerius Maximus, Frontinus and Aelian. One of these anecdote-mongers, named Polyaenus, is an authority for parts of Agathocles' life, and will be mentioned below.

If this paltry branch of letters had any serious aim, it was to supply tales and instances for the use of public speakers and students of oratory. Now whether Diodorus drew from such a collection or not, there are certainly ruses and stories in his work, that betray themselves firstly by their trifling nature, and again sometimes by their irrelevance to the narrative which they are meant to enliven. Such passages as Agathocles' escape from Gela, his flight from Acestorides, his make-believe shields and caged owls, the remarks on his bearing in public, and his jests in the assembly and out of it, besides the myth of his birth and childhood, are among the clearest examples[1].

With these stories there is only one safe way of dealing. Every case must be weighed on its own merits, without any foregone conclusions. All anecdotes are not false, and it is worth while at least to search for under-lying facts.

[1] Cf. pp. 26, 48, 49, 59, 112, below.

2. JUSTIN.

The second authority extant, far behind Diodorus in length and detail, is the abridgement of Trogus, drawn up by Justin. Pompeius Trogus lived in the reign of Augustus. He wrote a work called *Historiae Philippicae*. In name the book dealt with Macedonia, but all kinds of side-issues were entered upon, and the book was brought down to Roman times. The work is lost; but short summaries of the forty-four books remain. From these it is seen that Trogus devoted the end of his twenty-first book and most of the twenty-second and twenty-third books to the history of Agathocles. Justin himself wrote about Agathocles in his twenty-second and twenty-third books.

From a note of Justin at the beginning of his history it is easy to see in what spirit the summary was made. Disowning any serious aims, Justin says that he took from Trogus such passages as seemed to him specially interesting[1]. For this reason a good deal of purely rhetorical ornament, quite out of place in an abridgement, is allowed to stand, while a whole series of facts is summed up in a single phrase[2].

---

[1] Praef. § 4 *Horum igitur quattuor et quadraginta voluminum...cognitione quaeque dignissima excerpsi, et omissis his quae nec cognoscendi voluptate jucunda, nec exempla erant necessaria, breve veluti florum corpusculum feci.*

[2] The following are some of the obviously rhetorical passages in the Agathoclean books of Justin. xxii. 3, 2—5, Complaints to the Carthaginian senate about the conduct of Hamilcar. These are no doubt true, though the form is rhetorical. 4, 3, Agathocles' speech to the Syracusans before his start: also partly historical. 5, 2—13, Speech to the troops on landing in Africa; especially § 8, on a coming siege of Carthage, and §§ 12, 13, about glory—pure rhetoric. 7, 9, Bomilcar's speech. 8, 5, Agathocles' speech to the mutinous. 8, 9, Exclamations of the soldiers after Agathocles' flight. xxiii. 2, 6—13, Theoxena's farewell.

The style of Justin is clear and simple[1], so that in a few cases he is a more satisfactory guide than Diodorus. His frame of mind is always unfriendly to Agathocles[2].

Justin's own date is doubtful; but as he is mentioned by Jerome and by Orosius, he cannot have been later than the beginning of the fifth century.

3. POLYAENUS.

Polyaenus, the third authority, brought out a book of tricks or ruses, called *Stratagems*. In a high-flown address to the emperors, "Antoninus and Verus," that is, to Marcus Aurelius and Lucius Verus, Polyaenus deplored that old age no longer allowed him to share in the glories of the Parthian war. But he felt bound as a Macedonian to do something worthy of his warlike race, and so had put together some stratagems of the men of old to be a hand-book for Roman officers[3].

The true aim of the collection, however, was simply amusement[4]. Polyaenus begins with the ruses of Pan, Dionysus and Heracles: then he tells of the tricks of the Greek, Roman and foreign warriors; of cities, and lastly of women. Very few of these japes have any historical worth whatever. For not only was Polyaenus careless in

[1] On the style of Justin and Trogus cf. Teuffel-Schwabe, *Röm. Litteratur-Gesch.* I. 602. Peter, H., *Die geschichtliche Litteratur über d. röm. Kaiserzeit*, II. 224, 298.

[2] The fact that Justin sometimes says a good word for Agathocles (e.g. XXII. 1, 9) does not alter his general attitude.

[3] I. 1—3.

[4] The first "stratagem" of Agathocles is an example of the trifling nature of many of the anecdotes. Ἀγαθοκλῆς Σικελίας τύραννος ὀμόσας τοῖς πολεμίοις παρέβη τοὺς ὅρκους, καὶ κατασφάξας τοὺς ἀλόντας, ἐπιχλευάζων πρὸς τοὺς φίλους ἔλεγεν, " Δειπνήσαντες ἐξεμέσωμεν τοὺς ὅρκους." Pol. v. 3, 1.

following his authorities[1], but some of the "stratagems" may have been fastened upon the wrong man altogether. The chief use of Polyaenus to the historian is that he sometimes records stray facts that would otherwise have been lost. The order of arrangement of Polyaenus' stories on Agathocles is chronologically inverted[2].

4. LESSER AUTHORITIES.

Outside the works of Diodorus, Justin and Polyaenus, the only other historical account of Agathocles is found in the writing of Orosius, *Against the Heathen*. This tract was meant to prove that the disasters of the Roman world in the fourth and fifth centuries, so far from being aggravated by the wrath of the Pagan gods whom the spreading of Christianity was believed to have angered, were in truth nothing but the continuation of those woes that had always been the lot of man. Orosius tried to make good his thesis by giving a summary of the world's history with special stress on all mishaps and calamities. The disasters of Carthage form the ground for the mention of Agathocles, whose African war is shortly related[3]. Although Orosius speaks of Trogus[4], as well as Justin, as an authority, it would seem from the likeness of his Agathoclean section to the latter's abridgement, that Orosius only took this matter from the earlier historian

[1] Example: Pol. I. 40, 5. It is related that Alcibiades devised the plan for enticing the Syracusans out to Catana. In Polyaenus' authority, Thuc. VI. 64, 2, the Athenian generals are the authors of the trick. Many other examples are given in Woelfflin's introduction (Teubner text).

[2] This is obvious in the case of 7 and 8 (relating to the same series of events), 5, 4, 3, 2. The context of 1 and 6 is uncertain.

[3] Orosius, *Adv. Pag.* IV. 6.   [4] *Ibid.*

at second hand. Hence for all practical purposes the
narrative of Orosius is worthless.

Besides these more or less formal accounts there are
a few notices of Agathocles elsewhere. Polybius makes
several remarks about him, and there are one or two
valuable notes in Strabo and Appian. Of these passages,
with such scattered observations as have been gleaned
from other ancient writers, use will be made in the proper
place.

THE EARLIEST WRITERS ON AGATHOCLES.

As our extant authorities, including even Polybius,
lived many years after the events of which they wrote,
it is the duty of the historian to trace, as far as can now
be done, the contemporary sources from which the existing versions may have been drawn. As far as is known,
four writers of Agathocles' own age made his life the
subject of historical treatment. Of these three were Sicilians, Antander, Callias and Timaeus, and the other,
Duris, was a Samian. A contemporary who seems to
have mentioned Agathocles was the well-known Athenian
orator and statesman, Demochares, the nephew of Demosthenes. He is quoted as an authority for Agathocles'
length of life, but it does not appear that he wrote
systematically on Agathocles in his history[1].

If there were other writers on Agathocles' history of
his own age, all account of them has perished.

---

[1] [Lucian] *Macrob.* 10 mentions Demochares with Timaeus as an
authority for Agathocles' age at his death: this does not imply more
than a passing reference to the event. On Demochares cf. Müller, *F.H.G.*
II. 445, and the article in Pauly-Wissowa, *Real-Encyclopädie d. cl. Alter-
tumswissenschaft, s.v.*

5. The Earliest Writers on Agathocles: Antander.

Antander was an elder brother of Agathocles, and early became one of the foremost men in Syracuse. Before Agathocles became tyrant, his brother was one of the leaders of a Syracusan force sent to help Croton against the Bruttians. Afterwards he was left by Agathocles as joint ruler of Syracuse, while the prince himself was warring in Africa. Antander wished to treat with Hamilcar in 310, on the news of the burning of Agathocles' fleet, but Erymnon dissuaded him. In 307 Antander was bidden by his brother to slay all the Syracusan kindred of the soldiers left in Africa; and he carried out this order with ruthless severity. No further details of his life are known, but he must have lived to a good old age, for in the time of Agathocles' early campaigns he was already a general of the Syracusan army, and yet he outlived Agathocles, who died at seventy-two.

In writing his history Antander was in a way playing Philistus to his brother's Dionysius. The book is only mentioned once. Diodorus says that Agathocles ruled for twenty-eight years, which number was given by Timaeus, Callias and Antander[1]. This one notice does not allow it to be settled whether Diodorus made regular use of Antander's book, or merely referred to it as an authority on particular points, or again knew it only from references in other works.

6. Callias.

The main source of knowledge of this historian is found in the comparison which Diodorus makes between him and Timaeus[2].

[1] D. xxi. 16, 5.　　　　[2] D. xxi. 17.

"Furthermore Callias of Syracuse most thoroughly and rightly deserves to be blamed. He was favoured by Agathocles, and for the rich presents that he received, sold his pen, which should have served the cause of truth, and lost no chance of heaping undeserved praise on his paymaster. Though Agathocles did many deeds of impiety towards the gods, and injustice to men, the historian declares that he was far above the average in godliness and humanity. In short just as Agathocles robbed the burgesses of their goods and wrongfully bestowed on Callias what he had no right to have, so in his books this astonishing historian showers all that is good upon the tyrant. For it seems an easy way of repaying favours, if the historian's readiness to bestow praise was equal to the eagerness with which he took bribes from the royal house."

Callias is also mentioned (in the place already quoted) as recording the death of Agathocles and the length of his reign, and as having written twenty-two books[1].

A further proof of the use of Callias by Diodorus is found in the likeness between Callias' third fragment and Diodorus' description of the march of Ophellas[2]. "The wilderness of the Syrtis swarmed with all kinds of snakes, most of them poisonous, and numbers of the people met their death in this way, the aid of friends and leeches proving useless; for many of the snakes had skins of the same hue as the earth on which they lay, so that their own nature was unsuspected; and many trod on the snakes and so succumbed to their deadly bite."

The Callias passage is as follows; it is taken from Aelian. "Callias in the tenth book of his history of Agathocles says that the snake-bites were deadly, and

---

[1] D. xxi. 16, 5.   [2] Müller, *F.H.G.* ii. Callias, 3 and D. xx. 42, 2.

carried off both men and beasts, until a Libyan of the Psellian race appeared." There follows the way in which he healed the snake-bites.

As the subject was not a matter of everyday knowledge, it cannot be reasonably doubted that Diodorus took his account from Callias.

Furthermore there are many signs that the Agatho-clean narrative of Diodorus has been enriched from the descriptions of an informant who had himself visited Africa at the time of the prince's inroad. The reports of the wealth of the country, the blooming gardens, and fine houses, and again of the men and beasts of the further south, are enough to prove this. The original recorder of all this detail cannot have been Antander, who was at Syracuse the while; nor yet Timaeus, whose ignorance of Africa, according to Polybius, was childish; nor yet Duris, who lived either at Samos or in Athens most or all of his life. Callias therefore must have been the author, and the careful and minute record is what would have been expected from his pen.

Again there are passages in Diodorus where the tone is very friendly to Agathocles, and some of these may well have come from Callias, though how far Diodorus' charges against him can be believed, is another matter.

Agathocles had certainly enriched Callias with es-cheated goods, and the historian had gone beyond other writers in praising Agathocles. That Callias sold his pen is an inference of Diodorus, and the whole passage is balanced by an attack on Timaeus for his too un-friendly view of the tyrant, and may therefore have been heightened for the sake of effect. Callias seems to have written all his twenty-two books on Agathocles alone [1],

---

[1] This is proved by Schubert, *Geschichte des Agathokles*, 2. If Book x. dealt with Ophellas, and if Callias mentioned the death of Agathocles,

and to have gone to work with great care and research[1].
This hardly suits the character of a mere hack-writer
bribed to sound the praises of his master. But Agathocles was not the man to bestow his gifts for nothing.
No lover of letters as a rule, he must have wished his
deeds to have been worthily recorded, and therefore
secured the goodwill of an able historian; Callias, indeed,
may have taken the money rather as a travelling allow-
ance than a bribe. But in any case he was bound to
deal mildly with his lord's misdeeds. The mention of
Agathocles' death by Callias only proves that the book
was not brought out in its final shape during the king's
life-time. It is impossible to suppose that Agathocles
was unaware of the progress and contents of a work so
interesting to himself.

Whether Diodorus used Callias at first hand, or merely
quoted him from other books, is quite uncertain. But it
cannot fairly be doubted that a large part of his account
is embodied in Diodorus' history.

7. TIMAEUS.

Timaeus was the son of Andromachus, the ruler of
Tauromenium, and was born about 350. Whether he
afterwards lived at Syracuse is uncertain[2], but he was
banished from Syracuse or Tauromenium by Agathocles
himself. He then settled at Athens where he lived fifty
years and very likely to the end of his life[3].

whom he cannot long have outlived, this would have been near the end
of the work. The first nine books on this scale would have been amply
taken up with Agathocles' early career.

[1] Example: fr. 4 dealt with the volcanic nature of the Lipari islands;
fr. 5 with the origin of the Romans.

[2] This seems likely, as he is called a Syracusan in D. xxi. 16, 5.

[3] D. xxi. 17, 1 φυγαδευθεὶς γὰρ ὑπ' 'Αγαθοκλέους ἐκ τῆς Σικελίας ζῶντα

Athens was his new home, and Polybius blames Timaeus for not travelling widely nor wishing to see for himself the places where the events had befallen[1]. His history is quoted up to the thirty-eighth book, and probably ended there: the latter part of the work dealt with Agathocles.

Timaeus seems to have been used by all three of our extant authorities. Sometimes his influence can be traced both in Justin and Diodorus in the same context. Consequently when Justin and Diodorus happen to agree on any particular point, this may often be due to the use of Timaeus in both cases[2].

For the history of Agathocles Diodorus quotes Timaeus by name in three places[3]. Justin shows no trace of the use of any other original authority for the period: this would account for his always hostile attitude towards Agathocles[4].

Opinions in antiquity were divided as to the goodness

μὲν ἀμύνασθαι τὸν δυνάστην οὐκ ἴσχυσε. It is uncertain when Timaeus was driven out: perhaps in 312 (cf. p. 67 below), but anyhow early in Agathocles' reign, as he lived at least 50 years after his flight. Polyb. XII. 25[h] ὅτι Τίμαιός φησιν...ὅτι πεντήκοντα συνεχῶς ἔτη διατρίψας 'Αθήνησιν ξενιτεύων...ἐγένετο. Cf. Schubert 5.

[1] Polyb. XII. 28, 6, and 28[a], 4.

[2] The account that made Agathocles the son of a potter must have been started by Timaeus. Thus Polyb. xv. 35 (cf. XII. 15) ὁ δὲ 'Αγαθοκλῆς, ὡς Τίμαιος ἐπισκώπτων φησί, κεραμεὺς ὑπάρχων, καὶ καταλιπὼν τὸν τροχόν, τὸν πηλὸν καὶ τὸν καπνόν, ἦλθε νέος ὢν εἰς τὰς Συρακούσας. Justin xxII. 1, 2... Quippe in Sicilia patre figulo natus. D. XIX. 2, 7 (Κάρκινος)...πένης δ' ὢν ἐδίδαξε τὸν 'Αγαθοκλέα τὴν κεραμευτικὴν τέχνην ἔτι παῖδα τὴν ἡλικίαν ὄντα.

[3] D. xx. 79, 5, xx. 89, 5, xxi. 16, 5.

[4] At the same time it would be unsafe to say dogmatically that Trogus was unacquainted with other authorities. That Polyaenus used Timaeus, mediately or otherwise, is proved by Woelfflin in his introduction to Polyaenus (Teubner text), p. xii. But it would be hard to trace all the sources of so late a writer.

of Timaeus as a historian. Cicero praises both his learning
and style[1], while Polybius loses no chance of attacking
Timaeus, of whose popularity he seems to have been jealous.
But even he grants him two good points, firstly his care
for dates[2], and secondly his zeal for finding original documents[3]. The main charges made by Polybius against
Timaeus are three: that he was uncritical and super-
stitious[4]: that he had not had enough share in the making
of history to write it with insight[5]: and that his hatred
of Agathocles led him to make unfair accusations against
the king.

Timaeus' superstition seems to have taken two special
forms. He believed that sacrilege was visited by a direct
blow from heaven and that punishment by the gods for an
ill-deed took such a shape as clearly to show for what crime
it was inflicted. His care for dates led him to seek co-
incidences between the day of the year of the commission
of a crime and the day of its punishment. In fact all
kinds of curious analogies in the matter of dates seem
to have been interesting to Timaeus. He noted that
Euripides was born on the day of Salamis and died on

[1] Cic. de Orat. II. 14 Longe eruditissimus et rerum copia et senten-
tiarum varietate abundantissimus, et ipsa compositione verborum non
impolitus.

[2] Polyb. XII. 10, 4 λέγω δὲ κατὰ τὴν ἐν τοῖς χρόνοις καὶ ταῖς ἀναγραφαῖς
ἐπίφασιν τῆς ἀκριβείας, καὶ τὴν περὶ τοῦτο τὸ μέρος ἐπιμέλειαν.

[3] In Polyb. XII. 11 Timaeus is praised for finding an inscription which
was hidden away at the back of a temple.

[4] Polyb. XII. 24, 5 ἐν δὲ ταῖς ἰδίαις ἀποφάσεσιν ἐνυπνίων καὶ τεράτων καὶ
μύθων ἀπιθάνων καὶ συλλήβδην δεισιδαιμονίας ἀγεννοῦς καὶ τερατείας γυναι-
κώδους ἐστὶ πλήρης· οὐ μὴν ἀλλὰ διότι γε συμβαίνει διὰ τὴν ἀπειρίαν καὶ
κακοκρισίαν πολλοὺς ἐνίοτε καθάπερ εἰ παρόντας τρόπον τινὰ μὴ παρεῖναι
καὶ βλέποντας μὴ βλέπειν ἐκ τῶν εἰρημένων γε νῦν καὶ τῶν Τιμαίῳ συμβεβη-
κότων γέγονε φανερόν.

[5] Polyb. XII. 25[h], in reference to Timaeus' long stay at Athens.

the birth-day of Dionysius¹. Elsewhere he stated that
the Carthaginians had stolen an Apollo from Gela, and
sent it to Tyre. There the Tyrians had paid scant worship
to it; and as a punishment Alexander took Tyre on the
same day of the year and at the same hour of the day as
the image had first been stolen². In Diodorus' account of
the history of Agathocles several passages bear an unmistakable likeness to those just mentioned. In one case
the Carthaginians take two Greek freight-ships and cut
off all the sailors' hands. But the wrath of heaven followed the sinners. For some (seemingly quite separate)
Carthaginian ships were taken by Agathocles' men off
the Bruttian coast, and their crews were treated with the
same cruelty³. The next case occurs where the burning
of the Carthaginian camp in 307 is treated as a direct
visitation on the Carthaginians for sending their captives through the fire to Moloch⁴. Lastly the death of
Agathocles' sons is held to be heaven's punishment of
Agathocles for the murder of Ophellas; for both slaughters
were done on the same day of the year; and heaven like
a good lawyer had taken vengeance twofold⁵. It is easy
to believe that Diodorus took these instances, with others
which will occur in course of this history, from the work
of Timaeus⁶.

The passage where Diodorus speaks of Timaeus' bitterness against Agathocles is noteworthy not only because it

¹ Plut. *Symp.* 1, *Quaest.* 717 c (*F. H. G.* I., Timaeus 119) ἅμα τῆς
τύχης τὸν μιμητὴν ἐξαγούσης τῶν τραγικῶν παθῶν, καὶ τὸν ἀγωνιστὴν
ἐπεισαγούσης.

² *F. H. G.*, Timaeus 120.   ³ D. xix. 103, 4—5.
⁴ D. xx. 65, 2.   ⁵ D. xx. 70, 3—4.
⁶ On this point however it is unsafe to speak too confidently. For
such beliefs were very common, and might have occurred to other
historians as well as Timaeus.

contrasts the view of Timaeus with the partiality of Callias, but also because the whole place has been carried over from Polybius with changes in the words alone.   Diodorus says, "For this historian, who bitterly attacked the mistakes of earlier writers, was most careful about the truth himself except in his account of Agathocles; there most of the statements are falsely made, owing to the historian's personal feud with the tyrant.   He was banished from Sicily by Agathocles; unable to harm the king in his life-time, after his death he blackened his reputation for all time.   In short the existing faults of the king were increased by others of the writer's own making.   Agathocles' successes were slurred over, and his mishaps, many of them due wholly to chance, were undeservedly reckoned up against him.   Though Agathocles was admittedly a true general in laying his plans, and alert and dauntless in face of danger, yet the historian throughout his work does not cease from calling him a weakling and a coward.   Who does not know that of all princes Agathocles from the meanest beginning rose to the widest dominion?   In boyhood need and low birth forced him to work with his hands[1], who afterwards by his own merits not only mastered the greater part of Sicily, but also brought much of Africa and Italy under the power of his arms.   What again can be more astonishing than the historian's folly ?   In all his work he praises the bravery of the Syracusans, and yet he says that the man who was master of them all was the most dastardly of mankind.   It is quite clear from these invectives that the writer has thrown over that fearless truth-telling proper to the historian, for the sake of venting his own ill-feeling and spite.

"Hence the last five books of this writer, in which the

[1] In Polybius XII. 15 these statements are simply quoted from Timaeus: Polybius himself does not seem to have believed them.

acts of Agathocles are comprised, ought not to be accepted as truthful history."

On this passage two things are to be noted. Firstly that Diodorus has amplified the statements of Polybius to suit his own views of Timaeus, which proves that he was aware of Timaeus' errors and did not follow him blindly. Secondly that though Diodorus seems to charge Timaeus with purposely writing what was untrue, there is no reason to believe anything of the kind. Timaeus' perceptions were clouded by his intense hatred of Agathocles, and he was unfair to him without meaning it.

Timaeus was also charged with ignorance of the country of Africa[1]. "Timaeus, it may fairly be said, was not only ill-informed about the state of Libya, but childish and utterly unreasonable. He was quite unable to escape from the old tales that we have heard, saying that the country is all wilderness, sandy and unfruitful. Timaeus' account of the beasts in Africa is no better. All the abundance of horses, oxen and sheep, besides the numbers of goats (unmatched to my mind in all the world), are not even mentioned by Timaeus: with the result that his account is exactly the reverse of the truth."

Now it has already been seen that Justin's account rests chiefly on the work of Timaeus, and yet in spite of Timaeus' ignorance of Africa, there will be found in Justin a better knowledge of Carthaginian politics than appears in Diodorus. The simplest explanation of this seems to be not that Timaeus had special informants from the Carthaginian side[2] (for such men would surely have told him something about the land as well as the politics) but that these matters came easily to the ears of the Greeks,

[1] Polyb. xii. 3. (Abridged in translation.)

[2] As Schubert supposes; the cases to which this applies will be discussed as they occur.

and were recorded by Timaeus because they interested him, while the other historians were more concerned with the acts of Agathocles himself. That these notices of Carthaginian affairs are fictions of Trogus[1], and no part of the report of Timaeus, I should be unwilling to believe.

8. DURIS.

Born a Samian, but boasting himself the offspring of Alcibiades, Duris spent most of his youth away from home. He is said to have won an Olympian boxing-match in his boyhood, and to have studied in Athens at the feet of Theophrastus. In 324 the Athenian settlers were driven out of Samos, and Duris with many of his countrymen came back. Some unknown stroke of luck raised him to be prince of Samos, but the date and nature of his rule are doubtful.

Like another Hellenistic ruler, Demetrius of Phalerum, Duris was a man of letters and a ready writer. Three historical works from his pen are mentioned; a history of Greece from 370 to 281, a Samian Chronicle, and a Life of Agathocles[2]. Besides these Duris wrote some literary essays, "On Tragedy," "On Euripides and Sophocles," some books on art, "On Relief-carving," "On Painters," and a book "On Contests." Verses from Duris are also quoted.

Duris was one of the historians consulted by the Rhodians in the award on the boundary strife between Samos and Priene[3].

---

[1] So Beloch, *griech. Gesch.* III. 1, 193 and Meltzer, *Gesch. d. Karth.* I. 359, seem to think. I would however make an exception in rejecting Bomilcar's dying speech. See p. 154.

[2] The two latter were called Σαμίων ὧραι and τὰ περὶ Ἀγαθοκλέους.

[3] Cf. *Anc. Gr. Inscr. in British Museum*, Part III. Section 1, CCCCIII. 120, and Introd. 4, 5. The date of the award was about 240.

Diodorus speaks of Duris sometimes[1], but it is not always clear to which of his works he is referring. A remark on the battle of Sentinum in 295 might for example have come either from the Life of Agathocles or from the general history[2]. Diodorus knew the latter work, as he speaks of its opening in the year 370[3]: and the likeness of two of the fragments of Duris' Life of Agathocles to passages in Diodorus proves that he made use of the latter also. The first instance is the account of the African myth of Lamia, whose den the men of Ophellas believed themselves to have found on their march to Carthage. " Duris, in the second book of his ' Libyca,' relates that Lamia was once a lovely woman, but owing to the envy of Hera she lost her offspring. Thus she became disfigured through grief, and used to snatch away the children of others[4]." Diodorus speaks of the haunts " where legend says dwelt Queen Lamia, who was once a woman of surpassing beauty; but from her cruelty of heart her look was changed, and thereafter she became like unto a beast. For when all her own children had died, she was cast down by this sorrow, and, being envious of other women, who were happy mothers, she had the babes torn from their arms and at once put to death[5]."

Although Diodorus has somewhat modified the tale, perhaps by comparison with other versions, yet the likeness between the two pieces is unmistakable.

The other fragment of Duris comes from Athenaeus[6],

[1] The use of Duris by Diodorus is discussed by Roesiger in his dissertation *De Duride Samio Diodori Sic. et Plutarchi auct.*

[2] D. xxi. 6. A fragment with no clue to context.

[3] D. xv. 60, 6.

[4] *F. H. G.* ii., Duris 35: from Schol. Aristophan. *Vesp.* 1035.

[5] D. xx. 41, 3.

[6] Athenaeus xiii. 605 d, where the speaker says ἐμοί γε κατὰ φύσιν δοκεῖ πεποιηκέναι Κλεώνυμος.

and relates to the action of Cleonymus at Metapontum in
taking two hundred maidens of the leading families as
hostages. The passage of Diodorus states the same fact[1];
and the agreement on this rather trifling matter makes it
likely that the later historian drew from the earlier.

This remark, according to Athenaeus, came from Duris'
third book of the Life of Agathocles, and, as the account
of the Lamia was in the second (for " Libyca " can hardly
mean anything but the history of Agathocles), it may be
gathered that the whole work on this scale would have
filled at most four books: and the fourth book is actually
mentioned[2]. Thus Duris' Life of Agathocles was a short
work of a more popular nature than the twenty-two books
of Callias.

As Duris was himself a prince he was not likely to
judge a fellow-ruler harshly, so that his account seems
to have been favourable to Agathocles.

It was hardly to be hoped that a man so devoted to
the play, to poetry, and to art, as Duris was, would have
shone in the more sober qualities of the true historian.
Duris held, as his own words show, that history ought
above all things to be pleasant reading. "Of all my
foregoers, Ephorus and Theopompus were the most un-
satisfactory. For they were utterly lacking in dramatic
effect and charm of style, indeed they cared only for bare
narration[3]." These are the words of Duris, and Photius,
who quotes them, adds: "Yet Duris, in the very matters

[1] D. xx. 104, 3.

[2] Cf. Schubert 14.

[3] Οὔτε γὰρ μιμήσεως μετέλαβον οὐδεμιᾶς οὔτε ἡδονῆς ἐν τῇ φράσει
(or ἐν τῷ φράσαι) αὐτοῦ δὲ τοῦ γράφειν μόνον ἐπιμελήθησαν (fr. 1). Μίμησις
seems to be used here in the technical sense that it bore since the
Poetic of Aristotle: that is the enforcing and vivifying of the events and
characters presented by Nature, without leaving Nature so far as to be
unconvincing.

where he finds fault, did far worse than the other historians."

The truthfulness of Duris was strongly attacked by Plutarch. In speaking of the treatment of Samos by Athens, which Duris had made out to have been far worse than would appear from Thucydides, Ephorus and Aristotle, Plutarch adds[1]: "Even where Duris had no personal feeling in the matter, he seldom kept his account within the bounds of truth; so that it is all the likelier in the present case that he should have blackened the sufferings of his country to the discredit of the Athenians."

Again in his Life of Alcibiades Plutarch charges Duris with making Alcibiades' home-coming like a drunken pageant with music and flying colours[2]. It is possible however that Plutarch had a grudge against Duris for slighting some of the heroes of old Greece, whom Plutarch wished to exalt as examples of moral perfection[3].

The eighty-three fragments of Duris are most of them as foolish as history can well be made. But here again the critic must be wary, for it is only natural that the wisdom of any historian should be added to the bulk of accepted knowledge, while such childish sayings as had not been believed by other writers should be lastingly attached to their author's name. It has already been seen that Timaeus was on the whole a wise and painstaking historian; yet most of his fragments are quite as foolish as those of Duris himself.

Duris' remains however are enough to show the way

---

[1] Plut. *Pericles* 28.   [2] Plut. *Alc.* 32.

[3] Plutarch was just the man to be irritated by such aspersions; his whole complaint against Herodotus, in the *De Malignitate*, is that Herodotus was too outspoken as to the shortcomings of the Greeks, that Plutarch wished to idolise.

in which he tried to give dramatic life and charm to his work. He set himself to trick out the plain facts of history with all the gear and apparatus of the stage. Music and costume were often specially mentioned[1]. Both these are found in the passage about the return of Alcibiades, already noted. In another place Duris says that Polysperchon, when mellow, used to dance in a saffron robe and Sicyonian slippers[2]. Elsewhere the dresses of Pausanias, Dionysius, Alexander and Demetrius are given in the richest detail[3]. In all, ten of the fragments deal with clothes.

It has also been thought that the use of disguises was characteristic of the anecdotes related by Duris, although none of his known fragments afford an example[4].

---

[1] Cf. a fragment in Athenaeus IV. 184 d: Δοῦρις δ', ἐν τοῖς περὶ Εὐρι-πίδου καὶ Σοφοκλέους, 'Αλκιβιάδην φησὶ μαθεῖν τὴν αὐλητικὴν οὐ παρὰ τοῦ τυχόντος ἀλλὰ Προνόμου τοῦ μεγίστην ἐσχηκότος δόξαν.

[2] Fr. 24.   [3] Fr. 31.

[4] One use of disguise, which is supposed to have specially interested Duris, was the trick whereby a man by changing clothes with some-one else could escape pursuit and let the substitute die in his stead. Four examples of this ruse are related from Hellenistic times. The first story has been ascribed to Duris on purely general grounds, and on the strength of this we are asked to believe that all the tales are his own invention.   The cases are (1) Polyaenus VIII. 57. Arsinoe, wife of Lysimachus, escaped from Ephesus in the garb of a beggar, leaving a handmaiden to wear her dress and to lie in the queen's litter. Mene-crates, one of Seleucus' captains, burst into the palace and slew the maid, thinking that she was Arsinoe. (2) Plut. *Pyrrhus* 17. Pyrrhus, after his defeat at Heraclea, changed clothes with Megacles in the course of the flight.   He was saved and Megacles killed. (3) Cornelius Nep. *Datames* 9.   Datames saved his life by changing clothes with one of his guardsmen. The outcome was the same as in the last case. (4) D. XIX. 5. Agathocles, in his flight from Syracuse, guessed that Acestorides meant to murder him; he therefore dressed up one of his slaves in his own clothes and clad himself like a beggar.   The slave was killed and Agathocles escaped. (Grote notes the likeness to no. 3.)   The theory that all these stories are fictions of Duris is put forward by Schubert

When such means failed Duris did not disdain a romance or a piece of gossip. Of his extant fragments ten deal with some kind of love-story. Even the characters of Athena and Penelope were besmirched[1].

As the history of Agathocles gave little scope for this kind of embellishment[2], it has been supposed that Duris adopted other means to enliven his story. It has already been seen that there is an anecdotal element in Diodorus, and some critics wish to dispose of the tales in a summary way by treating them all as fictions of Duris. There is no doubt that Duris had an eye for a telling situation, and he may sometimes have improved on his facts for dramatic effect. But of the more general view there is no proof. That Duris invented ruses at all is a bare supposition, and hence to trace all the ruses in Diodorus to his pen is unwarrantable[3].

17—18. But it must be noted that tricks of this kind are so common throughout literature and history, that it would be a mistake to treat them as the property of one historian. It would be easy to find many examples. Thus in Greek myth Heracles took the dress of Omphale, and she took his club and tiger-skin. In the *Frogs* of Aristophanes Dionysus changes clothes with his servant Xanthias; but the trick is wittily made to fail. In the Old Testament (1 Samuel xix. 12) Michal, David's wife, put an image in David's place in case Saul should seek to slay him. This is a trick of much the same character. In Teutonic legend there is an example in the ruse of Hiordis, widow of Sigmund, who changes clothes with her maid (cf. Morris, *Sigurd the Volsung*, Book I. p. 71). Lastly, in English history it is said that when Lord William Russell was imprisoned in 1683, his friend Cavendish offered to change clothes with him, and to let Russell escape, while he went to death; but Russell would not.

[1] One love-story, that of Antiochus and Stratonice, seems at least in Droysen's beautiful German (cf. *Gesch. d. Hell.* II. 2, 293) to be a pleasing romance. (Most critics, though not Droysen himself, have traced this tale to Duris.) The others are mere balderdash.

[2] The scandal about Alcia (D. xx. 33, 5 and 68, 2) and the account of Eurydice, wife of Ophellas (D. xx. 40, 5), are the only alleged cases.

[3] Cf. Schubert 20, 21. Schubert's account of Duris is a spirited piece

Justin's work does not, as far as can be judged, show
any trace of the use of Duris. But Polyaenus seems to
have used him, at first hand or otherwise. The story of
Agathocles' dancing in a saffron robe[1] is a fairly safe
example, as it closely resembles Duris' account of the
behaviour of Polysperchon, already mentioned.

*   *   *   *   *   *

On the strength of this plainly incomplete knowledge
of the earliest writers on Agathoclean history, some modern
critics have claimed to settle in almost every passage of
Diodorus, Justin, or Polyaenus, the precise source from
which the account before them has been drawn.

The fruits of this so-called higher criticism would be
worth more, if its exponents were better agreed in their
results. But as every possible view seems to be held with
equal assurance[2], it might after all be wiser and more

of writing, but it will readily be seen that he has found no absolutely
certain example of a " stratagem " invented by Duris. His assumption
that Duris used to enliven his history with fictitious bugle-calls is also,
as far as can be seen, devoid of circumstantial proof. (On page 43 he is
arguing in a circle.) Dr Evans in his notes to Freeman has followed
Schubert, but Niese (*Gesch. d. griech. u. maked. Staaten*, 455, etc.) and
others have taken more moderate views.

[1] Polyaenus v. 3, 3.

[2] The following dicta will show the hopeless disagreement of the
leading authorities on these matters. Grote xii. 610, n. 1. " Diodorus
cites Timaeus by name occasionally and in particular instances, but he
evidently did not borrow from that author the main stream of his
narrative. He seems to have had before him other authorities—among
them some highly favourable to Agathocles—the Syracusan Callias, and
Antander, brother of Agathocles."

Freeman iv. 525. " Diodorus...is, I imagine, mainly following Antander; he would doubtless have other books before him as well: he uses
Timaeus, but he clearly does not at this stage take him as his chief
guide." For the rise of Agathocles, Meltzer i. 522 (following Roesiger,
De Duride Samio) holds that Duris used Timaeus and Callias, and that
Diodorus drew his Agathoclean history wholly from Duris, and thus
knew Timaeus only at second hand. Schubert holds that Diodorus used

honest to admit freely that there are some things not to be known about the history of Agathocles, than to make too many assertions and to support them by polemical methods. The truth of any ancient account is best gauged by its inherent probability: beyond this there is no appeal.

Duris and Timaeus (p. 15); he knew Callias only through Duris (p. 148); it is doubtful whether he used Antander (p. 1). Beloch believes that Diodorus, Justin and Polyaenus are all hostile to Agathocles throughout his history. The article in Pauly-Wissowa, *s.v.* Diodorus, holds that Diodorus used Duris for the main account, but referred to other historians in particular cases. Droysen (II. 2, p. 90, n. 2) holds that Diodorus and Justin *both* rest on the work of Duris.

CHAPTER II.

AGATHOCLES AS AN ADVENTURER.

1. STORY OF AGATHOCLES' BIRTH AND CHILDHOOD.

THE greatness of Agathocles was a thing at which the world was astonished. Living in an age of great men he gained by his own mighty deeds such a hold over men's minds as few of his fellow-princes ever won. To those coming after it seemed as if his life had been a fable and a wonder; and it is the crowning proof of the fame of Agathocles that legend tells anew in his honour the ancient tale of the birth of Cyrus[1].

Diodorus thus relates[2]:

"Carcinus of Rhegium had been banished from his home and settled at Thermae, the town being at that time under Carthage. There he became the lover of a woman of the place, and afterwards was troubled by dreams as to the child which should be born unto him. He therefore charged some Carthaginian envoys, who were going to Delphi, to ask the god about the babe. They carefully

---

[1] For the birth of Cyrus cf. Herodotus I. 107 ff. The story passed on to Romulus, and in a weakened form to Hiero II (J. xxiii. 4, 4 ff.). Hiero is there said to have been cast out and fed by bees: and sundry tokens from heaven foretold his greatness. The parallel between Agathocles and Romulus is noted as early as Perrinchiefe, *The Sicilian Tyrant* (London 1676). The myth is old and far travelled: Ion is an early Greek example, while the same tale appears in *Cymbeline*.

[2] D. xix. 2.

carried out his bidding, and the answer was, that the young child would be the cause of great ills to the Carthaginians and to all Sicily. Then Carcinus, hearing this and fearing the Carthaginians, cast out his babe openly and set watchers by it that it should die. But after some days, as the babe lived on, the guards grew heedless. Then came the mother by night, and took up the child by stealth and carried him away, not to her home, for fear of her husband, but to her brother Heracleides; and she called the child Agathocles, after her own father. And the child grew up at Heracleides' house, and he was comely to look upon and strong in frame beyond his years.

"Now when the boy was seven years old, Carcinus was bidden of Heracleides to a sacrifice, and seeing Agathocles playing with some of his playmates, he wondered at his strength and beauty. And his wife said that their son would now have been that age, if he had lived; whereupon Carcinus repented of his deed and wept without ceasing. Then his wife, seeing that her husband's mood was favourable to what she had done, told him the whole truth. And he heard her with joy and took back his son. But fearing the Carthaginians he moved to Syracuse with all his house; and being needy he taught Agathocles the potter's craft, while-Agathocles was still a lad. It was about that time that Timoleon of Corinth, after smiting the Carthaginians at the Crimisus, gave the citizenship of Syracuse to any that wished it. And Carcinus, being enrolled with Agathocles, lived a short time longer, and then died. And Agathocles' mother set up a stone likeness of her son in a shrine, and a swarm of bees settled upon the image and made honey on the hips. And when this token was told to those who were learned in such things, they all said that Agathocles would come to great glory, and this indeed came to pass."

Beside this legend the sober account of Justin must be set[1]:

"Agathocles, tyrant of Sicily, who succeeded to the greatness of the elder Dionysius, reached the rank of a prince from a base and mean origin. He was born in Sicily, the son of a potter, and his boyhood was not more respectable than his birth....Some time afterwards he moved to Syracuse, and was enrolled among the burgesses, but for a long time had no reputation."

A remark of Polybius on the same subject is also worth quoting[2]:

"Agathocles, as Timaeus scoffingly says, was originally a potter and, leaving the wheel, the clay and the smoke, he came as a young man to Syracuse."

It has already been seen that Timaeus was the original source of the account that made Agathocles a potter; and such a statement from so unfriendly an authority is not to be taken without suspicion. Polybius himself (who after all lived much nearer to the time of Agathocles than our other historians) does not seem to believe it. Again so far from Agathocles' family being of low estate, they are presently seen on the best of terms with the nobles of Syracuse; Agathocles himself becomes the chosen friend of the wealthy Damas, and ends by marrying his widow, while Agathocles' brother holds high command in the Syracusan army[3].

When Agathocles forsook the side of the oligarchs to become a popular leader and a popular tyrant, it was

[1] J. xxii. 1 §§ 1, 2, 6. The charges against Agathocles' own character cannot be discussed here. These seem to have been handed down by Timaeus: cf. Polyb. xii. 15, cf. also *F. H. G.* i., Tim. 149. Suidas, *s.v.* ᾿Αγαθοκλῆς, has copied all the unpleasant details through Polybius, without adding that the latter disbelieved them.

[2] Polyb. xv. 35, cf. xii. 15, 6.

[3] See below, pp. 40—1.

natural for his enemies to cast discredit on his birth, and
to find shameful causes for his quick rise to power. This
is in fact the spirit of Justin's account[1].

Of course it is easy to compromise the question by
saying that Agathocles' father was a master-potter who
for safety in time of party-strife or for hope of gain moved
his workshop from Rhegium to Thermae and thence to
Syracuse[2]. But even so he would hardly have been a
welcome friend to the Syracusan nobles. On the whole,
considering how easily the story of Agathocles' trade could
have been made up, and how ready the world has always
been to improve on tales of that kind, the modern reader
must incline to disbelief.

Still less ground is there for taking seriously the
picturesque details of Agathocles' childhood. The asking
of the Delphic oracle, the recognition-scene, the token of
the bees, are all essential parts of the legend, and probably
have no historical foundation.

[1] An example of the same kind of slander is seen in Plutarch,
Eumenes 1, where it appears that Duris made Eumenes the son of a
coachman, and ascribed his rise to athletic prowess, whereas in truth
the house of Eumenes had long been guest-friends of the kings of
Macedonia (cf. Schubert 31). Likewise Hiero II was made the son of a
slave-woman (Justin XXIII. 4, 6). The same class of tale made the Emperor
Philip the son of a robber, and Theodora, the wife of Justinian, an
actress.

[2] So Beloch III. 1, 186, n. 3. The supposed humble trade of Agathocles is very often spoken of by later writers, whose witness on such
a point is clearly worthless, e.g. Plutarch, *Reg. et Imp. Apophth.*, Agathocles I. "Agathocles was a potter's son. When he became master of
Sicily, he used to put earthen cups on his table beside the golden: then
he would point them out to the young men and say: τοιαῦτα ποιῶν
πρότερον νῦν τοιαῦτα ποιεῖ διὰ τὴν ἐπιμέλειαν καὶ τὴν ἀνδρείαν" (cf. D. xx.
63, 4). Also Suidas, *s.v.* Ἀγαθοκλῆς,—Photius, p. 530 (ed. Bekker),—
Amm. Marcellinus XIV. *fin.*, *Haec fortuna mutabilis et inconstans fecit
Agathoclem Siculum ex figulo regem.*—Athenaeus XI. 466 a, who gives
the same tale as Plutarch, on the authority of Caecilius of Calacte,
a rhetorician.

Undoubtedly Agathocles was born at Thermae, but whether his father really came from Rhegium or whether Agathocles' later relations with that city led to the invention of this detail is uncertain. Even the name of Agathocles' father is not altogether above suspicion.

The names of several of Agathocles' sons and grandsons are known, and it is strange that not one of them should be called after Carcinus, the founder of the house. Diodorus himself seems to be at pains to account for this departure from custom in making Agathocles' mother name him after her own father. He also gives Heracleides as her brother, and this was the name of one of Agathocles' sons. It is not easy to believe that such a matriarchal system of names can have been in use in the fourth century; and the truth may be that Diodorus, in trying to make the legend more reasonable, has mistaken the father's side for the mother's in Agathocles' ancestry. In so doing he did not trouble to correct the doubtful expression that he had already used about Agathocles' mother in calling her a " woman of the place." Was she a Greek or a Carthaginian?

The legend very likely made her a Carthaginian, for otherwise there is no possible sense in her concern in the Carthaginian embassy to Delphi; but Diodorus, though he gave her father and brother Greek names, seems hardly aware that he has made her into a Greek also.

In reality the supposed Punic descent of Agathocles, and the hint that his mother and father were living out of regular wedlock, are no more to be believed than the rest of the myth. It is therefore quite possible that Heracleides was not the foster-father but the real father of Agathocles, so that the prince took his name from his paternal grandfather. In this way the family-tree would bear a more reasonable aspect. But the whole matter must remain uncertain and it is not worth while discussing it further.

The tale of the bees seems to be a modified form of part of the Cyrus-legend. Cyrus was said to have been suckled by a bitch, as Romulus was by a wolf. Only with Agathocles the miracle is given a more rational turn by the exchange of the man for his statue—so that the bees which feed the living Hiero[1] are only allowed to make honey on the stone Agathocles.

2. STATE OF THE WEST.

The year of Agathocles' birth was 361. Before the historical account of his acts at Syracuse begins, it will be well to review shortly the condition of the states with which he afterwards had dealings[2].

ITALY. The parties concerned in the great struggle between Rome and Samnium had definitely taken sides. Rome had found allies in Lucania and Apulia, and thus harassed her foes continually in the rear. The Lucanians were the natural enemies of the Tarentines and other south Italian Greeks, and hence the latter tended to support the Samnites. But in the fourth century the strength and greatness of Tarentum were lost, and love of ease hindered her from sharing worthily in the great encounter which she might perhaps have decided. Her only known act during the second Samnite war was a feeble attempt at peacemaking after the disaster of the Caudine Forks; to this offer Rome would not listen. Otherwise Tarentum cared only for her own comfort, and

[1] Justin *ibid.* : cf. Schubert 30.

[2] In this general survey it would be needless to give references for all the statements made, which can be verified in any history-book.

while the Lucanians were busy with the Samnites she was
the more likely to be left in peace. On the other hand
when the Samnite war slumbered, Lucania was free once
more to harry her southern neighbours, and Tarentum
then resorted to outside aid to keep out the raiders.

Thus in 338, when Rome and Samnium were at peace,
Archidamus, king of Sparta, had fought in vain against
the Lucanians. Again about 334 Alexander the Molossian
helped Tarentum against the Lucanians, who were then
in league with the Samnites. At that time Rome was too
much taken up with the Latins to do anything in south
Italy; and she made a treaty with Alexander. His
championship was more effective, and, even after his
murder in 331—0, Tarentum was able to keep back the
Lucanians, and in 327 the outbreak of the second Samnite
war drew off their forces to the north. What has been
said of Tarentum applies also to the other Greek states in
Italy, which usually sided with her when a deliverer was
in the field. The Bruttian league, which had at one time
threatened to drive the Greeks out of Italy, was much less
dangerous after the campaigns of Alexander of Molossia,
although the native tribes were sometimes troublesome to
their near neighbours.

The years following Alexander's death were a time of
respite for the Greeks in Italy. Rome was already the
leading power in the country; but until the Samnites
were crushed, the south of the peninsula was no more to
her than a field for intrigue. She had no fixed policy
of enmity against the Greek states, for Naples and other
Campanian cities were already among her allies;—but
any useful friend would have been welcome to her. If
Rome did not then hope to bring all Italy under her sway,
still less did she dream of embroiling herself in Sicilian
politics or of becoming a Mediterranean power. Her

fleet scarcely existed, and her treaty with Carthage, the mistress of the sea, was a confession that Rome's ambition did not overstep her own shores.

Meanwhile the Greek cities were disunited, and the usual party bickerings took up most of their strength. There was no common aim or fixed policy : and therefore the cities were bound to become the prize of the strongest power,—Rome, Samnium, or a conqueror from Old Greece, as the case might be. The Italiots were no longer masters of their own destiny.

CARTHAGE had been inactive after her great disaster at the Crimisus, which led to the peace with Timoleon. In spite of the cruel death of Hanno in 343, the strife of parties was only temporarily at rest, and fresh troubles soon broke out. Timoleon had left Carthage mistress at sea, so that she could renew her attack on Greek Sicily, as soon as it suited her. Her commercial treaty with Rome, renewed in 348, showed her naval superiority, but was of no immediate political importance.

The GREEK EAST. The years of Agathocles' youth were the time of the rise of Macedonia, and the establishment of the new order, where the kingdom replaced the city as the unit of power. At the same time the depression of Greece under the Macedonian rule led men to look westward for a wider field for ambition and conquest,— and many deliverers, of whom Timoleon himself was the type, set out to fight for the Greek cause against the Italians and the Carthaginians. This was a direct effect of the Macedonian overlordship. With the course of Greek history itself Sicily was little concerned. The wars of Alexander and the strife following his death did not touch her : and it was not for many years yet that Sicily took her place among the Hellenistic kingdoms. But still the conquests of Alexander and the advance of military

spirit and tactics in his time must have had some effect
upon movements in the west. There indeed the work had
been partly forestalled by Dionysius I., whose imperial
policy and standing armies were far in front of the
conceptions of his own age. Sicily, it may fairly be said,
always afforded the materials out of which a great power
could be made. She had only to wait for her leader.

One of Alexander's unfulfilled plans had been the
conquest of Libya and Carthage, and although his death
relieved the city from her worst fears, so grand a project
cannot have been altogether forgotten. It will be seen
hereafter that Agathocles began and almost achieved an
enterprise of the same kind: and Ophellas, one of the
most ambitious of Alexander's followers, had hopes of
winning fame in that quarter also. What Alexander
planned, it was open to any daring soldier to attempt.

SICILY. It remains to speak of Sicily herself. Although
Timoleon's work of restoring the old freedom of the city-
states might seem at first sight to be a setback towards
a condition of things that the Greek world had outgrown,
it must be remembered that in the distracted state of the
country immediate deliverance followed by rest was the
most pressing need. Timoleon did not come to found an
empire. He had quite a clear notion of the government
which he thought best suited to Sicily. The cities were
to enjoy their full freedom in peace time under a moderate
republican rule. If a great war threatened, the Greeks
were to unite under another deliverer from Corinth.

If all things had fallen out as Timoleon wished, the
welfare of Sicily might never have been wrecked. But,
as it happened, the turn of fortune set against his plans.
The new republican governments soon lost their moderation; the cities would not live in peace, but began once
more to make war on one another or within their own

walls. They refused to unite when the danger of invasion came, and the deliverer from Corinth failed to deliver.

Thus the work of Timoleon was soon undone; but still he had tided Sicily over her worst peril, and to his settlement are due not only the twenty years peace following his death, but also, to a great degree, the wealth of the island in the later years of Agathocles. For the tyrant reaped what the deliverer had sown.

These matters will become clear if the state of Sicily be observed more in detail.

Timoleon after the deliverance of Sicily from foemen and usurpers had taken every care to ensure the lasting peace and safety of the island. He left Syracuse to be the leader but no longer the mistress of the Greek cities; although it is now almost impossible to tell which states were put under her overlordship, and which were merely in alliance with her. Gela and Acragas had been built up by Timoleon, and with Acragas Syracuse is soon found at war. Messena also appears later as a free city holding out against Agathocles. Camarina again, received fresh settlers from Timoleon. On the other hand he made the Agyrians citizens of Syracuse, and moved thither the whole people of Leontini, although that town is later seen once more independent[1]. The leading position of Syracuse is shown by the part which she afterwards took in helping Croton against the Bruttians, and thus acting as champion of the Greek cause. But it can hardly be doubted that the other Greek cities, of which no special mention is made, had their full liberties given back, and they seem

---

[1] The references are: for Acragas, D. xix. 3, 1, and below; Messena, D. xix. 65; Camarina, D. xvi. 82, 7. For the Agyrians, 83, 3; Leontini, 82, 7. The league of cities is called συμμαχία, 82, 4.

to have profited by later strife to break loose from the
Syracusan league[1].

There can be no question but that the years of more
or less unbroken peace following Timoleon's settlement
led to a renewal of wealth and prosperity among the
Siceliots; and Diodorus gives a glowing picture of the
happy time which now set in. "Altogether the restora-
tion of peace throughout Sicily by Timoleon led to a
great increase of prosperity among the cities. For many
years, owing to the strife and civil wars and the constant
rise of tyrants, the cities were empty of indwellers and the
fields lay fallow from want of tillage, and yielded no
cultivated crops. But now from the number of settlers
and the long peace that had set in, the fields were once
more brought under cultivation by fresh tillage, and bore
all kinds of crops in plenty. The Sicilian Greeks sold
their produce to the merchants at a profit, and their own
wealth grew fast. A sign of the ample means which they
won in this way, was the number of grand monuments
set up about that time[2]."

For all this, it is clear that the old policy of disunion
still held the field, so that the first strong power that
should appear in the west was not likely to be met by
any properly concerted measures.

The Syracusan commons were given back their power
at home[3], but the unruliness of the mob was checked by

[1] Thus in J. xxii. 2, 1, Morgantina chose Agathocles from hatred of
Syracuse, to be general.

[2] D. xvi. 83. One of these monuments was the house of Agathocles,
of which mention will be made below. For the state of Sicily at this time
cf. Freeman iv. 333 ff., 362; Beloch ii. 588.

[3] The assembly elected the military officers, D. xix. 3, 4: and offenders
were impeached before it, among them Timoleon himself (Plut. *Tim.* 37).
Agathocles afterwards brought his opponents to trial before the assembly,

the awe of a new office. The high-priest of Olympian
Zeus became the chief magistrate in the state[1]. Chosen
yearly from among three clans to this lofty place of civil
and religious dignity, he was expected to be beyond the
fear of popular clamour, while the sacred nature of his
function, disqualifying for leadership in the field, kept
far from him the desire or at least the means of grasping
unlawful power.

The authority of the generals did not go beyond the
army itself[2]; they held a joint command and were popularly
elected[3]. But as divided counsels are fatal in a great war,
it was laid down by Timoleon that whenever a barbarian
foe was threatening, a general should be sought from
Corinth[4].

Every care had thus been taken to ward off the danger
of another tyranny; and indeed the tyranny did not come
until a long course of party strife had cleared the way.
It was from an oligarchic faction that the state-fabric of
Timoleon had its first blow. Some of the richest and
foremost men in Syracuse formed themselves into a
political club called the Six Hundred; and this body soon
became the chief power in the state. Of the steps by
which the nobles usurped this position we are quite
uninformed. In name the commonwealth lived on un-
changed, but the leaders of the Six Hundred, among
whom Heracleides and Sosistratus were the greatest,
could fill the offices of peace and war with their own

D. xix. 3, 5. These two functions, elective and judicial, would imply the
transacting of common civil business as a matter of course.

[1] D. xvi. 70, 6; Cic. *Verr.* ii. ii. 51, and iv. 61. (Freeman iv. 314 n.;
Beloch ii. 588 n. Beloch's remarks on the supposed προαγόρας are inconclusive.)

[2] D. xix. 3, 3, where military power is contrasted seemingly with civil.

[3] *Ibid.* cf. § 1.

[4] πρὸς ἀλλοφύλους, Plut. *Tim.* 38.

AGATHOCLES AS AN ADVENTURER

creatures, and guided the policy of Syracuse as they
pleased[1]. The behaviour of this cabal was high-handed
and selfish, but the government seems to have been carried
on in a vigorous manner, so that the position of Syracuse
among the Greek cities was kept up[2].

3. AGATHOCLES' FIRST DOINGS AT SYRACUSE.

Agathocles was eighteen years old when Timoleon
issued his invitation for the re-peopling of Syracuse[3]; his
proposals attracted numbers of settlers from all over the
Greek world; and among the newcomers was Agathocles'
father. It was no doubt the desire of belonging to the
greatest city in Sicily, and not fear of the Carthaginians,

[1] D. XIX. 3, 3, and elsewhere. On the vexed question of the true
position of the Six Hundred in the Syracusan constitution, see note on
p. 92. Diodorus himself says that his 18th book dealt with this oligarchy.
If so it must have been in a digression now lost, or perhaps never written.

[2] At least their defence of Croton against the Bruttians (D. XIX. 3, 3)
does them credit. Diodorus himself gives two very unlike accounts of
their character. He first calls them *l.c.* ἄνδρες ἐν ἐπιβουλαῖς καὶ φόνοις καὶ
μεγάλοις ἀσεβήμασι γεγονότες τὸν πλείω τοῦ βίου, and in XIX. 71, 4, Sosistratus is called δραστικὸν ἄνδρα καὶ δυνάμενον ἐφεδρεῦσαι τοῖς κακῶς προιστα-
μένοις τῆς ἡγεμονίας.
We may have here a trace of Diodorus' careless use of two different
sources. The first is strongly on the side of Agathocles, and may have
been Duris or Callias. The second favours Sosistratus, and was no
doubt Timaeus. But the general character of Sosistratus as an overbearing, factious man, is clear from either.

[3] Polyb. XII. 15 = *F.H.G.* Timaeus 145 εἰς τὰς Συρακούσας παρεγενήθη
...περί τε τὴν ἡλικίαν ὀκτωκαίδεκα ἔτη γεγονώς; J. XXII. 1, 4 *Annos pu-
bertatis egressus.* Diodorus in making Agathocles only seven years old at
the time (D. XIX. 2, 6) is merely retailing the Cyrus-legend, and has not
yet begun his serious history; for the same reason he ignores Antander,
Agathocles' elder brother, and brings him in casually later on.
For the re-peopling of Syracuse cf. D. XVI. 82, 5...κηρύξαντος δὲ αὐτοῦ
διότι οἱ Συρακόσιοι διδόασι χώραν καὶ οἰκίας τοῖς βουλομένοις μετέχειν τῆς
ἐν Συρακούσαις πολιτείας, πολλοὶ πρὸς τὴν κληρουχίαν Ἕλληνες ἀπήντησαν.

as Diodorus says, that led him to move. He took with
him Antander, his elder son, and Agathocles his younger,
and all three were enrolled among the Syracusan burgesses
in the year 343[1].

Agathocles' father died soon after[2].

At the time of the resettling of Syracuse, the warfare
in Sicily was by no means at an end; and there is reason
to believe that Agathocles' first active service was in the
ranks of Timoleon's army. Justin says that the first
campaign of Agathocles, in which he gave signal proof
of his valour, was fought against the men of Aetna[3].
This can hardly be other than the war of 339, when
Timoleon marched against the Campanian soldiers en-
trenched in Aetna and smote them[4]. Agathocles, it is
said, was conspicuous for his bodily strength; he wore
a harness that no other man could carry and used
weapons too heavy for any of his mates[5].

His warlike valour was seconded by political influence,
which under an oligarchic government would naturally
be essential to success. Although Agathocles' own feelings
leaned rather towards the popular party, he entered active
life as a servant of the nobles.

His chief hopes in these early years were for glory in
war, and he was fortunate in finding a patron who could
help him; for on the whole it would seem that the ruling

---

[1] D. xix. 2, 8; J. xxii. 1, 6.   [2] D. *ibid.*

[3] J. xxii. 1, 11. *Primo bello adversus Aetnaeos magna experimenta
sui Syracusanis dedit.* Cf. § 8 *gregariam militiam sortitus.*

[4] D. xvi. 82, 4 (Timoleon)...τοὺς δ' ἐν Αἴτνῃ Καμπανοὺς ἐκπολιορκήσας
διέφθειρε.

[5] D. xix. 3, 2. Diodorus does not mention the share of Agathocles
in Timoleon's campaign, but says that Agathocles even before the war
against Acragas (which will be recounted later) was πολύσεμνος διὰ τὸ
μέγεθος τῶν ὅπλων, κ.τ.λ. It was naturally part of the legend to endow
Agathocles with uncanny strength; Justin merely calls him *manu strenuus.*

oligarchy stood for the cause of the old burgesses of
Syracuse as against newcomers such as Agathocles[1].
The patron's name was Damas[2], and he must have been
on good terms with the Six Hundred if not among their
number[3]. It is quite possible that some hereditary friendship was the reason that led this wealthy and distinguished
man to take up the cause of the two brothers from Thermae,
although Diodorus speaks as if Agathocles' personal
qualities were his only recommendation[4]. Damas seems
to have made a close friend of the young soldier[5], and the
two men went to the war against Acragas together :
Damas as general, Agathocles as an inferior officer. But
when one of the Captains-of-thousands fell in battle, the
influence of Damas gained the vacant commission for
his friend[6].

This war against Acragas is mentioned quite casually
by Diodorus, and it is not known when or why it was

[1] This view, though only a conjecture, is fairly probable. Niese holds
the same opinion.

[2] Called Damascon by Justin.

[3] This can hardly be doubted, for (a) the Six Hundred included
all the wealthiest and foremost men in Syracuse; (b) the dominant
cabal would never have allowed a rich and influential man to hold such a
high office as that of στρατηγός, if he had been opposed to them in
politics.

[4] Agathocles' powers of mob-oratory are mentioned by both authorities
(clearly from the same source since the very words correspond) without
any reference to date (D. XIX. 3, 2; J. XXII. 1, 9). But any exercise of
these powers at this time would have brought Agathocles under the
suspicion of the oligarchs, and it may therefore be gathered that the
words apply to his later democratic days.

[5] D. XIX. 3, 1 where it is even said Δάμας...ἐρωτικῶς διετέθη πρὸς τὸν
'Αγαθοκλέα. This does not sound very likely.

[6] D. ibid.; J. XXII. 1, 10 Brevi itaque centurio ac deinceps tribunus
militum factus est.

Tribunus Militum no doubt stands for χιλιάρχης ; but the Greek for
centurio in the Syracusan army is unknown.

fought. Possibly the Six Hundred wished to send help to the oligarchs in that city, as they afterwards did in the case of Croton and Rhegium. Of the result of the campaign we are also uninformed.

Damas died not long after, and Agathocles married his widow, thus becoming one of the richest men in Syracuse[1].

The next war was waged in Italy, the Syracusans sending a large force to help Croton against the Bruttians, who were beleaguering the city. Antander was one of the generals, and Agathocles himself had been re-elected a Captain-of-a-thousand. It is possible that Heracleides and Sosistratus also took the field[2]. The date of the war is not known; but in the life-time of Alexander the Molossian Croton would not have needed help from Syracuse. Alexander was killed in 330, after which date the present war should accordingly be placed.

The Syracusan army fought well, and seems to have freed Croton from danger, though peace was not made with the Bruttians until 317.

Agathocles himself did many doughty deeds, but the oligarchic leaders began to grow jealous and withheld from him the meed of his prowess. Enraged by this injustice and perhaps by intrigues of the commanders

---

[1] D. xix. 3, 2. Justin (xxii. 1, 13) says *cujus uxorem adulterio cognitam post mortem viri in matrimonium accepit.* Here is another unlikely piece of gossip.

[2] D. xix. 3, 3, 4, where it is carefully noted that Agathocles was elected by the people. This statement comes from the side friendly to Agathocles, and tends to slur over the obvious fact that he was still the servant of the oligarchs. His " election" was only a matter of form. Diodorus does not seem quite to know whether Heracleides and Sosistratus went on this campaign or not. He first contrasts the function of the generals with the ἡγεμονία τῶν ὅλων, which was in the hands of these men; but then says that Agathocles συνεστρατεύετο δ' αὐτοῖς.

in favour of the oligarchic party in Croton[1], Agathocles
forsook his partisans and became the bitter and desperate
foe of the nobles' cause.

The misunderstanding had doubtless been growing
for some time, and Agathocles, who had served under
Sosistratus rather as a patriot than a political follower,
hoped to find allies among the commons, for whose
leadership his own ready tongue and bold address
thoroughly fitted him.

He began by impeaching Sosistratus and his followers

[1] It is quite likely that not only did these two politicians take the
field, but that they also helped to set up an oligarchy in Croton; for
in D. xix. 10, 3, mention is made of Crotonian oligarchs who were
banished for intriguing with Heracleides and Sosistratus. (Diodorus says
that the details of these doings were in his 18th book. This again refers
to the lost or unwritten part already mentioned.) This misconduct of the
chief leaders would supply another ground for the next acts of Agathocles,
for which wounded vanity hardly accounts.

Justin's account of the campaigns of Agathocles is confused, and not
easy to reconcile with Diodorus'. He first speaks of the war against
Aetna, already given. Then xxii. 1, 12 *Sequenti Campanorum tantam de
se spem omnibus fecit ut in locum demortui ducis Damasconis sufficeretur.*
This war of Justin can be taken in three ways.

1. As the Acragantine campaign (Schubert). In this case "*Damasconis*" would be a kind of mistaken "gloss" on "*ducis*," the latter
meaning the fallen "chiliarch" in whose room Agathocles was chosen.
This view is perhaps too drastic in its treatment of Justin, whose foregoing sentence seems to be right.

2. As the Bruttian war. "Campanians" meaning Italians generally
(Freeman). This would go against Diodorus in putting Damas' death
during the Bruttian war instead of before it.

3. As a different war from either, but before the Bruttian campaign.
Against this it must be said that to make Agathocles $dux = \sigma\tau\rho\alpha\tau\eta\gamma\delta s$
here, and only *tribunus* $= \chi\iota\lambda\iota\acute{\alpha}\rho\chi\eta s$ in the later Bruttian war (as D. says
was his rank then) is not what would be expected under an oligarchic
system with regular promotion. But if the technical sense of "*dux*"
need not be pressed here, then the third view is not unlikely: for between
339 and at least a campaign after 330 there was plenty of time for another
war.

on the charge of high treason¹. The case was heard in the assembly², but either the popular party was too weak to take action or else it failed to recognise its new leader in Agathocles. Anyhow the charge fell to the ground³, and Agathocles was forced to leave Syracuse altogether.

Nor was this all. Sosistratus carried a decree of banishment against the friends of Agathocles, and a thousand men were obliged to make their way out of the city. An escort of horse and foot was sent with them, and on the road the soldiers, by the secret bidding of Sosistratus, fell on the exiles, taking or slaying a great number. The rest were doomed to death by proclamation.

The way to undisguised oligarchy was now clear. Sosistratus had all the outlaws' wealth escheated, and used it to hire a body of Greek and foreign spearmen, some of them evil-doers taken from the quarries: with this force the Six Hundred could keep the whole government of Syracuse in their own hands⁴.

¹ D. xix. 3, 5, where the charge is vaguely called "tyranny" (ὡς δι-εγνωκότας ἐπιθέσθαι τυραννίδι).

² Ibid. ἐν τῷ δήμῳ. This seems to mean that Agathocles came home to make the charge, in spite of D.'s statement (ibid. c. 4) that he stayed in Italy.

³ Ibid. οὐ προσεχόντων δὲ τῶν Συρακοσίων ταῖς διαβολαῖς. This remark is very unfriendly to Agathocles, for his charge was perfectly just, as the very same sentence shows.

⁴ Ibid. and Polyaenus v. 37. Diodorus says οἱ μὲν περὶ Σωσίστρατον ἐδυνάστευσαν τῆς πατρίδος μετὰ τὴν ἐκ Κρότωνος ἐπάνοδον. This puts the case against the Six Hundred as mildly as possible; but the use of ἐδυνάστευσαν in the aorist tense can only mean one thing. After the home-coming from Croton the followers of Sosistratus became the supreme unconstitutional rulers of Syracuse. Freeman's view (iv. 518) that "δυναστεία is clearly consistent with the regular outward action of a democratic assembly" seems therefore impossible; and here the aorist ἐδυνάστευσαν would be out of place if the Six Hundred merely went on ruling as they had ruled before the trial.

Diodorus only gives a bare outline, but the details have been filled in

4. AGATHOCLES' FIRST EXILE.
c. 326—322 B.C.

Agathocles gathered such forces as he could from the
downfall of his party, and began a run of wild adventures
in Italy. His first attempt was a surprise attack on Croton,
no doubt in league with the banished democrats of that
city. The stroke however was a failure; the exiles were
routed and Agathocles with a few survivors fled to
Tarentum[1].

There he was thankful for a commission among the
hired soldiers, for the Tarentines, as always, were readier
to declare war than to wage it[2].

from Polyaenus; for there is no doubt that the "stratagem" (Pol. v. 37)
belongs here. The mention of the enrolling of the convicts from the
quarries—a point which would never have been invented—proves that
genuine information underlies the story. It was no doubt the version
of the party friendly to Agathocles. (The statement that Agathocles'
friends were already plotting to make him tyrant, though of course untrue, has obviously been added by Polyaenus to make his story intelligible
out of its context, and can therefore be ignored altogether.)

[1] D. XIX. 4, 1 καὶ καταλαμβάνεσθαι τὴν τῶν Κροτωνιατῶν πόλιν ἐπιχειρήσας
ἐξέπεσε καὶ μετ᾿ ὀλίγων εἰς Τάραντα διεσώθη. Where ἐξέπεσε would imply
that the attacking force broke into the city, and was then driven out;
probably not, as Dr Evans thinks, that attack was made from within.

In D. XIX. 10 (date 317), the following further details on Crotonian
affairs are given. § 3 "The Crotoniates made peace with the Bruttians,
but against the citizens that had been banished for intriguing with
Heracleides and Sosistratus (which matter I have given in detail in the
book before this), they elected as commanders in the second year of the
war Paron and Menedemus, both men of note." § 4 The oligarchs tried
in their turn to surprise Croton, but were beaten back and in the end cut
to pieces. (The reference is again to the lost digression to Bk. XVIII.)

The war here mentioned thus began in 319, so that Agathocles' stroke
must have been made at any rate some time before then. Menedemus is
supposed to be the man mentioned in D. XXI. 4, as prince of Croton and a
friend of Agathocles. If so he may have been acting with the latter in
the present case.

[2] D. XIX. 4, 1. Tarentum was a thankless paymistress to her Greek

Against the foemen of Tarentum, no doubt as usual the Lucanians, Agathocles did many deeds of great daring. But soon he was suspected of plotting against the government, and was discharged from the army. Or it may be that the oligarchic party, which in Tarentum stood for peace with her Italian neighbours, as later for friendship with Rome, now gained the upper hand, and got rid of Agathocles as no longer needed for active service[1].

He was not however long idle, but soon found himself at the head of a strong body of outlaws, democratic exiles in fact from various parts of Italy and Sicily. Rhegium was being besieged by the forces of Sosistratus' oligarchy, and Agathocles marched to its relief[2]. Of the course of the war on land, which may have been accompanied by some roving cruises on the part of Agathocles' men[3], no account has come down. But the result is certain. The oligarchs lost not only their hope of taking Rhegium, but even their position in Syracuse itself. They fled from the city, and Agathocles came home the leader of the restored and triumphant democracy[4].

deliverers. She turned against Alexander of Molossia and her support of Pyrrhus was half-hearted, while she did little for Hannibal. Her people seem to have hated any kind of land fighting. Cf. Strabo VI. 3, 4 (p. 280) ἐν δὲ τῶν φαύλων πολιτευμάτων τεκμήριόν ἐστι τὸ ξενικοῖς στρατηγοῖς χρῆσθαι. καὶ γὰρ τὸν Μολοττὸν 'Αλέξανδρον μετεπέμψαντο...οὐδὲ ἐκείνοις δ' εὐπειθεῖν ἠδύναντο, οὓς ἐπεκαλοῦντο, ἀλλὰ εἰς ἔχθραν αὐτοὺς καθίστασαν.

[1] Or perhaps the course of the Samnite War, begun in 327, drew off the Lucanian forces.

[2] D. XIX. 4, 2. Rhegium itself must therefore have been democratic.

[3] This, if anything, should be the meaning of J. XXII. 1, 14: *Nec contentus quod ex inope repente dives factus esset, piraticam adversus patriam exercuit.* The war around Rhegium would give Agathocles a better scope for roving than his later fighting in Sicily itself. I therefore venture to place Justin's statement here. Justin's own arrangement gives no clue to the order of events.

[4] D. XIX. 4, 3, where as little as possible is made of Agathocles' victory. It is possible that we have a memorial of the deliverance of Rhegium in a

5. AGATHOCLES UNDER THE DEMOCRACY.
c. 322—319 B.C.

Although the popular government was set up, Agathocles was by no means free from difficulty and opposition.
A charge of piracy indeed, no doubt brought against him
by friends of the nobles, fell to the ground. This political
case for which the events of the last war may well have
afforded a pretext, merely shows the comparative strength
of the two parties at the time. Agathocles, who was likely
enough to have preyed on his enemies' ships if he had had
the chance, was bound to be acquitted as long as the
democrats had the upper hand[1].

The real danger however was from outside. Not only
had the nobles raised a strong force of their own, but
Carthage had an army in Sicily taking the oligarchic
side[2].

The Carthaginian government had at last learned that
the old policy of fire and sword only served to rouse the
Greeks to heroic defence. Now a craftier plan of stirring
up discord among her foes afforded Carthage a better
hope of widening her own influence. All the feelings of
the Punic senate were bound to be on the nobles' side, and
it was in their cause that the invading army was acting.

coin published by Larizza, P., *Rhegium Chalcidense*, 109, n. 74. On the
reverse a seated figure of the Demos is recognised, with the inscription
PHΓΙΝΩΝ.

[1] J. XXII. 1, 15 (following the sentence last quoted) *Saluti ei fuit
quod socii capti tortique de illo negaverunt*. The questioning of (I suppose)
Agathocles' slaves implies a regular trial. This must have taken place
when Agathocles was at home and could be punished. Before his first
exile he would have had no occasion for piracy, and after his second exile
no one would have dared to charge him. The present period is therefore
the only time to which the trial can belong. (Cf. Schubert 39. Most
historians have ignored the passage.)

[2] D. XIX. 4, 3 ; Trogus, *Prol.* XXI.

Of the war which followed very little is known. Diodorus merely says that great forces were pitted against

Gela (Terranova); Remains of Temple.

each other, and that Agathocles filled all kinds of posts with unfailing valour and resource[1].

In one case only has a detailed account reached us, telling of a night attack on Gela attempted by Agathocles

---

[1] D. xix. 4, 3 ἐγένοντο κίνδυνοι συνεχεῖς καὶ παρατάξεις ἁδρῶν δυνάμεων, ἐν αἶς Ἀγαθοκλῆς ποτὲ μὲν ἰδιώτης ὤν, ποτὲ δὲ ἐφ᾽ ἡγεμονίας τεταγμένος, ὑπελήφθη δραστικὸς εἶναι καὶ φιλότεχνος ἐκ τοῦ πρὸς ἕκαστον τῶν καιρῶν ἐπινοεῖσθαί τι τῶν χρησίμων. Where in spite of Schubert 41, Holm's translation of ἰδιώτης as "private soldier" (*Gesch. Siciliens*, ii. 222) seems most likely. Schubert finds that this passage of D. is continuous with xix. 3, 4, both belonging to the account friendly to Agathocles (=Duris), while all that lies between came from Timaeus. This is surely carrying ingenuity too far.

and of his hairbreadth escape from the oligarchs who held
the city.   Diodorus relates this as follows,—

"Agathocles broke into the town with 1000 men.   But
Sosistratus' followers met him with a large and well-
ordered force, and turned the party to flight, slaying 400.
The rest were trying to escape through a narrow place,
and had given up hope of safety, when Agathocles unexpectedly saved them.   He had fought heroically himself
and was wounded seven times, nearly fainting from loss of
blood.   Then as the foe pressed on he ordered the buglers
to go to two different parts of the wall and sound for
battle.   This was quickly done, and the attacking army
from Gela could not see the truth in the darkness, but
thought that a fresh force from Syracuse was about to fall
on them from two sides.   They therefore gave up pursuit
and parting into two bodies, ran in the direction of the
call.   Meanwhile Agathocles' men won a respite and made
good their escape into the trench[1]."

The foregoing feat must be taken rather as an example
of the resource and bravery of Agathocles than as a
weighty event in itself.   The issue of the war would
hardly have turned on an attack made with only a
thousand men.   How the war ended is not told, but the
upshot must have been failure for the democrats.   Gela
did not fall, and Agathocles' own credit was shaken.

The Syracusan democrats seem to have been ill pleased
with Agathocles and his conduct of the war.   For this
reason and perhaps because the danger from Carthage
was greater than would appear from extant authorities[2],

[1] On this story see note on p. 94.

[2] In Trogus, *Prol.* xxi., it is even said that the Carthaginians were
besieging Syracuse; but the epitomist confuses the later action of
Hamilcar (cf. *Mortuoque Sosistrato*) with this war.

it was thought fitting to use the last resort of Timoleon's constitution, in seeking from Corinth a dictator and a peacemaker. This at least seems the only possible explanation of the next events. One Acestorides came from Corinth and was voted full powers. Of most of his acts we have no knowledge; he does not seem to have fought against the Carthaginians, but rather tried to reconcile the parties in Syracuse. No doubt all peaceable citizens were weary of the strife, and the commons were quite ready to throw over Agathocles for the sake of quiet. At any rate the banished nobles came home, and Agathocles fled almost alone into the midlands.

A romantic tale was afterwards told of his escape. Acestorides, says Diodorus, wished to murder Agathocles on the road, but Agathocles guessed his plan and out-witted him. He took the slave most like himself in height and looks, gave him his horse to ride and his harness to wear, and sent him out along the highway. Agathocles himself put on beggar's rags and slunk away over pathless places. Now they that came to do the murder judged that the slave was Agathocles; for in the darkness they could not tell the truth. They therefore slew the slave, while the master escaped.

This story, like so many others, is meant to show the cunning and resource of Agathocles in the sorest straits; it cannot be taken as serious history. It is likely enough that Agathocles feared an attempt on his life; but it can hardly be believed that Acestorides ever made it. For one thing if the Syracusans did not object to the banish-ment of Agathocles, they would certainly, had Acestorides so demanded, have allowed his death-sentence in fair trial. Secondly, it must be believed that a man chosen to be a peacemaker at a political crisis, would have borne too high a character to have stooped to murder. Agathocles

T.   4 did perhaps escape in disguise, but the other details were probably added to give point to the story[1].

The flight of Agathocles was naturally followed by the recall of Sosistratus with his party, and by peace with Carthage. The constitution of Timoleon was doubtless restored in outward form, while the reality of power rested with the nobles[2].

6.   AGATHOCLES' SECOND EXILE.
319 (?)—317 B.C.

Agathocles had now made two attempts at gaining a leading place in Syracuse; the first had been thwarted by the jealousy of the nobles, and the second had miscarried through the weakness or moderation of the commons[3]. Now he found himself once more friendless and a wanderer; and it is no wonder that he should have forsworn his old allies, and sought help among his country's foes for plans which henceforward were purely selfish.

The smaller cities of Sicily, chafing under the over-

[1] D. xix. 5, 2 f.   Schubert's view on this ruse has already been mentioned (p. 22).   Without going so far as to agree with him, I would still note that the charge against Acestorides is based on one single piece of evidence, the supposed murder of one slave.   Now this is just such a detail as the story-teller would add to give a dramatic end to his tale. Without this addition the action of Agathocles is cowardly, not to say ridiculous; with it, his course becomes masterly.   I therefore believe that the murder of the slave, and consequently the charge against Acestorides, are both false.

Acestorides is introduced quite casually by Diodorus as some one already well known.   It is quite possible that the regular account of him was to be sought in the lost digression to Book xviii.; for the present chapter is still part of Agathocles' own life, and the annalistic order is not regained until the year 316.

[2] D. xix. 5, 4.

[3] J. xxii. 1, 16 *Bis occupare imperium Syracusanorum voluit, bis in exilium actus est.*

lordship of Syracuse, were not unwilling to make war against her under the command of Agathocles[1]. At Morgantina, his first place of shelter, he was quickly chosen an officer in the army and soon promoted to the rank of general[2]. He then took Leontini[3], and it seems likely that many cities were emboldened by this stroke to rise against their mistress. Syracuse herself was threatened with invasion; but now stoutly guarded by Hamilcar's Carthaginian troops, she defied the attack of Agathocles. The latter, finding himself outnumbered, was obliged to give up the attempt, and resolved to try more peaceful means of settlement. He sent envoys to Hamilcar, begging him to mediate between himself and the Syracusans, and assuring Hamilcar of his own good offices in return for so marked a service.

This offer was instantly accepted. Hamilcar came forward as peacemaker between the Syracusans and the partisans of Agathocles, and the war was at an end. This sudden change of front on Hamilcar's part is one of the strangest events of the times, and it is worth considering what led him to make it.

It is well known that the ruling oligarchy at Carthage was always confronted with an opposition. This party was never effective without a strong leader, but when

[1] Cf. D. xix. 6, 3.

[2] J. xxii. 2, 1 *A Morgantinis, apud quos exulabat, odio Syracusanorum, primo praetor mox dux creatur.* What these ranks in the Morgantian army were is uncertain, perhaps χιλιάρχης and στρατηγός. The other details also come from Justin, *ibid.* Diodorus only says Ἀγαθοκλῆς φυγὰς ὤν, ἰδίαν δύναμιν ἐν τῷ μεσογείῳ συνεστήσατο.

[3] J. *ibid.* § 2. The ruse told in Polyaenus v. 3, 2, which Freeman (iv. 520) places here, must certainly belong to a later date. Freeman's own doubts on the matter leave no uncertainty as to the wrongness of his course. A slaughter of citizens at this stage would have dashed all Agathocles' hopes at a moment when he sorely needed allies. The deed must belong to the time of the final crushing of Sicily (305—4).

such arose there was bound to be some unrest.   Either the
nobles were forced into a forward policy of conquest by
the election of popular soldiers to high commands, or the
people's favourite, after the failure of lawful means,
would be led to plot the overthrow of the government.
To an able general the temptation was strong; the
authorities at home were jealous, and if the war miscarried, he was likely to pay for their mismanagement
with his life.   If he shrank from being a scapegoat, he
was forced to turn traitor[1].

Now Hamilcar was in just such a position as this.   He
had saved Syracuse, but Agathocles with growing forces
was still in the field.   Another campaign might make his
own ground untenable.   The Carthaginian senate no doubt
longed for some ground of charge against him, for the
house of Barca, to which he, like other Hamilcars, seems to
have belonged, had a lasting feud with the nobles.   From
such judges neither justice nor mercy could be expected,
and death on the cross would be the only reward of loyalty
and obedience.   Thus the offer of Agathocles must have
been very tempting, and a secret league was formed
between the two leaders.   Each undertook to lend troops
to the other: and so Agathocles would become undisputed
lord of Syracuse, while Hamilcar could defy his home
government or overthrow it when the fair moment came.
These secret dealings are known only from Justin; still
there is every reason for accepting his version.   Diodorus,
who seems here to be following an account friendly to
Agathocles, does not mention the plot at all; but merely
says that Agathocles was persuaded to come home[2].

Hamilcar thus openly came forward as peace-maker

[1] Most of these points are mentioned by Diodorus in a later chapter,
xx. 10, 2 ff.

[2] J. xxii. 2, 5—7; D. xix. 5, 4.   On these matters see note on page 95.

between Agathocles and the oligarchs. The latter, finding themselves helpless without Punic aid, were obliged to lend ear to his words.

A treaty was made by which the parties were to be reconciled in Syracuse and Agathocles to come home as the leading man in the state. But he was so dreaded by the citizens that it was resolved to secure his loyalty by the most awesome of all pledges. He was taken to the temple of Demeter, the holy emblems were set out, and there he swore to do nothing to overthrow the commonwealth, and to keep the peace with Carthage[1]. He was forthwith elected general and guardian of the peace; he was to hold office until the ill-feeling of factions was laid to rest. Hamilcar then left Agathocles 5000 of his own troops and marched out of the city. Outwardly he might claim to have furthered the Punic cause by his demonstration in Syracuse; for when had a Carthaginian leader stood with his army inside her walls[2]? And had not Agathocles, at his bidding, sworn to stand by the terms of peace? But in truth Hamilcar had given Syracuse a master and Carthage a rival, whose hatred would not long slumber: for an oath in the mouth of Agathocles was worth no more than the broken pledge of Callippus[3].

[1] D. xix. 5, 4; J. xxii. 2, 7—9. The words "*in obsequium Poenorum jurat*" hardly imply more than an undertaking to keep the terms of Timoleon's treaty. (So Niese 433.) If Agathocles had promised submission to Carthage, he must have given hostages and handed over most of his forces. As a matter of fact, he received 5000 men, and was left free to do what he pleased. (Beloch 193 chooses to disbelieve the leaving of the 5000 men, but gives no reasons.)

[2] Once only before this, when Mago was called in to guard the city against Timoleon. Hamilcar's position as arbitrator was far more imposing than Mago's (cf. Freeman iv. 310).

[3] For Callippus cf. Freeman iv. 285.

7.   AGATHOCLES BECOMES RULER OF SYRACUSE.
316 (?) B.C.

Agathocles was now established in Syracuse, but he
could not feel sure of his ground until the forces of
opposition had been crushed. Although the nobles might
no longer dare to speak against him in open assembly,
their clubs and secret meetings were a standing threat to
his power. Syracusan society at this time was honey-
combed by these secret bodies, of which the Six Hundred
was the best known, and Agathocles now resolved to
sweep all such elements of disaffection from the city.

The more wary among the nobles had already fled
with Sosistratus, and Herbita was for the moment their
place of shelter. This town Agathocles made ready to
attack. His former friends from Morgantina and elsewhere found him 3000 men, and he held a levy among the
lowest class of Syracusans. But instead of marching at
once against Herbita he struck the first blow at his foes at
home[1].

Agathocles, as general, had control of the current
business of the state; and, seemingly three days after his
election to office[2], he gave orders to his troops to muster at

---

[1] D. xix. 6. For the date see note below. Cf. J. xxii. 2, 10—12;
Polyaenus v. 3, 8.

Owing to the distance of Herbita from Syracuse, Freeman thinks that
Herbessus may be meant. But the further from Agathocles Sosistratus
could go, the safer he would be.

Of the slaughter which followed all our three authorities have something to say. Diodorus shows great confusion and must have tried to
reconcile a version friendly to Agathocles, which has also been given by
Polyaenus, with another account where the horrors were magnified.
Justin as usual is unfriendly to Agathocles. It is hopeless to try to
reconcile all the statements in detail.

[2] This time can be gathered from Polyaenus v. 3, 7: see note below,
p. 57.

the Timoleonteum on the morrow. He also sent to three of the oligarchic leaders, Tisarchus, Anthropinus and Diocles[1], and appointed them to commands in the march against Herbita[2], desiring them to appear on the morrow in the same place. At the same time an assembly was called to meet in the theatre[3].

The fatal day dawned, and Agathocles, after sending a small body of troops to overawe the assembly, joined the main company at the Timoleonteum. The three oligarchs, fearing nothing, had also come with forty friends[4]. Agathocles rose, and in a fiery harangue charged them with plotting against his own life. His men shouted to him to make no delay in striking down the traitors. Thereupon he bade the trumpet sound[5], and called on the soldiers to slay the guilty and plunder their goods. Hearing the signal the men rushed in upon the oligarchs, and slew all that were there[6].

[1] Polyaenus alone gives all three names: this is enough to prove that he is here following a good guide. He adds that these men were said to have been plotting against Agathocles;—doubtless Agathocles' own excuse for the slaughter.

[2] Polyaenus does not give the name; he says, "to help a city of their alliance against its enemies." This must mean Herbita, and it was natural enough for Agathocles to call the oligarchs the "enemies" of a city hitherto democratic.

[3] The meeting of the assembly, though mentioned only by Justin, seems to be right.

[4] Justin's words, "*contracto in gymnasio senatu*," are most likely put carelessly, meaning the chief oligarchs. By *Gymnasium* he seems to mean the Timoleonteum.

[5] The trumpet-call, mentioned both by Diodorus and by Polyaenus, is rejected by Schubert 53 as a fiction of Duris. The reasons for this course are not very strong.

[6] In Polyaenus 200 nobles, as against Diodorus' 40, are cut down at the first onset. That in the tumult of bloodshed the exact numbers should have been forgotten was likely enough. In Pol. the men are shot down by a shower of darts.

From the Timoleonteum the maddened soldiery
swarmed out into the city, and fell upon all who withstood them or who were suspected of being oligarchs. In
this way at least six hundred of the foremost citizens met
their death[1]. Then the confusion spread, and all Syracuse
was filled with bloodshed and rapine. The soldiers and
rabble no longer knew the guilty from the guiltless, no
shelter was safe, neither age nor sex was respected.
Escape there was none; for Agathocles had let shut the
city gates, and many who tried to leap from the walls
were dashed to the ground[2]. The fall of night only made
the boldness of the destroyers more fiendish. For two days
the slaughter raged until four thousand men had fallen[3].

After these deeds Agathocles ordered into his presence
such oligarchs as had been taken alive. Among these were
some of his bitterest foes; these he put to death, but
Deinocrates, a shifty partisan, who had once been his
friend, he spared. Five or six thousand remaining
enemies were driven from Syracuse and found shelter
at Acragas[4].

[1] This number is mentioned by Polyaenus. Justin, after "*senatum
trucidat*," says, "*ex plebe quoque locupletissimos et promptissimos inter-
ficit*," perhaps meaning the same set of men.

[2] D. xix. 8, 1. This alone is enough to prove that Agathocles had
planned his butchery in deadly earnest.

[3] So Diodorus, *ibid.* The total of Polyaenus only reaches 800. We
thus have the extreme limits, but otherwise the matter is uncertain.
Diodorus, if he followed Timaeus, would give the highest possible number;
and Polyaenus, if he drew from Duris or Callias, the lowest. It seems
clear, however, that the slaughter was immense. (Cf. Polyb. ix. 23,...
Agathocles...δόξας ὠμότατος εἶναι κατὰ τὰς πρώτας ἐπιβολὰς καὶ τὴν
κατασκευὴν τῆς δυναστείας. As this was Agathocles' first stroke of the
kind, the relevance of Polybius' words here cannot be doubted.) The
view of De Sanctis, followed by Beloch, that there was nothing more than
a street fight brought on by the oligarchs, is therefore untenable. (Justin
gives no numbers.)

[4] 5000 in Polyaenus, 6000 in Diodorus xix. 8, 2. Here at least there

Agathocles now called another assembly, and addressed a set speech to his followers[1]. "This," he said, "is the day for which I prayed. The city is purged of her tyrants, and the burgesses can enjoy their freedom undisturbed. My work is done: all I now desire is to rest from toil and to live among you as a private citizen."

So saying he put off his cloak of office, laid aside his sword, and stood before the meeting in civil dress[2]. But the mob, seeing no hope of enjoying their plunder but in the continuance of his rule, shouted in answer that he must not leave them in the lurch. At first Agathocles held his peace: the shouts grew louder, until at last he came forward, and consented to rule, if he might rule alone; he could not, he said, be answerable for the misdeeds of any colleague. The assembly asked nothing better, and at once raised Agathocles to be general with full powers[3].

is no hopeless disagreement. The flight to Acragas, and the shelter afforded there, are mentioned by Diodorus, *ibid*.

[1] The report of this assembly is given by Polyaenus (v. 3, 7) and by Diodorus (xix. 9) in much the same terms. The former puts the last batch of executions and the banishment of the five thousand after the present event. This seems unlikely. Polyaenus says that six days after the meeting Agathocles banished five thousand; so that the writer may be confusing the earlier election of Agathocles as guardian of the peace with his final elevation.

The number of six days may well be sound, and helps in arrangement of the order of events.

[2] I am unwilling to follow Schubert 55 in rejecting these picturesque details as fictions of Duris. With an excitable southern audience a little "posing" would be very effective. A similar proceeding is told of Gelo (D. xi. 26): αὐτὸς δὲ οὐ μόνον τῶν ὅπλων γυμνὸς εἰς τὴν ἐκκλησίαν ἦλθε, ἀλλὰ καὶ ἀχίτων ἐν ἱματίῳ προσελθών...ὥστε μιᾷ φωνῇ πάντας ἀποκαλεῖν εὐεργέτην καὶ σωτῆρα καὶ βασιλέα.

[3] Στρατηγὸς αὐτοκράτωρ.

CHAPTER III.

AGATHOCLES AS A SOLDIER-PRINCE IN SICILY.

THE ghastly means used by Agathocles in grasping supreme power are evïdent enough from the account just given. There is no need to enlarge further on such horrors, and no ingenuity has been able to palliate them. Henceforward the tyrant's sway in Syracuse was unchallenged and he found it easy to wear a look of greater mildness. Agathocles' own nature had less of the calculating cruelty of a despot than of the hasty wrath of a rough soldier. In anger he had a fiendish eagerness for the sight of death and torture; at such times a bloodthirsty fury robbed him of all foresight or care for the outcome of his own deeds. But in calmer moods Agathocles had his generous impulses and a frankness that endeared him to his followers; where nothing crossed his path, the savage nature within might long smoulder unmarked: and in Syracuse at least his worst acts were over[1]. The few nobles still left at home were cowed into silence. The

---

[1] D. xix. 9, 5 f. The passage (Polyb. ix. 23, 2), where it is said that Agathocles, when once his rule over the Sicilians was secure, became the mildest and gentlest of men, can hardly apply to the period now opening. The tyrant's rule was by no means yet safe, and his worst acts of bloodshed are still to be recorded. Polybius seems to be thinking of Agathocles' years of undisputed sway after 304. Thus he does not here confirm the partial statement of Diodorus, which in any case only applies to the prince's behaviour in Syracuse itself.

mob was glutted with plunder, and devoted to a popular ruler. Agathocles had begun his reign by promising a remission of debts and grants of land to the poor, though how far this undertaking was carried out is uncertain. For all democrats he had fair words and a courteous bearing. He did not wear the diadem, and was easy of access to all that sought him. It is even said that he went about the city without a body-guard. This may mean that he contented himself with an escort of common soldiers; he can hardly have been rash enough to walk out altogether unshielded[1].

How far the machinery of the republican government still ran on is again a doubtful point. It is usually taken that the assembly met as before for routine business, and that the wonted officers were elected. This view is quite unwarranted. Diodorus, speaking of later events, says that Agathocles was often escorted by a crowd to the assembly, but went in alone; and that during the meetings he could not refrain from mimicking members of the audience, his sallies of wit delighting his hearers[2]. To say nothing of the trivial nature of the passage, it must be noted that Diodorus says nothing of the activities of the assembly itself, there or anywhere else. It is likely that Agathocles, as the Roman Emperors later did, announced important acts to the people; but all their administrative

[1] This point is again mentioned with other picturesque details in D. xx. 63, 2. In reality no Greek tyrant could have foregone an armed guard without the certainty of losing his life. Either the account is false or the view in the text must be taken. (Beloch here accepts Diodorus, but Schubert and Niese have taken the opposite opinion.)

[2] D. ibid. Freeman iv. 383, boldly argues, on the strength of this one passage, that Agathocles "kept on the usual assemblies of the people."

In D. xx. 4, 6, and perhaps in Polyaenus v. 3, 6, are cases of Agathocles' making announcements to the people.

functions were probably swallowed up in his own office of
general with full powers.

He strengthened the resources of Syracuse, the revenue
was carefully husbanded, arms were made ready, and new
ships of war set building. The new despotism was above
all things military[1].

1. AGATHOCLES' WAR AGAINST THE GREEK CITIES. 316—314.

For nearly two years after Agathocles' elevation he
was busy with small wars and intrigues with the lesser
towns of the Sicilian midlands—a tiresome undertaking
that gave no opening for great deeds. Some of the cities
had already been in league with him, and may have bowed
to his rule without more ado: the others were easily
crushed[2]. No details are known. Hamilcar, who was still
in Sicily, naturally let Agathocles work his will.

At this time the three cities that had set themselves
most firmly against the power of the prince, were Gela,
Acragas, and Messena. In these the banished nobles
were sheltering, and when the smaller towns were crushed,
it was their turn to feel the tyrant's hand.

Messena was the first object of his attack[3]. He had
a Messenian outpost in his power, and undertook to
give it up for thirty talents of silver. The money was
paid, but Agathocles, so far from handing over the stronghold, made ready a surprise-force to strike at Messena

---

[1] D. xix. 9, 7; J. xxii. 3, 1.

[2] D. xix. 9, 7 προσελάβετο δὲ καὶ τῶν ἐν τῷ μεσογείῳ χωρίων καὶ πόλεων
τὰς πλείστας. This would include both conquest and peaceful acquisition.
Cf. J. xxii. 3, 1 *finitimas civitates nihil hostile metuentes ex improviso
aggreditur.*

[3] All the details come from D. xix. 65.

herself.   Hearing that part of the city walls was in ruin,
he took a squadron of ships and fell on his foes by night.
But the Messenians had news of his plan and the stroke
failed.   He then sailed off to Mylae, where the guard,
after a short siege, opened the gates; and, satisfied with
this small success, Agathocles went home to Syracuse.

All this seems to have happened in the early spring;
and about the time of harvest, Agathocles took fresh
forces and pitched near Messena.   He led his men to
attack the city; but the storming parties were beaten
back again and again, for the exiles from Syracuse, who
helped to man the walls, fought with desperate bravery,
being nerved by their fierce hatred of the tyrant.   Meanwhile an embassy from Carthage landed and called upon
Agathocles to give up his siege.   His action was contrary
to Timoleon's treaty[1], and he was now bidden to hand
over the stronghold which he had wrongfully withheld,
and to withdraw to Syracuse.   Agathocles, still unready to
risk going to war with Carthage, was forced to obey.   He
withdrew to the allied city of Abacaenum[2], where the
hope of Punic help may have made his enemies restless.
To crush any stirrings of revolt, he took the strong
measure of taking forty leading citizens on a bare
suspicion of treason, and putting them all to death.

In the following year the outcasts at Acragas, and
other foemen of Agathocles, made a determined stand

----

[1] Diodorus says παραβαίνοντι τὰς συνθήκας : and Timoleon's treaty,
which as we have seen (p. 53) Agathocles most likely swore to observe,
and which guaranteed the freedom of the Greek cities, is doubtless meant
here (so Niese 436).   Schubert refers it to a treaty between Messena and
Agathocles; but this is less likely.

It is worth noting that Hamilcar took no part in thwarting Agathocles.
It was in fact the doing of the opposite party (senatorial) in Carthage
itself.

[2] The site is near the modern Tripi.

against his growing power[1]. They persuaded the Acragantine assembly to declare war and to join in league with Gela and Messena. A tried leader of unswerving truth was not to be found in Sicily, so some of the exiles were sent to Sparta to find another deliverer for western Greece. At Sparta they found a young soldier who was ready enough for adventure abroad. This was Acrotatus, the son of Cleomenes[2]. He had incurred the bitterest hatred of the Spartans by speaking against the remission of disgrace for the survivors of the Lamian war. For this bigotry he had been roughly handled by some of the runaways, and lived in fear of his life. The offer of a command abroad gave him grounds for leaving Sparta with honour, and he was so eager to sail that he started without even asking the ephors' leave.

His small squadron was driven up the Adriatic to Apollonia, which he found beleaguered by Glaucias, king of Illyria. His coming raised the siege, and Glaucias was induced to make peace[3].

Acrotatus then sailed to Tarentum, and urged the people to join with him in freeing Syracuse from Agathocles. The Tarentines listened readily to a prince of the royal blood of Sparta, and voted twenty ships to help in his undertaking. Acrotatus did not wait for this reinforcement, but hastened on to Acragas, where the full command was put in his hands[4].

Great things were hoped from his leadership, and his own boasting seemed to foretell the speedy overthrow of Agathocles. But all came to nothing. Acrotatus, as his

---

[1] D. xix. 70.

[2] For Acrotatus cf. Paus. iii. 6, 1; Plut. *Agis* 3. The tale in Plut. *Apophth. Lac.*, *s.v.* Acrotatus, may be an indication of his headstrong nature.

[3] D. *ibid.*   [4] D. xix. 71.

past record might have led men to expect, was high-handed and overbearing. His success in the field was trifling, and he was more dreaded by his followers than by his foes.

Men said that his character, unused to the temptations of luxury, became corrupt; that he lived more as a Persian than a Spartan, wasting the war-funds in feasting and amusement. How far the blame should rest on Acrotatus, and how much was provoked by the disobedience or invented by the hatred of the allies, cannot be settled [1]. The failure of Acrotatus alone is certain. At last he quarrelled with Sosistratus and had him stabbed as he sat at meat. This was the final blow. The allies met, and deposed Acrotatus from the command; then the mob made as if they would stone him, so that he had to flee for his life. He slipped away one night and sailed home to Sparta. Tarentum recalled her ships when she heard that the Spartan leader was gone, and the Sicilians gave up the struggle as hopeless [2].

Hamilcar once more came forward as peace-maker, and again furthered the cause of Agathocles. He took Heracleia, Selinus, and Himera in the name of Carthage, and it was agreed that the rest of the Greek cities were to

---

[1] D. *ibid.* Beloch holds that in view of Acrotatus' acts at Sparta the truth may have been that his discipline was too strict for the allies, who therefore turned against him. This may be right, but would not palliate the murder of Sosistratus. Diodorus gives here his note on the character of Sosistratus already quoted (p. 38).

[2] The whole war is summed up by Justin xxII. 3, 2 *Poenorum quoque socios, permittente Hamilcare, foede vexat.* This does not refer to the Phoenician cities; Agathocles as Hamilcar's friend had not so far touched them. The reference is to Acragas and the other Greek cities with whose oligarchic governments Carthage was officially in alliance.

Acrotatus himself had evidently nothing to do with making the peace: it was his flight that led to it.

be free under the overlordship of Syracuse. This was
another way of saying that the league of Gela, Messena,
and Acragas was broken up, and that Agathocles could
crush them in detail and at his leisure.

2.   OUTBREAK OF THE WAR AGAINST CARTHAGE.
313—312.

For the moment the allies yielded; but they sent
messages to Carthage, bitterly complaining of Hamilcar's
double-dealing and of his desertion of their cause. "The
tyranny of Agathocles," they said, "is less galling than the
treason of Hamilcar. By his pretended mediation he has
left your allies at the mercy of their deadliest foes. He
began by allying himself with Syracuse, your oldest and
fiercest rival, and now by this treaty of peace the cities of
your allies are enslaved to the same master."

The Carthaginian government, which may have been
too much hampered by party strife at home to take earlier
action against its disobedient general, was fully alive to
the danger involved in such growth of Agathocles' power.
At such a perilous moment, hidden counsels were deemed
the wisest, and a secret vote was taken on the fate of
Hamilcar. The government did not even dare to publish
the award until Hamilcar, son of Gisgo, another officer
from Sicily, should have reached Carthage with his
tidings. Whether Hamilcar himself would have gone
home to stand his trial, or whether he would have dared to
defy his own government and risk a civil war, can only be
guessed. Death carried him off in the midst of the crisis,
and saved the Carthaginian senate from the need of
knowing its own mind[1].

[1] All these details rest solely on Justin XXII. 3. All Diodorus says is
that the Carthaginians were displeased with Hamilcar about the treaty

Agathocles for the time being had a free hand in Sicily. But the death of Hamilcar and the attitude of the Carthaginian government warned him that fresh trouble from that quarter would soon arise. He therefore raised a body of 10,000 picked mercenaries, and 3500 horsemen, besides the regular forces of Syracuse and her allies; and made ready arms of all kinds.

The war in Sicily was carried on with great vigour: it must have consisted mainly of small sieges, of which no account has reached us. By the end of 313 nearly all the Greek states were in the prince's power[1].

In the next year Agathocles felt himself strong enough to strike at Messena. That city had long been a rallying-point for outcasts and malcontents of all kinds, and it was of the utmost weight for Agathocles to make short work of so dangerous an enemy, before the war with Carthage broke out again.

His plans were craftily laid. He first sent Pasiphilus with a strong force to make a sudden inroad into the land of Messena. Much booty and many prisoners were taken, and Pasiphilus then called on the besieged to give up the Syracusan oligarchs and to make peace.

The Messenians, who were now suffering in a cause not their own, lent ear to the proposals, which were

(XIX. 72, 2). Historians who, like Beloch (III. 1, 193), hold that Hamilcar was loyal to his own government and merely made a scapegoat, have to explain away the clear sense of Justin. The report of Hamilcar, son of Gisgo, was not about the conduct of Hamilcar, for the vote on him had already been cast. It must have related to the strength of Hamilcar's position, and to the advisability of publishing the award, and, if need were, of enforcing the sentence. Some of these points are discussed by Schubert 63 ff. (v. note on p. 95, below).

[1] D. XIX. 72, 1. Acrotatus had fled in 314; the present sentence of Diodorus covers the whole of 313, which must have been spent mainly in these small sieges.

enforced by the arrival of Agathocles himself with fresh troops[1].

The story of these dealings is enriched by a pleasing anecdote[2].

One Megacles had long been a bitter foe of Agathocles; he had warred against him in mid-Sicily, and even set a price on the tyrant's head. Now when Messena was besieged, Agathocles called on the citizens to hand over to him Megacles who was sheltering there; otherwise, he said, he would storm the city and enslave the burgesses. Megacles did not fear death, and said that he would go himself and treat with Agathocles. When he was brought before the prince he said: "I am come, Agathocles, as an envoy from Messena and I am ready to face death. First however call thy friends that ye may hear the charge of the Messenians." Then Agathocles called his friends, and Megacles pleaded for Messena, saying that no man did wrong to fight for his own country: "Wouldst not thou, Agathocles, fight for Syracuse if the Messenians lay under her walls?" At this the prince smiled, and some friends of Megacles persuaded him to spare the envoy and to make peace with Messena.

Peace in this case meant little less than surrender. The gates were opened, and Agathocles marched in with his troops. He used fair words to all; and the Messenians, who had already sent away the Syracusan outcasts, were now induced to take back their own. Many of these had been banished from Messena in course of law, and had since taken service under Agathocles[3].

The tyrant then threw off the mask; he summoned all

[1] D. xix. 102.

[2] Polyaenus v. 15. Although all the details of this tale may not be true, the main account is not unlikely.

[3] D. *ibid.*

his political enemies from Messena and Tauromenium, and
slaughtered them in cold blood to the number of six
hundred.

Among the Tauromenians that escaped from this
butchery may have been the young Timaeus. We know
that he was banished by Agathocles, and fled to Athens,
where he never forgot the cruelty of his country's
oppressor[1].

The Messenians now bitterly rued their mistake; for
by trusting to the fair words of the prince, they had lost
their best citizens, and recalled their worst[2]. But it was
too late for further resistance; Messena was crushed.

Agathocles then resolved to fall upon Acragas; but at
that moment a fleet from Carthage came in sight, sixty
ships in all. These saved the town, and Agathocles had to
be content with an inroad into Punic Sicily, which land,
now that Hamilcar was gone, he no longer cared to
respect. He took a few strongholds and gathered much
booty[3].

The sight of the Carthaginian fleet raised the hopes of
Agathocles' enemies. They now saw that the policy of
Hamilcar had been disowned, and if they could only hold
out for a few months, the help of an overwhelming force

[1] Polybius merely says that Timaeus was banished by Agathocles, and
as he was a native of Tauromenium, the view above given is not unlikely
(cf. Schubert 68). But cf. above, p. 12, n. 2.

E. Pais, *Ancient Italy*, 157, would bring into connexion with these
events the ruse in Pol. v. 3, 6. See p. 87 below.

[2] Diodorus is here following a source unfriendly to Agathocles: the
words used of the recalled exiles, τοὺς ἐπὶ κακουργίᾳ καταδεδικασμένους,
are no doubt too sweeping. Many of them must have been democrats
ousted for party reasons. Besides the 600 killed, many oligarchs must
have fled, so that Agathocles could safely leave the city under its restored
popular government.

[3] D. xix. 102, 8.

might be expected. Urgent messages were sent to
Carthage, begging the government to trifle with Agathocles no longer[1].

Meanwhile Deinocrates took the lead of the available
forces, now strengthened by the outcasts from Acragas,
and a desultory warfare began in midland Sicily.   Centuripa[2] was in the hands of Agathocles; but now some of the
citizens sent to Deinocrates, and offered to betray the
place, if the state might afterwards be allowed its freedom.
Deinocrates sent Nymphodorus with a few soldiers for
a surprise attack.   They broke into the town by night,
but the alarm was given, and the guard fell upon the
party, killing Nymphodorus, and such of his party as
were caught within the walls.   When Agathocles heard
the news, he came to Centuripa, and, accusing the citizens
of treason, had all suspects put to the sword.

The Carthaginian fleet, finding that Acragas was no
longer threatened, had sailed on to the great Harbour of
Syracuse.   Although they were fifty sail, they did nothing
more daring than to attack two freight-ships: one of
these, an Athenian, they sank, and the crews of both were
taken and had their hands cut off.   This cruelty did not go
unpunished; for Agathocles' captains took some of the
Carthaginian ships off the Bruttian coast, and treated
their sailors as they had treated the Greeks.   This of
course was meant as a repayment in kind, such harshness
not being usual among the Greeks: but Diodorus speaks of
it as a special judgment of heaven on the Carthaginians[3].

Deinocrates, in no way downhearted from his failure at
Centuripa, now put his whole forces on the march for

---

[1] D. XIX. 103.   [2] Now Centuripe or popularly Centorbi.

[3] Diodorus in this pious sentiment may be following Timaeus, who
was very much given to such remarks.   Caesar (as noted by Grote)
punished some of the Gallic " rebels " in the same way (B.G. VIII. 44).

another enterprise[1]. He had been called in by the enemies
of Agathocles in Galaria[2], and with his host, given at 3000
foot and 2000 horse[3], he threw himself into the city, and
drove out the partisans of the prince. He then pitched
outside the walls and awaited the coming of Agathocles'
army. The Syracusan leaders, Pasiphilus and Demophilus, forthwith marched up with 5000 men, whereupon
Deinocrates and Philonides, sharing the command, hastened
to give battle. Both sides fought in the old Greek way,
the whole line going into action at once. The balance was
even, until Pasiphilus, who seems to have been posted on
the right with the pick of the Syracusan troops, routed
Philonides' men and slew their leader. Deinocrates was
thus threatened in the flank and had to withdraw[4]. Many
of the oligarchs were cut down in trying to flee, and
Galaria was left open to the tyrant's troops. Pasiphilus
marched into the city, and it is stated that he punished all
who had shared in the revolt. This can hardly mean less
than the slaughter or banishment of most of the nobles.

The Carthaginians had been gathering their forces in
the meantime, and now took up a position on Mount

[1] D. xix. 104.

[2] Now Gagliano. The place was not betrayed, as Schubert 70 believes,
but the secession was openly resolved upon, and the friends of Agathocles
naturally fled when they saw Deinocrates coming.

[3] The large number of horse is not easy to explain. Either (1) there
were among the exiles many wealthy men who served on horseback
(Holm), or (2) Deinocrates, in making a surprise attack, left most of his
foot-men behind (Schubert). But in this case these would have marched
up later. Or (3) the number of horse is corrupt.

[4] The fighting here is not on the lines of Epaminondas' tactics, but
in the old Greek way. Each army puts its best troops on the right, and
whichever right can be the first to rout the weaker troops facing it, is
bound to win the day by taking the enemy's still unvictorious right wing
in the flank.

Ecnomus[1]. This point was the chief height on the southern coast of Sicily, it had a good landing-place near, it was within striking-distance of Gela, and it overlooked the road from there to Acragas. From this stronghold the Punic army secured the last refuge of the oligarchs against any Syracusan attack.

Although the summer was nearly over, Agathocles marched down southwards and offered battle to the Carthaginians. But the latter, who were awaiting fresh forces in the spring, did not choose to hurry on the encounter: and Agathocles, seeing that they would not come forth, withdrew to Syracuse, and hung up his spoils in the chief temples like a conqueror[2].

3.   THE CAMPAIGN OF THE HIMERAS.   311.

Carthage had spent the winter in gathering stores and raising forces with the utmost vigour, and by the spring she had a huge army ready to take the field[3]. A hundred and thirty warships had been fitted out, and now put to sea. The army was made up of 2000 Carthaginian citizens, many of noble birth, 10,000 Africans, 1000 hired soldiers and 200 war-chariots from Etruria, and 1000 Balearic slingers[4]. Hamilcar, son of Gisgo, one of the leading men in Carthage at the time, was in command.

[1] Now Monte Cufino above Licata. The geography of this part will be spoken of below. Ecnomus was the traditional site of the brazen bull of Phalaris: D. xix. 108, 1.

[2] D. xix. 104 *fin.*

[3] D. xix. 106. The careful details of the numbers, and the note of the public mourning (see p. 71), must have come from a good authority. The custom has already been mentioned by Diodorus xi. 24. Speaking of the behaviour of Carthage after the war against Gelo, he says: ἥ τε πόλις ἐπένθησε κοινῇ. It will be seen that many of these Carthaginian uses were a matter of common knowledge among the Greeks.

[4] The common reading is ζευγίππαι, but ζευγῖται, "cars," is more likely. (So Niese 442.)

The host set sail with fleet and convoy; but on the high seas a storm sprang up, in which 60 men-of-war and 200 corn-ships are said to have been sunk. Many of the leading citizens were drowned, so that Carthage hung her walls with black, and mourned for her lost sons.

Hamilcar at last landed his men, and took over the troops already in the island. The allies sent their contingents, and fresh mercenaries were hired, until the total reached 40,000 foot and 5000 horse. Hamilcar's vigour in command went far to hearten the allies, and struck terror into the minds of his foemen[1].

A piece of ill luck befell Agathocles at the beginning of the campaign. Twenty of his ships were sailing in the strait of Messena, when part of the Carthaginian fleet fell upon them and took them all[2].

The nearness of the Carthaginian host made Agathocles fearful of treason among his subjects. It was above all things needful for him to make sure of Gela, for the field of war was to be the plain of the Himeras, and Gela would have to serve him as a base.

This city had lately been at peace with Agathocles, although no guard of his was quartered there. Still no doubt the old hatred rankled in his mind. His actions are thus related: "Agathocles resolved to secure Gela by a garrison, but did not dare to lead a force into it openly, fearing to be forestalled by the Geloans, who only wanted an excuse to revolt....He therefore sent in his soldiers a few at a time, on one errand or another, until their numbers were more than a match for the burgesses. Soon after he came himself, and charged the Geloans with

[1] D. xix. 106 *fin.*

[2] D. xix. 107, 2. This section breaks into the account of the punishment of Gela, which is taken up in § 3. Diodorus may here be using different sources. Gela had not fought against Agathocles since 314.

treason, either because they really had some idea of the kind, or because Agathocles had listened to the slander of exiles, or because he wanted to raise money. He then slew more than four thousand of them and took their goods. He ordered all the other Geloans to bring in all their money and all the uncoined gold and silver, threatening to punish the disobedient. The Geloans in terror did as he bade, and in this way Agathocles got plenty of money and overawed all the states subject to him[1]."

In relating the punishment of Gela as a long-planned stroke carried out by a ruse, Diodorus seems to have placed the action of Agathocles in a false light. If the prince had suspected treason it would have been misguided ingenuity to send a few troops at a time into the city on various pretexts, for such an air of secrecy would have alarmed the Geloans and probably thrown them into the arms of Carthage. The fact that the Geloans, with the Carthaginian army at their doors all the winter, made no attempt to revolt, is enough to show their loyalty to Agathocles; and it is not likely that he doubted this until his own arrival in the city. He sent on his troops in detachments, as he naturally would, to the city that was to be his headquarters. The Geloans readily admitted them as friends, and not until Agathocles came did he find any signs of discontent. Perhaps the quartering of the soldiers on the Geloans, or the fear of a heavy war-tax, made the people restless, and Agathocles, as his way was, made such murmurs an excuse for a slaughter. The number of victims is perhaps overstated[2].

Leaving a strong guard in Gela, Agathocles marched

[1] D. xix. 108, 5.

[2] Schubert 74 holds that this supposed trick of Agathocles was a fiction of Duris. He makes the mistake of supposing that Gela was already garrisoned, while, as Niese 442 rightly notes, it was a free ally of

out and pitched his camp on Mount Phalarium, where the old king Phalaris once had a fort; the Carthaginians had their old position Ecnomus, likewise formerly a post of Phalaris, five miles away. The river Himeras, now Salso, flowed between the two camps.

The fight now to be related was one of the most memorable in Sicilian history: even the prosaic Diodorus rises to the occasion, and gives us an account not altogether unworthy to compare with the great battle-pieces of the older historians. His version therefore will be translated as it stands, and the difficulties arising therefrom can be taken later[1].

It had been foretold that a great number of men would fall in the coming fight, and therefore neither side dared strike the first blow, until a mere chance brought on the battle[2].

"The Libyans kept overrunning their enemies' land, and this emboldened Agathocles to send his own men out foraging. One day the Greeks were bringing in their plunder, and had driven off one of the baggage-beasts from the Carthaginian camp, when the Carthaginians rushed out from the stockade in pursuit.

Agathocles, foreseeing what would happen, set a picked body of his bravest men in ambush along the river. So as the Carthaginians chased the foragers and followed them across the stream, the liers-in-wait leaped up from their hiding, fell on the disordered foe, and routed them easily. While the Carthaginians were being cut down or

Agathocles. I believe that the facts are rightly given by Diodorus, but that he misunderstood the motives of Agathocles. Gela, as the large finds of vases in the burial-ground prove, was a populous city, and 4000 is not an impossible number of victims.

[1] D. xix. 108, 109.

[2] Schubert calls this "eine Local-tradition," which arose *after* the fight, and was recorded by the pious Timaeus. I doubt this.

were fleeing to their own camp, Agathocles, who now
thought that the moment for decisive action had come, led
out his whole force to attack the enemy's position. He fell
on them unexpectedly, quickly filled in part of the trench,
tore up the stockade, and threw himself forcibly into the
camp.

The surprise was complete.   Having no time to form in

Licata Summit.

battle-line, the Carthaginians had to fight whatever foe
they found in front of them. A fierce struggle raged
about the trench: and soon the ground was strewn with
dead bodies.   For the foremost of the Carthaginian army,
seeing the camp on the brink of capture, came up to the
rescue: while Agathocles' men were heartened by their
first success; and the hope of ending the war by one day's
risk lent fury to their attack on the Carthaginians.

But when Hamilcar saw that his own men were being overpowered, as more and more Greeks kept pouring into the camp, he brought up the slingers from the Balearic isles—a force not less than a thousand men. These slingers launched a shower of heavy stones at the foe, wounding many, hitting some and slaying them outright, while most of the assailants had their defensive armour battered in. The Balearic slingers, accustomed to throw stones of a pound weight, and trained from childhood to the use of their weapon, were a most important arm in face of danger.

In this way the Greeks were worsted and driven out of the camp. Again Agathocles' men tried to storm the position from other points: and once more the camp was in the very act of capture, when an unawaited force from Libya arrived by sea to help the Carthaginians. Therefore the defenders of the camp went on with their hand-to-hand fight with fresh courage, and the new comers began to surround the Greeks. This unexpected blow quickly turned the scale. The Greeks fled, some to the river Himeras, others to the camp, forty furlongs away. The middle space was flat, and the Carthaginian horsemen, in number at least 5000, followed in hot chase. In this way the whole field was covered with dead.

The river itself helped in the destruction of the Greeks. The season was near the dog-days, and the pursuit came about noon: many of the Greeks therefore were maddened with thirst owing to the heat and the exhaustion of flight, so that they drank greedily of the water, brackish as it was; with the result that as many dead were found unwounded by the river as had been cut down in the chase. About five hundred Carthaginians were slain in the fight, but of the Greeks there fell no less than seven thousand."

The chief points needing consideration in this account are the following: (1) The forces. (2) The field of battle. (3) The plans of the two leaders. (4) The fight.

(1) *The Forces.* Hamilcar, as already said, had 40,000 foot and 5000 horse. The latter number is again mentioned by Diodorus in speaking of the flight of the Greeks. Agathocles had raised a picked body of hired soldiers, 10,000 foot and 3500 horse[1], besides these he had the contingents of the allies. These may have amounted to a fairly large force, for in 317 the small inland towns sent Agathocles 3000 men[2]. It is indeed stated that his forces were fewer than those of Carthage, but in view of the equality of the struggle until the fresh troops poured into the field, we cannot place his army below 30,000 foot and 3500 horse.

(2) *The Field of Battle.* The place of encounter depends first of all on the place assigned to Gela. The common view was that it answered to the modern Terranova, but as early as 1753 Pizzolanti proposed to move the site westward to the modern Licata. This view has been adopted by Schubert. The chief grounds for holding it consist in the finding of four inscriptions at Licata which speak of the " People of the Geloans." Two of these are later than the overthrow of Gela by the Mamertines after the death of Agathocles. The Geloans had been given a new home by Phintias, and settled in the city that bore his name; but there is no reason why they may not have called themselves by their old name in official documents. The two other inscriptions, which are earlier, may have been rescued from the fall of Gela, and carried to Phintias, which the common view places at Licata.

---

[1] D. xix. 72, 2.   [2] D. xix. 6, 3.

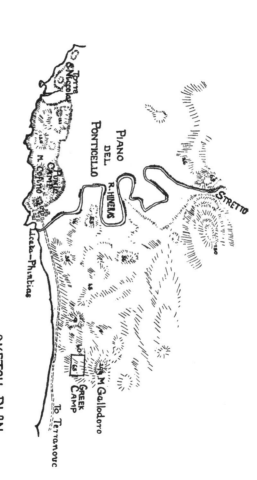

SCALE OF KILOMETRES.

SKETCH-PLAN
OF THE BATTLE OF THE
HIMERAS.

Torre S.Nicola

PIANO
DEL
PONTICELLO

M. Cofino

Licata-Phintias

R. HIMERAS

STRETTO

M.Gallodoro

Greek
Camp

To Terranova

The ancient remains found at Terranova prove that a city of some size stood there. At the eastern end of the long hill are the ruins of a massive Doric temple of the sixth or early fifth century[1]. On the western side a large burial-ground has been found, which has yielded many hundreds of vases. Some of these are now in the Museum at Syracuse, others in a large private collection in Terranova. The vases range from the black-figured to the later red-figured styles. These finds are just what would have been expected from a city that flourished in the fifth and fourth centuries, and fell in the third. On the other hand the few remains at Licata, chiefly Helle-nistic houses, and a large vaulted tank, do not point to any important settlement there in the fourth and fifth centuries. It may be added that Pizzolanti was himself a man of Licata, and his contentions ought not to be taken too seriously[2].

Schubert's remaining arguments rest on the events of the fight itself, and will be seen to be based on a mis-understanding of the site.

The camp of Hamilcar being above Licata, on Monte Cufino and the neighbouring heights, it follows that Aga-thocles would have pitched on Monte Gallodoro, a long and rather gentle slope, the highest point of which is in fact about five miles from Monte Cufino. Agathocles, in other words, found the enemy encamped in the strongest position in the neighbourhood, and took the next best for himself. Pizzolanti, having made Gela equal Licata, places Mount Ecnomus on Torre S. Niccola, the next height to the west. He then puts the camp of Agathocles

[1] Compare the view on page 47.

[2] Grote, Freeman, Holm, Meltzer, Beloch and Niese are all against Pizzolanti; as also is Schubring in his important geographical article *Rhein. Mus.* xxviii. (1873) 67 ff.

much further north, at a place called Racalmallina, north
of the Stretto, or narrow cleft through which the Himeras
(Salso) flows out into the plain. The river mentioned in
the battle-piece is not, he says, the Salso proper, but
a western arm of it flowing into the sea just east of
Torre S. Niccola. The objections to this are: (1) A narrow
gorge like the Stretto, which to-day does not seemingly
allow more than a mule-path to thread it, would be an
obstacle with which no general would hamper himself
willingly. It would have made advance slow and flight
disastrous. (2) This same gorge led to nowhere; while
for Agathocles to pitch in that neighbourhood would have
meant leaving the way to Syracuse open, save for the
paltry barrier of the guard in Gela.   (3) Pizzolanti in
claiming that the river can be forded easily near the
Stretto, overlooks the fact that in summer it is equally
passable much lower down.   (4) The "right arm" of the
Salso does not appear in the Italian staff-map; and from
the highest point above Licata, from which the whole
plain can be seen, I could not descry it. It may therefore
be taken that Diodorus in speaking of the Himeras meant
the principal stream of that name, and not a small brook
of which no one ever heard.   (5) Although, as Schubert
says, there is more flat ground west of the Himeras than
east of it, yet it is quite clear that the grassy slopes of
Monte Gallodoro would not have checked the pursuit
of the Punic horse.   (6) Schubert claims that his arrangement affords a clue to the meaning of Diodorus in men-
tioning two different lines of flight taken by the Greeks :
"They fled, some to the river Himeras, others to the
camp."   His explanation is; some fled along the brook
(the "right arm of the river"), others across the brook
to Licata-Gela. But if Diodorus really meant this, it
would have been strange to express it so indirectly.

Again this brook, if it existed, must have been quite dry in summer, and would not have tempted anyone to reckless drinking. (7) If Gela was so near, it is not easy to see why Agathocles did not shelter there instead of letting the Carthaginians chase him over five miles of level ground.

The following account seems more likely. Agathocles camped on Mount Gallodoro. In marching on the Carthaginians he did not take a straight line, for two reasons. (1) The mouth of the Himeras becomes choked up in summer owing to the silt; the stream forms a deep and very brackish pool near the sea, but about a mile and a half higher up it can easily be forded. (2) The natural place to attack the height of Licata was not the steep face near the mouth of the river, but the much gentler slope on the northern side.

Agathocles in attacking from this side could not of course see the Carthaginians sail up and put their men ashore. But Hamilcar, who must have had a watcher on the hill-top, cannot have been unaware of their coming. Where this surprise-force landed is uncertain. I believe that the ships were coasting along from Punic Sicily, and that Hamilcar may have signalled to them to land between Monte Cufino and Torre S. Niccola, and so to march round and take the Greeks in the rear. The flight of the Greeks is then easily explained : those that had any presence of mind made for the ford by which they had already crossed earlier in the day, hoping thus to regain their camp. But the Punic horse gave chase, and on the grassy slopes of Gallodoro naturally wrought fearful havoc. The rest, maddened by fright and thirst, rushed to the nearest point of the river, where it was deep and heavily salt. There many died either from exhaustion, from drowning, or from the deadly draught

of brackish water.   A few perhaps may have swum over
and reached Gela or the camp in safety[1].

(3)   *The Plans of the Two Leaders.*   That Hamilcar,
who knew that fresh troops were on the way to join him,
should not have wished to hurry on a battle, is natural.
It remains to be seen what led Agathocles to attack when
he did.   He doubtless knew that more Carthaginian

Licata ; harbour, and mouth of the Himeras (Salso).

troops might at any moment be coming, but he probably
miscalculated the time of their landing.   If he did know
this, he must have reckoned on taking the Carthaginian
camp before the new danger threatened.   But in that

[1] For much of the geographical information here used, I am indebted
to the kindness of H.B.M. Vice-Consul at Licata, Cav. A. Verderame,
who supplied me with valuable data on my visit there in February, 1906.

case he would hardly have forgotten to detach a small covering-force to check the new comers. His plan of ambushing a Carthaginian foraging-party was not intended to " mask" his attack, which it could not possibly have done[1], but to draw the enemy down to the plain to help their own men. Hamilcar however followed the wiser course of letting the Greeks attack him in his stronghold, and not coming out until he was sure of winning.

(4)   *The Fight*. According to Diodorus, the Carthaginians were taken by surprise. This I believe to be a mere inference, and a wrong one. The Greeks looked to their foe to form line and charge down the hill, and when instead they were allowed to reach the outworks of the camp, they naturally fancied that their onslaught was unexpected. But as a matter of fact Hamilcar's aim was to hold the Greeks in play until the fresh forces arrived : to have beaten them off too soon would have spoilt his plan. For the moment some of the Carthaginians may have been staggered by the fury of the onset, but Hamilcar was ready and brought up the arm best fitted to use the advantage of the hillside—his Balearic slingers. The Carthaginians only lost 500 men in the whole fight; and the smallness of this number proves that the defence of the camp cannot have been such a desperate matter as Diodorus believed. The Greeks seem to have thought after their victory at the Crimisus that they were bound to surpass the Carthaginians in hand-to-hand fighting; Hamilcar respected his foes, and laid his plans accordingly. We shall not be wrong in seeing in him one of the greatest of Carthaginian generals, by whose masterly

[1] Cf. Schubert 79. If he means that the whole Greek host could march over five miles of open country without being noticed by the Carthaginian generals, I cannot agree with him.

tactics the headlong rashness of Agathocles was fatally overreached.

How the fresh troops landed and assailed the Greek rear, has already been seen.   It is however uncertain why the Greek horse, which might have shielded the foot-soldiers in their flight, took little or no part in the battle.   Possibly the Greek knights, who in any case can hardly have shared in the assault on the Punic camp, rode off the field without delay, when they saw that the day was lost; for it is specially recorded in another place that nearly all of them survived[1].

The number of fallen on the side of Agathocles is scarcely overstated, for he was quite unable to fight in the open or to control his allies after his defeat[2].

4.   AFTER THE FIGHT.   311—310.

Agathocles had no longer any means of keeping the field, but at once set fire to his camp and threw himself into Gela[3].   There he was cheered by a trifling success. Three hundred Carthaginian horse on a false report that Agathocles had gone to Syracuse, rode up to Gela, hoping to be welcomed as friends.   There however they were all shot down[4].

The road to Syracuse was still open, but Agathocles waited in Gela, hoping to keep Hamilcar busy in the

[1] D. xx. 4, 2.

[2] The battle is briefly mentioned by Justin xxii. 3, 9 in these words : *Prima igitur illi cum Hamilcare, Gisgonis filio, proelii congressio fuit : a quo victus, majori mole reparaturus bellum Syracusas concessit.*   The second clause will be discussed below.

[3] D. xix. 110.

[4] Diodorus *ibid.* says that Agathocles had himself spread the false report to ensnare the enemy.   This I should think is rightly held by Schubert 84 to be a fiction of Duris.

neighbourhood until the Syracusan harvest, already delayed by the campaign, should be safely stored in the
city[1]. Perhaps too he feared to march out until his troops
had somewhat mended after their defeat.

Hamilcar indeed could have spared enough men to
harry the Syracusan harvesters and yet have been able
to hold Agathocles. But he had no wish to attack
Syracuse. Finding Gela too strong to take, he began
to bring the other Greek states to his side, hoping no
doubt that the revolt of Agathocles' subjects would soon
save Carthage from the need of any more fighting.

After personally visiting[2] and bringing over some
smaller places, and proclaiming freedom and good-will
to the Greeks, Hamilcar was met by envoys from Camarina, Leontini, Catana, and Tauromenium with offers of
alliance. Then from further-off Messena and Abacaenum
the same message came. In fact "the cities vied with
one another in going over to Hamilcar; such was the
outburst of feeling on the part of the commons after the
defeat, owing to their hatred of Agathocles[3]."

It has hitherto been found that the party opposed to
Agathocles was in every case oligarchic. Here however
the explicit words of Diodorus show that even the democrats were now ready to forsake the prince. Nor is this
hard to understand. As long as tyranny meant ease and
plunder it was welcome, but when the loans and levies

---

[1] Diodorus says ἵν' οἱ Συρακόσιοι πολλὴν ἄδειαν σχῶσι συγκομίσαι τοὺς
καρπούς, ἀναγκάζοντος τοῦ καιροῦ. This last clause might mean (1) That
the corn was becoming over-ripe; for the dog-days, that is the end of
June or beginning of July, would be very late for the Sicilian harvest; or
(2) That the corn was already reaped, but that there was no time to lose
in bringing it in to Syracuse, because the enemy was coming.

[2] D. ibid. 3 ἐπιπορευόμενος. That Hamilcar made a mistake in not
instantly striking at Syracuse can hardly be doubted.

[3] ibid. 4.

of a long war were impending, the allegiance of the people was bound to waver. It is also likely that the cruel treatment of Gela by Agathocles had opened men's eyes to the real nature of his rule. Now the call to freedom was eagerly taken up, and the mildness of Hamilcar carried on the work that his generalship had so gloriously begun.

These doings gave Agathocles a chance of drawing his forces together and slipping home to Syracuse[1].

Of the anxious months following his withdrawal little account has reached us[2], but there seems to have been fighting by land and sea. Justin speaks of a second defeat of Agathocles by Hamilcar after an engagement more serious than the first. This is certainly incorrect, but it is not impossible that some further battle took place; for Agathocles would hardly have given up his whole domain without a last struggle[3].

---

[1] D. *ibid.* 5.

[2] For the dating see note below, p. 97.

[3] J. xxii. 3, 9—10 (part already quoted) *Prima igitur illi cum Hamilcare, Gisgonis filio, proelii congressio fuit: a quo victus, majori mole reparaturus bellum Syracusas concessit. Sed secundi certaminis eadem fortuna quae et prioris fuit.*

This passage has usually been overlooked. It is noted but not explained by Niese 444, and by Wiese 37. Short of accepting Justin as I have ventured to do, two courses are open, (1) To disallow the whole place as a mistake or confusion; or (2) To identify the "*prima congressio*" with the parade before Acragas in 312, and *secundum certamen* with the battle of the Himeras. To this, however, there are two very strong objections, (*a*) The parade before Acragas was anything but a defeat for Agathocles, who, in fact, claimed the better by hanging up his spoils. That Callias and Timaeus should of the same event have made the one a success the other a defeat, is surely more than the most advanced critic would maintain; (*b*) During the year 312 Hamilcar was probably not in command of the Punic army in Sicily. He was sent for after the treaty of 314 to report to the Carthaginian Senate, and he sailed with the great host in 311.

The more distant allies were hopelessly lost, but Agathocles seems to have taken measures to secure or at least
to make harmless those nearer home. We hear later of
an outpost at Echetla, which may have been held as early
as this[1]. Against Tauromenium some action seems to have
been taken, if the following confused tale of Polyaenus
be worth anything[2]: "Agathocles called upon the Syracusans for two thousand soldiers in array, as if he were
about to cross over to 'Phoenice,' for, he said, some
traitors there had eagerly invited him. The Syracusans
believed him and granted the men. But when Agathocles
got the soldiers, he paid no heed to the Phoenicians, but
marched against the allies, and pulled down the strongholds round the land of Tauromenium."

It has already been seen that the order of the anecdotes
in Polyaenus is the opposite of that of the events themselves. Now this story, the sixth, would come before the
fifth, in which Agathocles' last acts at Syracuse and his
start for Africa are related, and after the seventh, in
which he first gains supreme power. Again it must
belong to a time when Agathocles feared a revolt of
Tauromenium; but as the city had been reduced in 312,
and before that was hardly an "ally," the present date,
when the secession was in full swing, seems the most
likely. That Agathocles made a sudden raid on the land
of Tauromenium, and pulled down the strongholds lest
Carthage should use them as bases against Syracuse, and
that for this small undertaking he raised 2000 men, may
fairly be believed. That he professed to be starting to
invade some Phoenician land, in western Sicily or in
Africa, is possible. But he can hardly have spoken of
Carthage, for Diodorus says that none of his men knew

---

[1] See below, p. 39.   [2] Polyaenus v. 3, 6.

that he meant to attack her, even when he actually
started. On the other hand it is absurd to suppose that
Agathocles, as general, could not raise 2000 men without
a vote of the assembly; if Polyaenus thought of the
matter at all, he must have meant that Agathocles called
for the men to enroll themselves, and they came forward. Still more improbable is the view that Phoenice
in Polyaenus means the Epirot town, and that Agathocles
might have attacked it, while he was at Corcyra about
296. Apart from the difficulty of upsetting the order of
Polyaenus, it is hard to see why Agathocles sent specially
to Syracuse for so trifling a reinforcement, and still
stranger that he should have used it in attacking a
subject city with which he had been many years at
peace[1].

[1] The connexion of this story with Phoenice in Epirus was suggested
by Droysen 242, and accepted by Freeman IV. 479, 529–30. Apart from the
historical unlikeliness of this view, there are two grammatical objections.
(1) Polyaenus speaks of τὴν Φοινίκην; this use of the article would be impossible with the name of a town; (2) below he speaks of Φοίνιξι, which
can only = Phoenicians or Carthaginians, and never the inhabitants of
Phoenice in Epirus, the proper name for whom is unknown. Cf. Schubert
200–1, who does not, however, suggest a better context for the story.

An ingenious theory is that of E. Pais, *Ancient Italy* (trans. E. D.
Curtis) XIV. 157, who holds that by Φοινίκη the town of Φοῖνιξ, a place on
the Sicilian coast about 20 miles N. of Tauromenium, is meant. (This
place is mentioned by Appian, *B.C.* v. 110; it is the same as Palma
or Tamaricium, Holm, *Beitr. z. Berichtigung d. Karte d. alten Sic.* Praef.
11.) Pais dates the attack between 317 and 312, regarding it as part of
the Sicilian war which involved the fall of Messena (above p. 67). This
view is open to the grammatical objections already mentioned; furthermore in the years 316–312 there seems to have been open war between
Agathocles and the Greek cities, which could hardly have been considered
as his allies. Also to pull "down the strongholds" of such a small city
as Tauromenium was not an adequate result of a surprise. Therefore,
while admitting the possibility that Pais may be right, I suggest the
above explanation as more likely.

Of the sea-fighting about this time no record has come down but a single tale in Polyaenus[1]. Hamilcar had a Greek pilot who used to betray his master's plans to Agathocles. At last Hamilcar found this out and thereupon told the man that he would surprise the Olympieum. This was passed on to Agathocles, who set out to defend it. Hamilcar meanwhile laid an ambush, and when the Greeks came, he fell on them and slew seven thousand.

This story can only belong to the time of which we are now speaking; for formerly the Punic fleet had only made surprise descents on Syracuse without Hamilcar, while the behaviour of the pilot shows that constant sea-fights were now going on; and later Agathocles did not come back to Syracuse until long after the death of Hamilcar. The number of victims is no doubt overstated, but the rest of the account can be accepted, and it proves that the Carthaginian fleet blockaded Syracuse after the battle of the Himeras, and that many small sea-fights took place, in which both generals joined. Of course we are not bound to believe all the details given by Polyaenus. Hamilcar may never have tried to deceive Agathocles[2]. Enough that the latter, on a false report of a Carthaginian attack, set out with his forces, and was so surprised and defeated. There is also here a clue to the order of events. Hamilcar would not have taken command by sea until the land force had done all it could for the time being. The sea-fighting may therefore be placed later than the last land-battle, and after the secession of the Greek cities had taken full effect.

[1] Polyaenus VI. 41, a passage hitherto, I believe, unnoticed. Of the Olympieum we shall hear again.

[2] The story-teller, who may of course again be Duris, seems to have followed the common plan of turning accident into design. The false report reached Agathocles and misled him; the rest of the tale may be fiction.

5. AGATHOCLES STARTS FOR AFRICA.   310.

Agathocles' dominion in Sicily was narrowed down to the compass of Syracuse itself. His plight was not hopeless, nor his cause lost. Dionysius had sat for months within the walls, until the gods and the fevers of the Anapus had done their work on his foemen. But Agathocles had not the dogged patience of the older prince. Either at the suggestion of the treasonable party in Carthage, or by the sheer boldness of his own genius, Agathocles formed the plan of leaving Syracuse with a strong guard, and crossing over with the pick of his troops to strike at the land of Carthage itself.

His first care was to raise men and funds[1]. He borrowed all the money held in trust for orphans, making himself their guardian, and saying that he could manage their property far better than the legal tutors. He then raised loans from merchants, took some of the temple-treasures, and even robbed the women of their jewels[2].

After that he gave out in the assembly that he had found a sure means of victory; let the people only wait patiently for a while; those who could not abide the siege might take their money with them and leave the city.

[1] D. xx. 4; J. xxii. 4.

[2] *ibid.* These acts were not altogether unexampled. Dionysius the Elder had resorted to the same means. Loans from merchants and from temples were quite common. The robbery of the Delphian hoard by Onomarchus was called a loan. Even Christian Heraclius borrowed freely from the Church for his Persian war. As for the taking of the jewels, a device of the same kind was carried out by Dionysius II. Cf. J. xxi. 3, 3. (The Locrians had made a vow to Aphrodite.) *Dionysius... hortatur ut uxores filiasque suas in templum Veneris quam possint ornatissimas mittant...certatim omnes feminae impensius exornatae in templum Veneris conveniunt: quas omnes Dionysius immissis militibus spoliat, ornamentaque matronarum in praedam suam vertit.*

Sixteen hundred rich men are said to have gone out; but Agathocles sent and murdered them all on the road, and took the money for himself. Whether Agathocles really meant to have the refugees slain—in revenge perhaps for a similar onslaught on himself or his friends—or whether the unwillingness of the rich to hand over their gold to the tyrant led him to take strong measures, is a question hardly to be settled[1].

In this way Agathocles raised enough money to store Syracuse with war-gear, and to spare fifty talents, in gold, which he put on board ship to pay his men.

He held a levy of troops and enrolled many freed slaves, taken perhaps from the rich men just slain. In picking the other troops, Agathocles chose them from as many households as possible, so that those who sailed might be hostages for the faith of their kinsfolk left at home. The horsemen, who, as has been said, had come out almost unscathed from the battle of the Himeras, were bidden to take saddle and bridle with them, but no mounts; for such were to be had in plenty in Africa. Two sons of Agathocles, Archagathus and Heracleides, set out with their father. His brother Antander, with Erymnon the Aetolian, was left to rule Syracuse. These two men, whose interests in the city were naturally bound up with those of Agathocles, were the most trustworthy regents that could possibly have been found.

In spite of Agathocles' public promise to make good his disasters, he had kept his real plans a dead secret[2]. His men thought that he would sail to Italy or Sardinia, or for a raid on Punic Sicily, but their hearts were downcast, for they regarded any such venture as foolhardy, and never hoped to come back alive.

---

[1] D. *ibid.*; Polyaenus v. 3, 5.   [2] D. xx. 5; J. xxii. 4, 3; Orosius iv. 6.

Everything was now ready, and the sixty ships of Agathocles were waiting in the harbour till a chance should offer of slipping past the Carthaginian fleet. For some days the blockade was strictly kept; but then a squadron of corn-ships drew near to the mouth of the harbour. The Carthaginians sailed out to attack them, when Agathocles, seeing the way open, rowed from the haven as fast as his men could pull. The enemy were already near the corn-ships, but when they saw the Syracusan fleet coming out of the harbour, they wheeled round and prepared to fight. Agathocles however turned out southwards and made off at full speed. The Carthaginians gave chase, and were only baulked of their prey by the fall of night. Meanwhile the freight-ships had made the haven of Syracuse, and the fresh supply of corn was a timely relief for the city, where famine was already threatening.

On the morrow the sun was darkened; day became as night and the stars were seen. This token brought dismay to the hearts of Agathocles' men, bound they knew not whither; and it took all the skill of their leader to reassure them. The portent, he said, was not given to withhold them from their venture, for if so it would have happened or ever they had set forth. The sign was for their enemies and foretold the downfall of Carthage[1].

---

[1] D. xx. 5, 5; and especially J. xxii. 6, 1—3. For the date see note below. This seems not to have been the only time that Agathocles had to hearten his men after an alarming token of the sky. We read the following story in Frontinus, *Strat.* i. 12, 9: *Agathocles Syracusanus adversus Poenos simili ejusdem sideris* (= *lunae*) *deminutione quia sub diem pugnae ut prodigio milites sui consternati erant, ratione qua id acciderit exposita, docuit quidquid illud foret, ad rerum naturam non ad ipsorum propositum pertinere.* As no place or date is mentioned, the story is of little use historically : nor was a lecture on astronomy the usual means adopted by Greek generals to reassure their men in face of a portent. We may therefore believe as much of this tale as we choose.

NOTE ON THE SIX HUNDRED.
(Cf. p. 38.)

It has been much disputed whether the Six Hundred were an association of an informal, perhaps secret, nature or a regular council with a place in the constitution. Freeman, after a long discussion (IV. App. vii.), declares for the former view, which Niese (I. 430) also holds. Beloch (II. 588) on the other hand goes so far as to believe that the Six Hundred were the actual Senate set up by Timoleon, although no such institution is anywhere attributed to him.

Most of the terms applied to the Six Hundred by Diodorus are quite vague :—thus XIX. 3, 3 τῶν δ' ὅλων εἶχε τὴν ἡγεμονίαν Ἡρακλείδης καὶ Σωσίστρατος. (The 18th book, he adds, dealt with their doings. This statement is again made in XIX. 10, 3 with special allusion to intrigues at Croton. The 18th book now extant gives none of the details promised. Either Diodorus forgot to write them, or else they stood in a special digression now lost. This arrangement of Diodorus may account for the rambling and dateless nature of the earlier Agathoclean chapters in book XIX.)

The commonest phrases used of the oligarchic faction are simply οἱ περὶ Σωσίστρατον and οἱ περὶ Ἡρακλείδη καὶ Σωσίστρατον (D. XIX. 3, 4; 4, 2, 3, 4; 5, 4). The expression "Six Hundred" occurs in D. XIX. 6, 4, and elsewhere. In XIX. 3, 5 Diodorus says οἱ μὲν περὶ Σωσίστρατον ἐδυνάστευσαν τῆς πατρίδος μετὰ τὴν ἐκ Κρότωνος ἐπάνοδον. The mention of the home-coming from Croton implies a change in the position of the Six Hundred at that date. Formerly they had been the leading men in the state (ἡγεμονία, above), now at a given moment (as shown by the use of the aorist) they gain supreme unconstitutional power (δυναστεία). In XIX. 4, 3 they are likewise spoken of as δυνάσται.

So far there is nothing to suggest that the Six Hundred had any official place in the republican constitution ; but in D. XIX. 5, 6 is a passage taken by Beloch to support such a view. Εἰς πολλὰ γὰρ μέρη συνέβαινε διαιρεῖσθαι τὰς ἑταιρείας τῶν συνιόντων καὶ πρὸς ἀλλή-λους ἑκάστοις εἶναι μεγάλας διαφοράς, μέγιστον δ᾽ ἦν ἀντίταγμα τοῖς περὶ τὸν Ἀγαθοκλέα τὸ τῶν ἑξακοσίων συνέδριον κατὰ τὴν ὀλιγαρχίαν ἀφηγημένον τῆς πόλεως· οἱ προέχοντες γὰρ τῶν Συρακοσίων καὶ ταῖς δόξαις καὶ ταῖς οὐσίαις ἐν τούτοις ὑπῆρχον καταλελεγμένοι. Beloch gathers from these words that the Six Hundred were a regular Senate set up by Timoleon with a property test. All that Diodorus says however is (1) The Council of the Six Hundred had ruled Syracuse at the time of the oligarchy (i.e. after the campaign of Croton already mentioned), and (2) The wealthiest and foremost Syracusans were among the Six Hundred. These statements are not nearly enough to prove Beloch's point, and the next passage tells strongly against it. In XIX. 6, 4 Diodorus says that Agathocles summoned Tisarchus and Diocles τοὺς δοκοῦντας προεστάναι τῆς τῶν ἑξακοσίων ἑταιρείας. Not only are the Six Hundred called ἑταιρεία (that is explicitly, a political club) but it seems that it was not officially known who their leaders were. The use of *Senatus* in the parallel passage, Justin XXII. 2, 10, 11, does not alter the case: the account is much confused, but Agathocles' first victims are called *potentissimi ex principibus*, while *senatum trucidat* comes later: what Justin meant by *senatum* is uncertain: he *may* have meant the Six Hundred, but if so he must have been mistranslating a word like συνέδριον : in any case his testimony here is outweighed by the clear statement of Diodorus.

There may have been a Senate in Timoleon's constitution ; of this we know nothing: but it cannot be the same as the Council of the Six Hundred. The Six Hundred were at one time the ruling body in the state, but their authority was unconstitutional, and rested on force. They were none the less a political club even when they stood at the head of the Syracusan government.

NOTE ON AGATHOCLES' ESCAPE FROM GELA. D. xix. 4, 4—7. (Cf. pp. 47—8.)

The story as given by Diodorus is believed by Grote, Freeman, Holm, and others, but has been called in question by Schubert (42) and following him by Dr Evans (notes to Freeman, IV. 367). As these two authorities seriously propose to reject all adventures and "stratagems" of Agathocles as fictions of Duris, it is worth while testing the case before us.

The points are :—(1) There are no passes or defiles anywhere near Gela. The town (=Terranova) stood on a long low hill, the only rising ground in the neighbourhood. But Holm's view that the "narrow place" was a street *in* Gela, solves the difficulty. (The fact that Sosistratus' men are called οἱ προσβοηθήσαντες ἐκ τῆς Γέλας, makes no difference. The preposition ἐκ is simply used vaguely of the defending force.) For in any case a besieged army would not be likely to give battle *outside* a city at dead of night. (2) The details are supposed to be contradictory. Agathocles loses 300 men before the last fight, yet at the end, in spite of a fierce hand-to-hand struggle, he still has 700 alive, the total having been 1000. Again how could the buglers escape if the rest of the force could not ?

The answer is that there *was* no more fighting after the fall of the 300. Agathocles got his seven wounds in the first mellay at the same time as these men were killed, that is at the first shock. (This is proved by the use of the aorist tense ἀγωνισάμενος and the contrasted μὲν and δέ clauses.) The 700 instantly fled, no doubt dragging Agathocles along with them. Diodorus does not say that they were surrounded, but only that they were in despair. Agathocles' ruse gave them breathing-space and diverted the pursuers. (3) "The bugle-call is pointless and stamps the whole story as Duris' invention." Certainly if the fight was going on outside the city, there would be no sense in having the call sounded at two points on the city wall. But if the fight was inside, such a course would be quite reasonable, the object being to draw the pursuers away from the gate or other point of escape for which Agathocles was making. The charge against Duris of inventing bugle-calls for all possible occasions is not by any means proved. (Cf. p. 24.)

This "stratagem" thus proves to be credible after all.

NOTE ON HAMILCAR'S AGREEMENT WITH AGATHOCLES. (Cf. pp. 51—2.)

Justin's account is as follows (XXII. 2, 5—7): *Sed Agathocles, cum videret fortius defendi urbem quam oppugnari, precibus per internuntios Hamilcarem exorat ut inter se et Syracusanos pacis arbitria suscipiat, peculiaria in ipsum officia sui repromittens. Qua spe impletus, Hamilcar societatem cum eo, metu potentiae ejus, junxit, ut quantum virium Agathocli adversus Syracusanos dedisset, tantum ipse ad incrementa domesticae potentiae recuperaret.*

Justin's version is accepted by most historians. It is questioned by De Sanctis (296) and by Beloch (III. 1, 187). Niese (439) is doubtful on the point. These writers seem to think that Justin knows too much about secret plots, and they prefer to suppose that Hamilcar was really acting for his country's welfare all along, but made a mistake in setting up such a dangerous ally as Agathocles, and in the end was made a scapegoat.

But (1) If Hamilcar was afraid of Agathocles, he would hardly have been so senseless as to make him the chief man in Syracuse in return for a bare promise of allegiance (which as a matter of fact was never given: cf. p. 53). (2) It is clear from later events that the Sicilian cities friendly to Carthage regarded Hamilcar as privy to the misdeeds of Agathocles; this would not have been possible if Hamilcar had forced Agathocles into a treaty favourable to Carthage. (3) In D. XIX. 65, 5 when Agathocles was attacking Messena, the town was saved not by Hamilcar, though he was still in Sicily, but by envoys from Carthage. (4) D. XIX. 71, 6. After the failure of Acrotatus, a peace very favourable to Agathocles was made by Hamilcar. This treaty roused the fury of the allies of Carthage and of the home government. (This point is mentioned by Diodorus XIX. 72, 2 as well as by Justin XXII. 3, so that it is impossible to overlook the matter.) This led to Hamilcar's recall. Henceforth all the acts of Carthage are hostile to Agathocles. (5) Bomilcar in his dying speech (J. XXII. 7, 10) is made to say that Hamilcar wished to secure for Carthage the friendship of Agathocles but was condemned for the offence. This passage is

pure rhetoric and might be made to prove anything : it is therefore
a waste of time to discuss it.

These points make it perfectly clear that Hamilcar's policy was
in opposition to the plans of his home government.

The support officially given by Carthage to Dionysius I does not
supply any sort of parallel to the present case ; for (1) Carthage was
then helping tyranny against democracy not oligarchy. (2) Dionysius
when first recognised, gave to Carthage not a bare promise, but
nearly the whole of Greek Sicily.

Here therefore the version of Justin must stand.

NOTE ON THE ORIGINAL SOURCES USED BY DIODORUS FOR THE BATTLE OF THE HIMERAS. (Cf. p. 73 ff.)

It seems that Diodorus having in this battle-piece a subject
quite to his taste, read all available versions and wrote a description
based on them all.   Beyond this I would not venture to go.
Schubert 79 however attempts to prove that the whole passage rests
on Timaeus, and that the latter drew entirely from an informant
on the Carthaginian side. His points are: (1) "The foremost of
the Carthaginian army," as well as the slingers and horsemen, play
parts in the battle "of which a Greek narrator would have been
unaware."   Against this it may be said (a) These bodies of troops
are just those that did most execution in the fight ; the Greeks
would therefore have known too much about them rather than too
little.   (b) The valour of picked bands of Punic troops had become
traditional among their Greek foemen (e.g. the Sacred Band).   It
would be absurd to suppose that every historian that speaks of them
was drawing from a Carthaginian source.   (2) Schubert thinks that
the failure of Diodorus to notice: (i) That Agathocles' attack on
the foragers was part of his plan of battle, and (ii) That the main
body of Carthaginians had not noticed the skirmish between the
foragers and the Greek party (such skirmishes being of common
occurrence)—also proves the Carthaginian standpoint of the narrator.

Against this it must be said (a) The statement that the Carthaginians were caught unready has already been disproved. (b) The
mere ambushing of a party of foragers gave Agathocles no opening
for an attack on the Punic camp. No doubt he hoped to draw the
whole force out to fight in the plain : but here his plan failed, and
therefore Diodorus very wisely says no more about it. It must also
be noted (3) The account is not over favourable to Carthage. As
much as possible is made of Agathocles' first success. He is con-
ceived as robbed of a victory already his, by a mishap on which no one
reckoned. (4) Diodorus has no idea that Hamilcar based his whole
plan on the knowledge that fresh forces would come up to help him.

That Timaeus or even Callias might have had some information
from Greeks serving with Carthage is of course quite possible. But
there is no reason for tracing Diodorus' whole account to that source.

NOTE ON THE DATES UP TO THE
AFRICAN WAR.

The fixed point from which our reckoning starts is the total
eclipse of the sun which happened on the day after Agathocles set
sail for Africa. The date has been fixed as Aug. 15, 310 B.C. (for
this compare Dr Evans' note, Freeman IV. 401 ; where the authorities
are all given).

Diodorus rightly dates the eclipse as falling in the archonship of
Hieromnemon, and in the consulship of C. Junius Bubulcus, and
Q. Aemilius Barbula.

This was in Agathocles' seventh year of rule (J. XXII. 5, 1), so
that he became tyrant between Aug. 317 and Aug. 316. Diodorus
places his rise in the archonship of Demogenes = 317/6 B.C.; but the
Parian Chronicle (Ath. Mitt. XXII. 187 and 197) gives the archonship
of Democleides as the date = 316/5. The early part of 316 may
therefore be taken as about the right time. The negotiations with
Hamilcar perhaps took up most of the winter, and if Diodorus is
really dating the beginning of them, this would account for his earlier
date, for, as will be seen below, his years are not archontic but consular.

Diodorus says that Agathocles ruled 28 years to the day of his
death. (D. XXI. 16, 5.) He must therefore have died in 289. At

his death Demetrius was still king of Macedonia, but he died in 289/8. So that the end of 289 is the latest possible year for Agathocles' death.

Agathocles died aged 72 (D. *ibid.*). This would give 361 B.C. as the date of his birth. Polybius says that Agathocles was 18 when he came to Syracuse. The occasion of his coming was the enrolment of the new citizens by Timoleon. This fell in 343, so that the date of Agathocles' birth is confirmed.

His first campaign, against the men of Aetna, is fixed as 339.

Following this comes a period of uncertainty. The Bruttian war must have been after the death of Alexander the Molossian in 331/0; but we cannot tell how long after.

Agathocles' first exile can only be roughly dated.

It must obviously have been two campaigns after 330, and some time before 319. This has already been proved (see note on p. 42).

Under 319 the Parian Marble has the following entry: "In this same year the Syracusans chose Agathocles as general with full powers for the defence of the inhabitants of Sicily." If this be accepted, it would appear that Agathocles was elected general three years before his final stroke. In other words we should have a blank of three years without any record whatever; for Diodorus lets only a few days elapse between the two events.

The sentence on the Marble can hardly refer to Agathocles' office before his second exile, when Diodorus says he was ποτὲ μὲν ἰδιώτης ποτὲ δὲ ἐφ᾽ ἡγεμονίας τεταγμένος, the latter phrase probably means no more than the chiliarchy.

I venture therefore to suggest that Agathocles' name is here an error of the Marble, and that we really have a notice of Acestorides. For his office 319 is a very likely date, and that the mason should have put the better known for the obscurer man is not impossible. The accuracy of the Marble is not by any means perfect, for the eclipse of 310 is there given under 313/2.

This view I put forward with all diffidence as the least unlikely supposition. Beloch, who boldly follows the Marble, makes no attempt to fill up the three years. Wilhelm (*Ath. Mitt.* l.c.) has no suggestion.

Eusebius under 323 B.C. (ed. Schoene, II. p. 117) has: *Agathocles Syracusanis tyrannidem exercuit.* This is perhaps a misunderstanding of Agathocles' position after the war at Rhegium (p. 45, above). It would be very rash to claim such a statement as a confirmation of the Marmor Parium with a view to discrediting the accepted dating.

The attack on Gela might thus have been made in 320 (D. XIX. 4).

For the years following Agathocles' elevation, which as already seen belongs to 316, we gain another fixed point from the history of Apollonia. This place fell to Cassander in 314 ; so that Acrotatus, who relieved it from an Illyrian siege, probably did so in the year before (D. XIX. 71). In 316/5 Diodorus has nothing on Agathocles, but no doubt the minor operations of XIX. 9 fin. fairly filled it. The attack on Messena would fall in 315, as Diodorus allows us to place it; during this time Acrotatus landed and prepared to fight. His campaign and departure belong to 314 (D. XIX. 70 f.). Diodorus has naturally placed all his account of Acrotatus in this one year for the sake of continuity. Peace was made at the end of the campaign.

The crossing to Africa being fixed as Aug. 16, 310, we must next discover whether the battle of the Himeras was fought in that year or the year before. The fight fell in the Dog-days and about the time of harvest, that is at the end of June.

Diodorus puts the battle in the archonship of Simonides = July 311—July 310, and the crossing in the archonship of Hieromnemon = July 310—July 309.

From this the "acute and ingenious" Clinton (*F.H.* II., anno 310) and Beloch (III. 2, 202 f.) have concluded that the fight was fought in June 310, and that Agathocles sailed about seven weeks later, in Aug. 310.

This view is entirely mistaken. Diodorus in Sicilian history does not follow the archontic division of the year. His arrangement is, as would naturally be expected, that of the solar years ; and as they answered roughly to the consular terms, it follows that Diodorus kept fairly closely to these also, while his archons are merely mentioned at the beginning of each calendar year as a matter of form. This can easily be proved by a comparison between Diodorus and Livy, whose consular arrangement is undisputed. The following table will prove the point more readily than pages of argument.

(The table has been compiled from the authorities, and from Matzat. *röm. Chronologie.* Cf. Fischer, *gr. u. röm. Zeittafeln,* Holzapfel, *röm. Chronologie,* Soltau, *röm. Chronologie.*)

TABLE OF CONSULAR AND ARCHONTIC YEARS
IN DIODORUS AND LIVY.

	Consular Year	Consuls (Livy and Diodorus)	Dated Events of the Year	Archon	Events of Sicilian History
A.	315 Feb. 1	Sp. Nautilus M. Popilius	Nuceria joins Samnites. D. XIX. 65, 7.	Praxibulus, 315/4	Coming of Acrotatus
B.	314 Jan. 23	L. Papirius Q. Publilius	Revolt of Sora to Samnites. D. XIX. 72. L. IX. 23.	Nicodorus, 314/3	Departure of Acrotatus
C.	313 Feb. 3	M. Poetilius C. Sulpicius	Dictator: C. Maenius. D. XIX. 76. L. IX. 26.	Theophrastus, 313/2	No details in D.
D.	312 Jan. 25	L. Papirius C. Junius	Colony to Pontia. D. XIX. 101. L. IX. 28.	Polemo, 312/1	Campaign of Messena
E.	311 Feb. 6	M. Valerius P. Decius	Colony at Interamna. D. XIX. 105.	Simonides, 311/0	B. of Himeras
F.	310 Jan. 27	C. Junius Q. Aemilius	Invasion of Samnium. D. XX. 26. L. IX. 31.	Hieromnemon, 310/9	Invasion of Africa

This table leads to the following course of reasoning[1]. Take for example the year marked D.

We have the datum:—Archon Polemo; that is 312/1. Now do the events assigned to year D. belong to 312 or to 311 or some to each ?

Besides the archon we have also assigned to year D. the consuls Papirius and Junius, who held office from Jan. 25, 312 onwards. To this year both Livy and Diodorus assign the settling of a colony at Pontia. Now the months of overlapping between the given archonship and the given consular year belong to 312, so that the rule of Diodorus seems to be to mention at the beginning of the consular year that archon who entered office in the following July. A similar reasoning gives the results tabulated above.

Thus it follows that the battle of the Himeras and the African invasion, which fall in different consulships, must therefore fall in different calendar years. If further proof were needed, we can also say (1) Between the battle and the start for Africa there are traces of more fighting besides long negotiations. (2) When Agathocles sailed there was already a dearth of food in Syracuse. This could not have happened after a few weeks' siege. The land of Syracuse raised huge quantities of grain (as the Romans afterwards used to draw their food-stuffs from there) and it is specially said that Agathocles had carefully provisioned the city[2].

These two points are given by Schubert and derided by Beloch. Now it appears that Schubert is right.

The battle of the Himeras being thus fixed as June 311, we can easily date the events before it. The outbreak of the war falls in 312 (D. xix. 104) and the downfall of Messena in 313 (a year to which Diodorus assigns no act of Agathocles). Thus the events may be summed up as follows.

[1] There is still some uncertainty as to the exact dates on which the consuls took office. But the table gives (after Matzat) an approximation near enough for our purpose.

[2] Another point is that Diodorus in xix. 1, 10, says that his narrative from the accession of Agathocles (placed by him, as we have seen, at the end of 317) to the battle of the Himeras included seven years—reckoned inclusively, this number would give 311 as the date of the battle.

TABLE OF DATES.

361   Birth of Agathocles.

343   Removal of Agathocles to Syracuse.

339   War against the Aetnaeans.

After 330 Bruttian War.

c. 326   Agathocles' Attempt on Croton.

c. 322   Agathocles' Homecoming.

c. 320   Agathocles' Attack on Gela.

319 (?)   Acestorides chosen General.   Flight of Agathocles.

317   Agathocles makes terms with Hamilcar.

316 (early Spring) Agathocles becomes Tyrant.   Minor Operations
           in Sicily.

315   Attack on Messena.   Acrotatus lands.

314   Failure and Flight of Acrotatus.

313   Minor Operations (D. XIX. 72).

312   Messena yields.   Outbreak of the War with Carthage.

311   Battle of the Himeras.

310   Agathocles sets sail for Africa.

CHAPTER IV.

AGATHOCLES' WARFARE IN AFRICA.

1. THE LANDING AND FIRST OPERATIONS. B.C. 310.

THERE can be no doubt that Agathocles, in the dangerous state of his fortunes, had chosen the only possible means of dealing a blow at the Carthaginians. Nothing could have been done in Sicily, and no help was forthcoming from outside. The Greeks of Italy had no wish to uphold a tyrant's cause, and the Greeks of the Near East were too intent on their own wars to find another deliverer for their western brethren. On the other hand the outroad to Africa had a good prospect of success, if enough forces could be landed in the country. The land was open, the natives chafed under Punic rule, and the fealty of the Numidian vassals was wavering. The untoward sight of an army in the home-country would frighten the Carthaginians, and the wasting of their fields might drive them to buy off the invaders with an offer of peace. Lastly the Senate of Carthage was hampered by a strong opposition party, which was suspected of being in league with Agathocles. The least that could be expected to follow from a brilliant campaign in Africa would be the relief of Syracuse by the recall

of Hamilcar's forces[1]: a lasting conquest on African soil
was no part of the invader's plan[2].

The Syracusan fleet after baffling the first pursuit
of the Carthaginians had sailed some way to the west
along the coast of Sicily. The ships then steered south-

Cape Bon.

wards and after a six days' sail the rocky Hermaean
headland[3], now Cape Bon, was sighted at daybreak. The
Carthaginians had guessed in the meantime the line taken

[1] The reasons that led Agathocles to plan his descent on the African
coast are given by Diodorus xx. 3 and Justin xxii. 5. The latter puts
them into Agathocles' mouth as a long speech, much of which, especially
§ 11, about the capture of Carthage, and §§ 12, 13, about glory, is pure
rhetoric.

[2] Agathocles in his address to Ophellas (D. xx. 40, 3) specially disowns
any wish to hold sway in Africa.

[3] Ἑρμαία ἄκρα.

by the Greeks and had been following in their wake, but now they once more caught sight of the enemy, and gave chase with all speed. It was a desperate race, but the Greeks had some start at the outset, and most of their ships got to land before the Carthaginians came near. The rear-guard however came within shooting range and some artillery practice ensued, until at last the Carthaginian van came to close quarters with a few of the Greek ships. But then the Greeks had the better, for their decks were crowded with soldiers, and the enemy were forced to sheer off to escape being boarded and taken: thus Agathocles landed his men undisturbed[1].

The place where he put in was called The Quarries, and there are still to be seen on the spot some huge underground caverns from which Carthage drew her building-stone. The anchorage was no better than a rocky creek, only practicable in calm weather[2].

There Agathocles beached his ships and threw up an earth-wall to guard them.

How long the Greeks lay in their camp is not known, but it seems likely that Agathocles only waited to make sure that no land force was ready to meet him, and then resolved to push forward with all speed. The first difficulty

[1] D. xx. 5—6; J. xxii. 6.

[2] This roadstead, as the nearest landing-place for boats coming from Sicily, seems to have been in fairly common use. Curio landed there: cf. Caesar, *B. C.* ii. 23. *Curio...appellit ad eum locum qui appellatur Anquillaria. Hic locus abest a Clupeis passuum* xxii. *milia, habetque non incommodum aestate stationem.* Regulus touched there, Polyb. i. 29. (The place was called Λατομίαι by the Greeks.)

Anquillaria or Aquilaria has given its name to the Arab hamlet of El-Haouria; this is about three miles from Cape Bon, and about a mile from the roadstead and the "rhar-el-Khebir," as the old quarry is now called. (Cf. Tissot, *op. cit.* i. 174, 5 and map in iii. Pl. VIII.)

Maltzan, *Reise in Tunis* ii. 312, notes that El-Haouria means "The Ruins"—it may still be a corruption of Aquilaria.

was the disposal of his ships; for he could ill spare men to guard them, and he would not brook their falling into the enemy's hands. He therefore made up his mind to burn the whole fleet, and to lessen the fear which such a deed was bound to cause in his army, he treated the destruction as an offering to the gods.

The scene is thus described by Diodorus[1].

" Agathocles called a meeting of his soldiers, and came forward to address them clad in a white robe with a wreath on his head. 'When the Carthaginians were pursuing us,' he said, 'I made a vow to Demeter and the Maid, the goddesses of Sicily, to burn all the ships in their honour. Now that we are come out unscathed it is time for us to pay our vow. Only fight well, and I will repay you many times what you have lost. For the goddesses have told me in the sacrifice that the victory in the whole war will be ours.' So saying, he took a lighted torch from the hand of a servant, and bade all the captains to do the same. Then he called upon the goddesses and ran to the flagship. There he stood on the prow and told the others to do as he did. So the captains fired all the ships, and the flames quickly leaped up, while the buglers blew a blast, and the host shouted, and all prayed for a safe homecoming at the last."

The pomp and solemnity of this rite led the men to forget for a while the plight in which they were now landed. But even before the flames died down, the exaltation passed, and they began to reflect how many

[1] D. xx. 7; J. xxii. 6, 4. Diodorus alone speaks of the sacred nature of Agathocles' act. Grote (xii. 558), regarded the account as based on the report of an eyewitness; but Schubert (98) holds that most of the details, especially the trumpet-calls, were made up by Duris. On the whole there does not seem to be enough ground for rejecting Diodorus here. Cf. Orosius iv. 6, *Illico unanimiter naves primum in quibus venere incendunt, ne qua spes refugiendi foret,* and Polyaenus v. 3, 5.

miles of sea cut them off from Sicily, and how recklessly they had trusted themselves to unfriendly ground[1]. Agathocles however was ready to march forward, and resolved to cheer his men by the taste of conquest and plunder.

The Quarries (Latomiae) near Aquilaria.

He led his men by a quick march to attack a Carthaginian town called Megalepolis, or the Great City. The way led through a wonderfully rich country, thickly grown with vines, olives, and all kinds of fruit, and dotted with homesteads and country-houses. The gardens were carefully watered by cuts leading from large store-tanks; the houses were well built and hand-

[1] Diod. xx. 8.

somely plastered, and everything showed the taste that
the wealthy Carthaginians had applied to the beautifying
of their homes. The pastures were grazed by large
numbers of sheep and oxen, and the low ground was full
of horses. Long years of peace had brought this land to
such a pitch of well-being, as the Greeks in their own
troubled island had never dreamed of; now they felt that
a rich reward awaited their valour[1].

The Great City was quite unready to withstand attack,
and was quickly stormed. The men were let loose to
plunder, and then Agathocles, who was for pressing on
towards Carthage, had the walls dismantled and camped
in the open.

The next city taken was White Tunis, which was
treated in the same way.

Our understanding of the course of this campaign
would be much clearer if it could be settled where the
first of the two places taken by Agathocles really lay.
The Great City must have been some way off the landing-
place, for otherwise the alarm would have been given and
the cattle and horses, which the Greeks found peacefully
grazing, would have been brought into a place of safety.
The suggestion of Barth to place the Great City at Missua,
about six miles from Aquilaria, must therefore be given
up. But there is little or no evidence to help the
geographer to find a more likely site. At the present
day the most important track from El-Haouria leads
south-east to Kelibia, and it is not impossible that Megale-

---

[1] This account (D. xx. 8, 3) is no doubt drawn from the description of
an eyewitness, who had perhaps himself enjoyed what he describes so
glowingly. It is interesting to note that the beauty of the scene appealed
to the narrator quite as much as its material wealth. For the defenceless
state of the country, cf. J. xxii. 5, 5; 6, 5. The mention of stucco
($\kappa o\nu\iota a\mu a$) on the Carthaginian houses is also noteworthy, especially as it
may refer to the whitewash still used everywhere in the country.

polis may have been in that region, as Wesseling suggested. This was a short day's march from Aquilaria. Agathocles himself founded Aspis in that neighbourhood, perhaps near the site of his earlier capture. The present state of the land through which Agathocles marched does not help to fix his road; for the dreary stretches of sand and scrub between El-Haouria and Kelibia may once have been blooming gardens, such as are now seen a few miles further south. The whole headland is dotted with small ruins, none of which afford means of identification. On the other hand there are easy tracks from Cape Bon nearer the western coast, leading to Soliman, and affording a shorter road to Tunis. The site of Megalepolis must therefore remain uncertain[1].

White Tunis is said by Diodorus to have been 250 miles from Carthage, but as this is nearly twice as far as the distance from Carthage to Cape Bon by the present roads, the number is almost certainly corrupt. The only known city of Tunis held the site of the modern town. Agathocles later on had his headquarters there, but it is nowhere related that he took a second Tunis. The most likely view therefore is that White Tunis is the well known city, and that it got its name from its white cliffs. This was the natural base for any force acting against Carthage, and it afforded almost the only passable haven on that coast. Regulus used Tunis in this way, and the leaders in the Mercenary war also held it[2].

[1] For the rival sites, cf. Tissot, I. 537.

[2] Holm and others have supposed that "White Tunis" was different from Tunis itself: while Schubert thinks that it may have been an outpost of the better known city. But these guesses seem to be needless. Agathocles may have sacked the place and still left enough standing to shelter his army later on. Tunis was 14 miles from Carthage.

The Carthaginian fleet had been hovering round Cape
Bon[1] and the seamen saw with astonishment and delight
that Agathocles had burned all his ships. But when the
prince was seen dashing boldly inland, the admiral felt
that it was time to warn the government of what had
happened. He had the prows of his own ships hung with
skins as a sign of disaster, and after picking up the brazen
beaks of Agathocles' boats, which the fire had spared,
he sailed to Carthage with all speed.

The alarm however had already been raised; and the
city was crowded with fugitives from the land, while the
utmost terror prevailed. Everyone thought that the host
in Sicily had been crushed, and the fleet driven off the
seas, so that the victorious enemy had come to invade
their country. There was no army ready to guard
Carthage, and Agathocles was hourly expected to show
himself under the walls. The Senate met in a panic.
Some counsellors were for sending envoys to treat with
the foe or at least to spy out his strength, others held
that it was better to wait for fuller news. In the midst
of this wild uproar the admiral's messengers landed and
told what had really happened. The people took heart,
and the Senate assembled to form a plan of defence.
A vote of censure was first passed on the sea-commanders,
for allowing Agathocles to land in spite of their own
greater numbers. Then it was resolved to send an army
to fight the Greeks, and two leaders of opposite parties,
Hanno and Bomilcar, were chosen to command it[2].
Bomilcar was a kinsman of Hamilcar the friend of
Agathocles, and his election now must have been meant

[1] D. xx. 9. The ships can hardly have been riding at anchor as
Diodorus says (ἐφορμοῦντες). Owing to the depth of water there can have
been no moorage out of range of the Greek weapons.

[2] D. xx. 10.

to satisfy the popular party: while good citizens tried to console themselves with the thought, that the jealousy of the generals would make each strive to outdo the other in valour[1]. This course, however, was unlucky for Carthage, for Bomilcar was already hoping to rise above the laws, and high command gave him an opening for treason[2].

The Carthaginian generals were anxious to meet Agathocles at once, and decided to raise such forces as the city could muster, without waiting for the levies elsewhere[3]. The foot soldiers amounted, it is said, to 40,000 men, the horse to 1000 and the chariots of war to 2000. Of the population of Carthage at this time nothing is known[4]; but it would seem that a great effort must have been made to arm so many men, and numbers of these would have been poorly trained and only fit to take the field near home; otherwise Agathocles would never have faced them with an army of half the size.

The camp was pitched by Hanno on a hill near the Greek position, and the host was set out in array. Hanno himself, as senior commander, took the right wing, where

[1] A similar sentiment is attributed to M. Livius (Salinator) in Livy XXVII. 35.

[2] D. *ibid.* 2. Diodorus here explains the jealous policy of the Punic Senate, and adds that it was only in times of unrest that leaders of the popular party had any chance of rising.

Hamilcar is called Bomilcar's *patruus* in J. XXII. 7, 10.

[3] Justin, however, says that Hanno brought 30,000 *paganorum* into the field (J. XXII. 6, 6). Unless *Poenorum* be the right reading, his account is probably a mistake. Meltzer took *paganorum* for a mistranslation of some such word as ἐγχωρίων. Orosius IV. 6 has, *Hannonem quemdam cum triginta millibus* POENORUM, *obviam habuit.* This tends to confirm the reading of *Poenorum* in Justin.

[4] Strabo (XVII. 3, p. 833) gives 700,000 before the last Punic War, but we cannot tell whether the number would have been greater or smaller so long before.

the Sacred Band, about a thousand strong, was posted[1].
Bomilcar stood on the left, where lack of room obliged
him to make a narrow front. The chariots and horsemen
were posted in the van to make the first onset.

Agathocles meanwhile had been setting his own men
in array. Instead of taking the post of honour on the
right wing, he gave this to his son Archagathus, and kept
for himself the more dangerous task of facing the best
troops of the enemy. Archagathus had 2500 foot under
his own command; then came 3500 Syracusans, 3000
Greek hirelings, and 3000 foreigners (Celts, Samnites and
Etruscans); on the left wing stood Agathocles himself
with a thousand picked men. The 500 bowmen and
slingers were placed on the wings: no horse is mentioned.

Owing to the small number of his forces—which, if
rightly given, were only 13,500 strong against 40,000—
Agathocles resorted to a curious plan to add to his
apparent strength[2]. He had some of his ships' crews
in camp besides his regular troops, but there were not
enough arms for them all. He therefore took the cases
of the shields and stretched them on wicker frames, says
Diodorus. These make-shifts were quite useless in action,
but from a distance the men equipped with them might
deceive the enemy into believing that Agathocles had
reserve troops in waiting. In spite of this contrivance
the Greeks, our account goes on, were still downhearted
in face of such overwhelming odds, and the ready wits of
Agathocles found yet more remarkable means to cheer
them. In several points of the camp he let fly some owls,
that he had long had in readiness for such an hour. The

----

[1] The Sacred Band had mustered 2500 men at the Crimisus (D. xvi.
80, 4) but in this present case it must have been weaker, since Agathocles
only set 1000 men against it.

[2] D. xx. 11, 2.

birds flew along the battle line and settled on the men's shields and helmets; and the soldiers, who thought this a fair token from Athena, at once regained their courage. Thus, says Diodorus, what seems a trifling device may often lead to great results.

Neither of these ruses can be fully believed. In the first place they break into the account of the battle, without having very much to do with it. The supposed reserves play no part in the action, and in the roll of the army they have no place. It is also unlikely that any large number of men lacked arms; Agathocles must have known that every oarsman would have to be a land-fighter later on, and therefore he would certainly have put on board enough shields for all. Again if any of these had been dropped in the fighting that had already taken place, the capture of two cities must have afforded means of making good the loss. The utmost that can be believed is that a few shields were missing, and that Agathocles had substitutes patched up of such stuff as was to hand.

The truth underlying the second story may be that a few of Agathocles' men happened to start some owls not long before a battle. The birds, being half blinded by the daylight, flew about aimlessly in the camp. This was taken as a token from heaven, and the victory was afterwards ascribed to Athena. The thought of Agathocles' carrying about an owl-cote on the march against such an occasion, is obviously ridiculous; and even the Greeks, when they saw the owls being let loose, would hardly have fancied that a goddess was giving them a sign. It has already been seen that in many of these ruses of Agathocles accidents are made the outcome of set purpose, and small details are overstated for dramatic effect. This has happened in the case in hand: neither story is altogether false, but neither can be believed in its present shape[1].

The fight began with a charge of the Carthaginian war-chariots. The Greeks stood their ground; some of the drivers were shot, some were let pass right through the ranks, but the more part were forced to wheel round and take shelter among the foot-soldiers. Then the horsemen charged; but the Greeks never wavered, so that these too had to flee with heavy loss. The onset of the infantry proved more dangerous, and a fierce fight began along the whole line. Hanno and the Sacred Band wrought a great slaughter among the Greeks, until the light troops came up to the rescue. The Carthaginians fought on under a rain of arrows till at last Hanno fell with many wounds. The Greeks now felt that the victory was theirs, and began to press hard on the enemy. Bomilcar meanwhile saw the discomfiture of the right wing, and withdrew his own troops, sending word to the rest to retire to the camp in good order[2].

Such a command naturally meant the ruin of the army, and Bomilcar was strongly suspected of treasonable designs in wishing to bring about the overthrow of the Sacred Band; for not only would the weakening of Carthage make it easier to upset the government, but

[1] Schubert (110—112) looks upon both these tales as pure fiction, the work of Duris. Most historians have related them without expression of belief or disbelief. Ferrari tried to support the story of the owls by the comparison of Louis Napoleon's eagle, let fly at Boulogne in 1840. Here the release of the eagle was symbolic, while Agathocles' men were not supposed to know that any human means had brought the owls. (Quoted by Schubert 111.)

Dr Evans (Freeman IV. 410, n. 2) refers to a figure of an owl on a gold stater of Agathocles, struck after 310, which may possibly be an allusion to some such omen of victory as has been described, but, as is shown by the same authority (*ibid.* 488), another explanation is more likely.

[2] D. xx. 12.

with the Sacred Band many of the staunchest oligarchs would perish[1].

The right wing, thinking from the withdrawal of Bomilcar that the battle was already lost, was swept away in headlong rout, in which the Sacred Band, from fear of being cut off, was forced to share, and nearly the whole army fled like a disordered rabble to the gates of Carthage.

The Greeks did not pursue far, but turned back to plunder the camp. There they were astonished to find, besides other booty, several waggon-loads of handcuffs, twenty-thousand pair, it was said. So sure had the Carthaginians been of the victory, that they meant to make a great number of captives, and to set them to work on their lands.

The numbers of the fallen were variously reported. Diodorus says that 200 Greeks were slain, and either 1000, or according to another account, 6000 Carthaginians. Justin speaks of 2000 Greeks and 3000 Carthaginians as slain. The smallest numbers, that is 200 Greeks and 1000 Carthaginians, seem the most likely[2]. This heavy defeat within sight of Carthage spread the utmost

[1] Diodorus goes into Bomilcar's motives at some length, xx. 12. 5, 6. Modern writers have disagreed as to whether Bomilcar's act was treason or cowardice. Meltzer and Niese, 448, besides De Sanctis *op. cit.* 307—8 incline to the latter view. Schubert 114 (although he regards the alleged motives of Bomilcar as Duris' fiction) seems to accept his treason. The remark of De Sanctis, that a *victory* would have been the best means of ensuring Bomilcar's rise to power, is quite against all our knowledge of Carthaginian history. On the whole, as the Carthaginians were always bold and desperate fighters, it seems to me unlikely that any loyal commander would have acted with such panic-stricken folly as Bomilcar must have shown, if we are resolved to clear him of the charge of treason.

[2] Orosius here has (Hannonem)...*quem cum duobus millibus suorum interfecit. Ipse autem duos tantum in eo bello perdidit.* The last number

fright and dismay among her citizens[1]. They believed that the wrath of heaven was smiting them, since the gods seemed no more to go forth with their hosts. The Carthaginians remembered with shame how grudging their own gifts to the gods had been, and turned with fearful haste to make good this shortcoming. From of old the wont had been to send to Melkart[2] at Tyre a tithe of every year's income; but when the wealth of Carthage grew, the greed of men would allow but a trifling share to their fathers' god. Now the anger of Melkart seemed to be upon them, and it was resolved to send a rich offering to appease him. Many costly gifts were brought together, and among them golden models of shrines, which were kept in the Punic temples. These offerings were taken to Tyre and there dedicated to the god.

Still more dreaded was the wrath of Moloch, whom the Greeks called Cronos. To his ruthless godhead the Semites used to make their own children pass through the fire. But ease and culture made the Carthaginians feel the horror of such rites, and the nobles used to buy slave-children and offer them to the god instead of their own[3]. Perhaps too the sacrifice itself had been in

is obviously absurd. Should *ducentos* be read? And if so, would this mean that Orosius for once went straight to Trogus?

I have honestly failed to understand Schubert's explanation (p. 113) of the disagreement between Diodorus and Justin.

[1] D. xx. 14.

[2] In Greek Heracles. The use of such Biblical names as Melkart and Moloch, if not quite scientific, is justified by precedent. (They are so used by Grote and Freeman.)

[3] Schubert's sneer (p. 116) that the Carthaginians, like true Semites, cheated their own gods, is needless. Every people whose beliefs have been unspiritual has been tempted to laxity in worship in time of weal, especially where the ritual is cruel or ugly : and every such people in time of stress has turned to degrading means to ward off the

abeyance. Now in the agony of remorse it was resolved
to take two hundred children of the highest rank and
offer them; while other three hundred, who were suspected
of having escaped unduly, came forward, by their own
will or their fathers', and gave themselves up to death.

The image of Moloch was brazen, and the hands
stretched out and sloped downwards towards the earth.
The children were laid one by one on the god's hands
and so rolled off into a deep pit filled with fire.

Having taken these means of appeasing the wrath
of heaven, the Carthaginian government sent orders
to Hamilcar to ship the best of his forces for Africa,
to help in the war against Agathocles.

2. HAMILCAR'S ATTEMPT ON SYRACUSE.

Hamilcar meanwhile had been besieging Syracuse,
and a complicated series of events now followed which
must first be given in the words of Diodorus (c. 15)[1].
The Carthaginians in sending their call for help to
Hamilcar, had despatched at the same time the brazen rams
of Agathocles' ships. "Hamilcar bade the messengers
hold their peace about the late defeat, but told them to
spread abroad the tidings that Agathocles had lost his
ships and his whole force. (§ 2) He sent some of the
messengers as envoys to the Syracusans, and with them

anger of heaven. The Athenians in their dark hour purified Delos
(Thuc. IV. 104). The Romans in the second Punic War made human
sacrifices (Liv. XXII. 57, 6). These customs of the Carthaginians were
a matter of common knowledge to both Greeks and Romans. Ennius
says, *Poeni sunt soliti suos sacrificare puellos*. In Plutarch's *Apo-
phthegmata* (*s.v.* Gelo I.) it is said that one of the conditions of peace
after the victory of Himera was that the offering of children to Moloch
should be stopped (ὅτι καὶ τὰ τέκνα παύσονται τῷ Κρόνῳ καταθύοντες).

[1] D. xx. 15. I have "englished" somewhat freely to save space.

the brazen rams; they were to demand the surrender of the city. The power of Syracuse, they were to say, had been overthrown by the Carthaginians: and her ships were burned. Those who doubted must be convinced by the sight of the rams. (§ 3) When the news came to Syracuse, most of the citizens believed it, while the rulers, who were at a loss what to do, kept watch to check any turmoil. Hamilcar's envoys were at once sent back, and an order was issued to drive out of the city all kinsfolk of the exiles, and any others who seemed to chafe at the government of the regents. No fewer than eight thousand were cast out; (§ 4) and this sudden flight filled Syracuse with bustle and din and the wailing of women. No house but mourned in that hour. (§ 5) The rulers wept for the fate of Agathocles and of his sons: some of the citizens bewailed their friends, whom they believed to have fallen in Libya, others sorrowed for those who were driven from hearth and home, who might not stay and who dared not go forth with the foe under the walls, and in whose flight so many helpless children and women were forced to share. (§ 6) But when the outcasts fled to the Carthaginian camp, Hamilcar gave them shelter. At the same time he marshalled his army and marched on Syracuse, hoping that the emptiness of the city, and the fright caused by the ill tidings, would make it easy to surprise the besieged. (c. 16) Hamilcar sent on an embassy and undertook to spare Antander and his fellow-rulers, if they handed over the city. A council met, and Antander, who was a coward and very unlike his brother, declared for yielding, but Erymnon the Aetolian, who had been chosen to aid Antander, took the other side, and persuaded the council to hold out until the truth was known. (§ 2) When this resolve was told to Hamilcar, he began to build all kinds of

siege-engines, meaning to storm the city. (§ 3) Agathocles had built two thirty-oared boats after his victory.
He sent one to Syracuse with his strongest rowers on
board, and Nearchus, one of his trustiest friends, to
carry the good tidings. (§ 4) The weather was fair,
and after five days' sail the boat drew near to Syracuse
at night[1]; and then, after crowning themselves, and singing
songs of triumph on the way, made a dash for the harbour at daybreak."

Diodorus then states that the Carthaginians on the
blockade espied the boat and gave chase. A desperate
race followed, which was eagerly watched by Greeks and
Carthaginians, who had gathered on the shore near the
harbour. In the end, the despatch-boat escaped by a
hair's-breadth, and came safely to land.

The account goes on (§ 7) "When Hamilcar saw that
the stir and expectation of news had drawn most of the
Syracusans to the harbour, he guessed that some part
of the wall would be unguarded, and sent the strongest
of his men with ladders. The party found a place
undefended, and climbed up unseen; they had already
taken the space between two towers, when the usual patrol
came up and caught sight of them. (§ 8) A fight
ensued; the citizens rushed to the rescue, and their
quickness hindered the army outside from helping the
storming-party. Some of the assailants were cut down,
and the rest were hurled from the walls. This failure
disappointed Hamilcar, who drew off his forces from the
city, and sent 5000 of his men to the help of the
Carthaginians."

[1] This express-boat thus took a day less in crossing than the fleet
of Agathocles had done, when the distance (Cape Bon instead of Tunis
harbour) was slightly less. Most likely therefore the boat took the same
line as the fleet: that is, it sailed to the nearest point of the Sicilian
coast and then worked round towards Syracuse.

Although Diodorus seems to speak of two embassies from Hamilcar to Syracuse, there can be little doubt that he is really describing the same event in different words. To prove this it need only be said that the council of the Syracusan rulers (placed by Diodorus after the second embassy) must have been held as soon as the news from Hamilcar came in; for the sending his envoys back with a refusal, and the banishment of the suspected partisans, are both the outcome of the resolve to wait for further tidings. In fact Diodorus says as much, in stating that the regents did not know what to do, but resolved to crush sedition at all costs, and not to treat with Hamilcar.

The order of events therefore needs setting right, and it seems to have been as follows.—Hamilcar probably heard of the burning of Agathocles' fleet long before any news of the land fight came to Sicily: and very likely both he and the Syracusans knew of the fate of the ships before the rams could have been carried across to Hamilcar's camp. It is not easy to believe that the whole tale of sixty ships'-beaks was ever brought to Sicily. The weight of the rams would have made their conveyance very costly, and the chance of deceiving the Syracusans was remote. One beak may perhaps have been sent, not to confirm the burning of the fleet, which the Greeks *ex hypothesi* believed already, but merely as a kind of symbol such as the Semites love.

Cheered by this news, Hamilcar called on Syracuse to treat: he offered fair terms; the exiles of course must have been taken back, and peace made with Carthage: the cause of Agathocles must have been given up, but the whole of the tyrant's party was promised safety. Whether Hamilcar really knew the issue of the land-fight when he sent his proposals may well be doubted;

for he must have seen that there could be little chance of a peaceful settlement with Agathocles victorious in Africa.

The council of war followed the coming of the envoys: and after Erymnon had carried his motion to await news from Agathocles, the Carthaginians were sent back, and it was resolved to purge Syracuse of all oligarchic elements. Perhaps the tale of Agathocles' destruction had caused restlessness among that party, which now found itself ruthlessly forestalled. The heart-breaking scenes of parting are drawn rhetorically, but must indeed have been painful, especially as the mildness of Hamilcar, politic as it was, seems to have been quite unhoped for.

Hamilcar of course had his siege-engines ready beforehand, and the return of his envoys, as well as the flight of the banished nobles with their wives and children, informed him of the stubborn mood of the Syracusans. There was nothing left but to storm the city, and Hamilcar chose the moment when the friends of Agathocles were making merry after the good news had come. The despatch-boat had met with fair weather, and crossed in five days where Agathocles' fleet had needed six. The account of the run into the harbour, though highly coloured for the sake of dramatic effect, is not altogether false. The race must have lain between the extreme end of the entrance to the Great Harbour and the point of Ortygia. The garrison there posted and the Carthaginians stationed on the shore could easily have followed the course of the pursuit. But as the distance is under a mile and the time can have been little over five minutes, it was therefore impossible for a large crowd to have gathered in time to see the finish of the race. The coming of the news is quite enough to account for the disorder of which Hamilcar tried to take advantage.

The strength of the walls was such as almost to defy storming, so that Hamilcar's failure cannot have surprised even himself. By that time he must have had the news of the Carthaginian defeat in Africa and wished to make a last try before sending home his best troops.

By the withdrawal of so large a part of Hamilcar's army Carthage virtually gave up hope of striking a telling blow at the power of Syracuse. But her act must not be judged hastily. Doubtless the crowded state of Carthage made food very scarce, and it was needful at all costs to keep the road open to the midland of Africa; for a city which drew all its food-supplies from its own fields would not have been able at such a crisis to feed its swollen population by means of its ships. Therefore until the crowd of runaways could be drilled and sent out to fight (as they were later on), the help of fresh troops could not be foregone.

3. THE WAR IN AFRICA. 310—309.

By his late victory over the Carthaginians Agathocles found himself master of the open country[1]. He now built a strong camp near Tunis[2], which, as we have seen, he had probably already taken; there he left a detachment of troops to watch Carthage, and to shut her off from the land to the south. The threatening nearness of this camp and the sight of burning crops and farms weighed heavily on the hearts of the Carthaginians in the city,

[1] D. xx. 17; J. xxii. 6, 8, 9.

[2] J. ibid. *Castra deinde in quinto lapide a Carthagine statuit, ut damna carissimarum rerum, vastitiamque agrorum et incendia villarum de muris ipsius urbis specularentur.*

Agathocles' camp cannot really have been less than twelve miles away from Carthage.

Cf. too Orosius iv. 6, who seems here to have copied almost word for word from Justin.

but until the troops of Hamilcar came, there were no means of checking Agathocles.

The latter marched to the eastern coast and fell upon the city of Neapolis. This place, which has left its name in the modern Nabel, stood on an open sandy beach in a rich neighbourhood. No doubt the pottery, now made there in large quantities, was a source of wealth to the ancient town. Agathocles took Neapolis by storm, but spared the indwellers, for like Hamilcar in Sicily, he wished to play the deliverer to subject cities.

Hadrumetum was next attacked, and, while Agathocles lay before it, he was greeted with an offer of alliance from Elymas king of the Libyans. The action of this powerful chief shows that the valour of Agathocles was becoming widely known, and that the allies of Carthage were ready to join him[1].

The Carthaginians seem to have taken heart when Agathocles' back was turned, and marched out in great force to surprise his camp. The stroke succeeded, and the Greek troops had to throw themselves into Tunis itself, which was at once besieged by the enemy with the aid of their engines. Many assaults were beaten off, and a call for help was sent to Agathocles outside Hadrumetum. He is said to have saved Tunis by a strange trick.

"He left most of his men to carry on the siege, and took his camp-followers and a few troops to a hill-top in sight of Tunis and also of Hadrumetum. There he made his men light fires over a wide stretch of ground, and thus led the Carthaginians to believe that he was coming to attack them with a large army. At the same time the Hadrumetans thought that a fresh Greek force was on its way to press the siege. Thus both were outwitted

[1] D. *ibid.*

by the ruse, and unexpectedly worsted. The besiegers of Tunis left all their engines and fled to Carthage, while the Hadrumetans yielded to the Greeks."

This story seems out of place at the present juncture[1]. Firstly, the distance between Hadrumetum and Tunis was too great for the fires to have been seen from both places at once. Hadrumetum, which seems to have held the site of the modern Susa[2], was at least seventy miles from Tunis; and even if with some travellers we place it at Hammamet, the distance would still be too great. At all events there would have been nothing more than a faint glow in the sky, which could hardly have frightened the Carthaginians into such headlong flight, that they forgot to move or even to burn their siege-engines. Still less would it have alarmed the Hadrumetans, who might just as well have thought that a Punic and not a Greek army was coming.

All that can be believed is that Agathocles in marching to the relief of Tunis surprised the Carthaginian camp: the men fled in a panic, and left all their artillery behind. Then Agathocles came back to Hadrumetum, which at once made terms.

The prince then marched southwards to Thapsus, which stood in a weak position on a flat headland; this he stormed[3]. After the taking of the three chief cities

[1] So Grote xxii. 568 n. and Schubert 125. Niese 451 also doubts the ruse. (See also note below.)

[2] So Barth and Tissot ii. 159. Davies chose Hammamet largely on the strength of the present passage, which cannot prove anything. For the ancient remains at Susa cf. Tissot *ibid.* 149 f. and plan, iii. Pl. IX.

[3] Thapsus is usually sought on the headland of Henchir-ed-Dimas, near Mkalta. The ruins consist of a Roman pier, and some large concrete remains. The fields are littered with marble-chips. A little further inland a Punic burial-ground has been found. Natural defences and a natural harbour are wholly wanting. (Cf. Tissot ii. 172 f. and iii. Pl. XI.)

in the coast-land the smaller towns could not withstand the Greek forces; most of them yielded, and the rest were carried by assault. At the end of the campaign Agathocles had two hundred places in his hands.

Although there is no break in the account of Diodorus, it can hardly be believed that Agathocles undertook in the first year of his inroad the operations now to be described. It will be seen that Diodorus only relates one trifling event for the year 309 in Africa, and there is good ground for thinking that the undertakings before us really belong to that year and not, as Diodorus implies, to 310[1].

[1] Agathocles had sailed on the 14th of August; he landed on the 20th, and must have waited two or three days before burning his ships: he marched, say, on the 25th. From Cape Bon to Tunis it would be at least four days march, and to this must be added the time for storming two cities. It is also clear that the army marched leisurely and took time to plunder. Thus the occupation of Tunis cannot have been before the 10th, say, of September. Several more days were needed for the Carthaginians to march out, so that the battle falls late in September. Then came the building of the despatch-boat and the making of the camp near Tunis: probably the beginning of October is not too late for Agathocles' start for the coast. Neapolis was nearly two days march from Tunis; this had to be stormed; Hadrumetum was two days further south, and here there was a long siege. Then at least three days march to relieve Tunis, and three to return; then a day's march to Thapsus and the time for storming it. This would bring us to the end of October. For the occupation of 200 places, November would not have been too long. Thus Agathocles had only one month left, and that usually cold and rainy in Tunisia. I believe therefore that he went into winter quarters after the winning of the 200 towns, and that the whole passage D. xx. 18 relates to the warfare of 309, excepting only the arrival of Hamilcar's troops, which took place at the close of the campaign of 310. These troops were too late to take the field that year, so that their coming is not mentioned until later.

The view here taken of the dating agrees with that of Niese 451. Schubert has followed Diodorus' arrangement, but has made this easier (as will be seen) by striking out a large part of the narrative as a "doublet."

Agathocles had now subdued all the civilized part
of the eastern coast.   He strengthened his hold by
founding a dockyard and haven at Aspis.   The new
harbour took its name from the neighbouring shield-
shaped hill which is a far-seen height along the flat
strand.   This rising made a safe stronghold and a good

Citadel of Aspis (Kelibia), with Arab Castle.

watch-tower, for it overlooked the whole coast from the
eastern shoulder of the Cape Bon cliffs almost to Neapolis
itself.   The Romans called the place Clupea, and the
modern Kelibia carries on the name[1].

[1] The gain to Agathocles of a fleet-station on the eastern coast is
clear: for it spared his ships the need of doubling Cape Bon and making
the difficult entrance to Tunis harbour.   There are remains of ancient
quays at Kelibia, but hardly any other antique relics.   The stronghold is

The prince then undertook a long march up country, but we are not told how he fared[1]. His absence emboldened the Carthaginians, now strengthened by Hamilcar's troops as well as by the long awaited levies from the interior, to make another attempt on Tunis. They laid siege to this and won back some smaller posts from the Greeks. The garrison of Tunis sent a hasty message to Agathocles, who at once turned back to relieve the place[2].

He crept up within a few miles of the Carthaginian camp and there halted, forbidding his men to light fires[3]. Then he made a night march and fell on the enemy at daybreak. Many of the Carthaginians were caught outside the camp and cut down; a pitched battle followed, in which Agathocles won the day. Over two thousand of the Punic soldiers were killed, and many were taken alive. This defeat was a great blow to Carthage; for it now seemed that her best troops were no match for the invaders.

Elymas, the Libyan prince who had joined Agathocles some months before, proved faithless when the new muster raised for a time the hopes of the Carthaginians; and Agathocles, after his victory and the relief of Tunis, set out to chastise this fickle ally. A fight was fought,

Arab. The view from the hill is very striking. Diodorus does not mention the building of Aspis, which comes from Strabo XVII. 3 (p. 834). Εἶτα ἄκρα Ταφῖτις καὶ ἐπ' αὐτῇ λόφος Ἀσπὶς καλούμενος ἀπὸ τῆς ὁμοιότητος, ὅνπερ συνῴκισεν ὁ τῆς Σικελίας τύραννος Ἀγαθοκλῆς, καθ' ὃν καιρὸν ἐπέπλευσε τοῖς Καρχηδονίοις.

[1] D. xx. 18.

[2] Ibid. 3.

[3] Diodorus says 200 stades, = 25 miles (xx. 18, 2). This must be a mistake, for no army would be ready to fight after a night-march of such length.

and again the Greeks had the better. Elymas fell, and
many of his subjects died with him[1].

Diodorus himself has only assigned two events of the
African war to the year 309[2], although it has already
been seen that others may properly belong to it. It is
first stated that after the sending of Hamilcar's head
to Agathocles (of which matter we shall speak below),
the Carthaginians were much cast down in heart, while
the Greeks were overjoyed, as they felt that Syracuse
was safe. This must have happened fairly late in the
campaign.

For the moment the fighting was at a standstill, but
the ill-feeling among the followers of Agathocles brought
on an outbreak of mutiny on the part of the troops.

It is said that Agathocles and his son Archagathus
sat at wine with one of the generals, named Lyciscus.
This man forgot in his cups the respect owing to his
leader, and reviled Agathocles recklessly. Agathocles
bore it patiently, but his son was wroth and chid Lyciscus
with threats. When the party broke up, Lyciscus taunted
Archagathus with being the lover of his step-mother
Alcia. Enraged at this charge Archagathus snatched
a spear from one of the guardsmen, and ran Lyciscus
through the chest. Lyciscus fell dead, and was borne
to his tent. On the morrow the friends of the murdered

[1] D. xx. 18, 3. Schubert 128 believes that Tunis was only relieved
once by Agathocles, but that Diodorus has repeated the same event.
His chief argument is that Agathocles would not, after once relieving
Tunis, have turned his back, while there was any likelihood of the Punic
attacks being renewed. But, as the two reliefs seem to have fallen in
different years, it is probable that the Carthaginians were led to make
the second attack by the arrival of Hamilcar's troops ;—of this Agathocles
knew nothing, and so did not take any steps better to secure Tunis.
Schubert's other arguments hardly alter the case.

[2] D. xx. 33.

man roused the whole army to wrath. It happened that
many officers feared punishment on one charge or another,
and the men's pay was owing: so that the ill-feeling
against Agathocles led to an uproar in the camp. The
mutineers called on the prince to give up his son to
justice, and when he would not, they chose leaders of
their own, set guards on the walls of Tunis, and kept
Agathocles and his sons closely watched.

These doings came to the knowledge of the Carthaginians, and they sent word to the mutinous troops
offering them gifts and high pay if they would forsake
the Greek side. This proposal found most favour among
the officers, who undertook to bring over the whole host
to the Carthaginians[1]. Agathocles, knowing well that no
mercy awaited him if he were carried over to the foe,
resolved to throw himself on the loyalty of the common
soldiers.

He came forward in a mean garb without his cloak
of office[2], and made a moving harangue to the crowd.
He professed his readiness to die if his men so wished it,
and ended by drawing his sword, as if to do the deed then
and there. The soldiers shouted to him to stay his hand,
declaring that he had done no wrong, and bidding him
put on his robe once more. He obeyed with tears of joy,
and the cheers of his troops assured him of their renewed
faithfulness.

The Carthaginians had no notion of the turn of affairs,
and are said to have been waiting outside the camp to
welcome all who would join them. Soon a large force
was seen marching from the Greek position: Agathocles
in fact had thought the moment favourable for another

[1] D. xx. 34.
[2] Diodorus (*ibid.* 3 and 5) carelessly calls this πορφύρα, and βασιλικὴ
ἐσθής.

attack. The army drew near to the Carthaginians, who feared nothing. All at once the bugles rang out, and the Greeks fell upon the enemy in a furious onset. The Carthaginians were routed with heavy loss and fled to their camp. Thus Agathocles once more saved himself and worsted the foe by his own bravery and cleverness. Only two hundred of the mutineers went over to Carthage.

Such is the substance of Diodorus' account, but there is reason for believing that he greatly overrates the importance of the mutiny[1]. Only the army actually in Tunis was concerned; the other bodies holding Hadrumetum, Aspis, and the rest of the posts, were guiltless. The cause of the upheaval seems to have been the jealousy of the officers against the sons of Agathocles: for, firstly, the charge of adultery against Archagathus would not have been so galling unless there was already great bitterness of feeling[2]; and again, the officers appear throughout as the chief agents. They stir up the men to rise, and they welcome the offers from the Punic side. The men on the other hand only think about their arrears of pay when the officers put them in mind of it: and when Agathocles appeals to them, they quickly forget their discontent. Doubtless the army of Tunis was the same body that had fought against Hamilcar's reinforcements; Agathocles very likely left them to rest after the fight, and took fresh troops from Hadrumetum to march against Elymas: for Hadrumetum seems to have been near that king's lands. Thus the men left behind had only weary and bootless garrison duty, while the other

[1] Cf. Niese 455. The anecdotal nature of the whole story is another proof of its small importance.

[2] Diodorus again refers to this scandal in xx. 68, 3. The charge was almost certainly false, as will be seen below.

army had the easy task of chastising and plundering an untrained desert-tribe.

In this way some discontent may have arisen. The fact of the Carthaginians' trying to buy over the Greeks with promises of high pay shows how much they felt their own weakness[1]. Agathocles' harangue to his troops, and his play-acting, may be overdrawn, but need not be disbelieved altogether[2]. It is also hardly likely that the Carthaginians would have let themselves be surprised quite so easily as Diodorus relates. No doubt the news of the mutiny made them careless, and Agathocles in some way found means of taking them unawares and of slaying many[3]. The two hundred traitors, who were very likely the ringleaders in the mutiny, must have gone over by Agathocles' leave. He did not wish to spoil the general rejoicing by harsh measures, and such an accession could not have been worth much to the Carthaginians. But there is reason to believe that these deserters one day felt the vengeance of Agathocles after all[4].

[1] Cf. the attempt of the Germans to buy over the men of Germanicus (Tac. *Ann.* ii. 13).

[2] Schubert 137 (followed by Evans, Freeman's *Sicily* iv. 440, n. 3) calls the whole scene "Blosse Erfindung"; but his only reason is that anything theatrical is *ipso facto* an invention of Duris.

The means used here by Agathocles have often been taken against mutinous troops. Dionysius I (Polyaenus v. 2, 1) was threatened by hired troops, and came forward in a mean garb with dust on his head, and bade them do with him as they would. His bearing moved the men to pity and they spared him. Grote gives another parallel, the case of Fabius Valens (Tac. *Hist.* ii. 29), which is a closer analogy than Schubert will allow. Another case is that of the Emperor Anastasius in a popular sedition (cf. Bury, *Hist. of the Later Roman Emp.* i. 297).

[3] Schubert and Evans both consider that the bugle-call mentioned by Diodorus is another mark of the hand of Duris.

Evans is surely mistaken in placing here the mutiny of J. xxii. 8, 4 which belongs to the time after Agathocles' return from Sicily.

[4] See below, p. 142.

4. THE DEATH OF HAMILCAR. 309.

Hamilcar seems to have left the neighbourhood of
Syracuse after his failure in the year 310. He spent the
winter in raising fresh troops to fill the place of the six
thousand that he had sent home; and by the next spring
it is said that the whole force amounted to 120,000 foot,
and 5000 horse; among these no doubt the Greeks were
reckoned[1]. With this great host he won over the remaining
towns or strongholds in the island, and then resolved to
make an assault on Syracuse[2].

The city was now in sore straits, for the Punic fleet
was closely blockading the harbour, and Hamilcar's army
wasted the fields utterly. But a bold plan favoured by
good luck brought a quick deliverance.

Hamilcar had set his army in march, and meant to
pitch his camp on the hill of the Olympieum, the natural
base for attacking Syracuse. To reach this point he had
to march right past the walls of the stronghold on Euryelus.
For some reason he chose the late evening to make the
passage. Perhaps he hoped to slip by unseen, and thus to
save his column from a tiresome flank-attack. Diodorus
says that he meant to surprise Syracuse on his march, and
that he had high hopes, because his seer had foretold that
he should sup the next evening in the city.

The Syracusans had wind of Hamilcar's plans, and
posted a picked body of 3000 foot and 400 horse in the
fort of Euryelus. Presently the Carthaginian army drew
near in the darkness. First came Hamilcar with his own
guards, then Deinocrates at the head of the knights. These
were followed by two huge columns of foot, one Greek, one
foreign. The regular troops were accompanied by a crowd

[1] D. xx. 30, 1.
[2] D. xx. 29, 2. The account of the march follows.

of camp-followers, who hoped to share in the plunder of
Syracuse. This rabble was a hindrance on the march, and
when the road became narrow and rocky, serious disorder
with shouting and quarrelling set in.

The Syracusans in Euryelus heard the noise and chose
that moment to dash out and fall upon the foe. This
sudden onslaught threw the Carthaginian host into confusion. The Greeks blocked up the road, and the enemy,
who had no notion of the small numbers of their opponents,
were seized with panic and tried to flee. But in the darkness there was little hope of safety; some fell down steep
places, others were trampled by the frightened horses,
while many struck out wildly at friend or foe and perished
in the fray. Hamilcar bade his followers stand firm, and
fought manfully himself, but when the alarm spread he
was forsaken by his men, and the Syracusans took him
alive.

Thus had three thousand Greeks routed an army of
twelve myriads, and Syracuse was saved[1].

The march of Hamilcar past the walls of Syracuse is
usually taken as a night-attack on a large scale, with the
same object as that of Demosthenes the Athenian[2]. But
in this case the acts of Hamilcar, whose generalship has
hitherto been of the highest order, would bear the stamp
of incredible folly. In the first place the works on Euryelus
and Epipolae were so strong that even a surprise could

[1] Some trite reflexions in D. xx. 30. Justin's account is (xxii. 7, 2)
*Nam post profectionem a Sicilia Agathoclis in obsidione Syracusarum
Poeni segniores redditi, ab Antandro, fratre regis Agathoclis, occidione
caesi nuntiabantur.* This may perhaps mean that Antander himself took
command of the band stationed on Euryelus.

Cf. Orosius iv. 6 *Nam et apud Siciliam deletus cum imperatore exercitus
nuntiatur; quem re vera incautum et paene otiosum Antander Agathoclis
frater oppresserat.*

[2] So Holm, Grote, Freeman, and Schubert.

not promise more than a momentary gain. Next it would
have been stark madness to take 5000 horse and a large
baggage-train on a night-attack; nor would any treasures
or costly objects, such as the Syracusans are said to have
picked up after the rout, have been much use in such an
undertaking.

The main body of Hamilcar's army, as Diodorus'
description quite clearly shows, was in marching order,
and there was no question whatever of its attacking
Syracuse. The comparison with the attempt of Demosthenes therefore falls to the ground.

As the main Carthaginian army cannot thus have
been trying to surprise Syracuse, some have thought that
Hamilcar detached a small body of troops for that purpose,
and that their repulse led to the rout of the whole force.
But so experienced a general as Hamilcar would never
have endangered his army so recklessly, especially as the
noise made by the main body would have warned the
Syracusans and thus foredoomed any attempt at surprise.
If he had meant to take the besieged unawares, he would
have needed above all things to keep the troops not
required for the attack as far away as possible; the
surprise-force must have gone forward by itself swiftly
and silently. The fact that Hamilcar on the night of the
encounter made no such dispositions is enough to prove
that he had no notion of surprising the city.

Diodorus says that Hamilcar had meant to attack
the walls on his march[1]; but does not state that the attack
was ever tried. In other words he was fully aware that
the action of the Syracusans was directed solely against
the marching column, and that the supposed plan of

[1] D. xx. 29, 8 εὐθὺς δὲ καὶ προσβάλλειν ἐξ ἐφόδου τοῖς τείχεσι
διεγνώκει. Niese 453 takes this as above.

surprise attributed to Hamilcar had no effect on the
course of events.

Why then was this unfulfilled design of the Punic
leader ever mentioned? The answer seems to be that
Diodorus found the story of the seer in one of his
authorities, and that in trying to work in this detail, he
has half implied that some kind of attack on the city
was intended—otherwise the prophecy would be pointless.
It is very likely in the nature of things that the whole
account of the soothsayer and his quibble is pure fiction.
The Syracusans were undoubtedly astonished at the
sudden downfall of their dreaded foe, and tried to explain
it by making Hamilcar a victim misled by the gods to his
own ruin. With the seer-story the night-attack will also
be struck out; and Hamilcar's mistake becomes a much
more intelligible one[1]. He did not dream that the Syracusans would show such desperate boldness as to attack
his huge column on the march; and probably they would
never have dared to do it but for the disorder in the
Carthaginian train. The camp-followers, who must have
been mostly Greeks, may have insisted on sharing in the
march without yielding obedience to Hamilcar, so that
Diodorus is right in the main in making them the cause
of the ruin of the whole host[2].

[1] So Beloch 199, who notes that Diodorus' words do not necessarily
imply that Hamilcar tried to surprise Syracuse at all, but only that he
meant to. The words of Justin (quoted above), though little can be made
of them, seem to show that the Carthaginians were beaten owing to their
own carelessness or rather contempt of the foe.

[2] Another form of the tale is found in Cicero, *de Div.* i. 24. "In
the history of Agathocles it is said that Hamilcar the Carthaginian,
when he was besieging Syracuse, dreamed that he heard a voice
announcing to him that he should sup on the succeeding day in
Syracuse. When the morning dawned, a great sedition arose in his
camp between the Carthaginian and Sicilian soldiers. And when the

The victors gathered rich spoils from the baggage left by the routed foemen, and made their way back to the city with Hamilcar in bonds[1]. There no mercy awaited him. The rulers are said to have handed him over to any that had lost kinsfolk in the war, and these heaped every kind of insult and cruelty upon him as he was led in chains through Syracuse. In this hideous manner Hamilcar met his end. The rulers, it is said, then cut off his head, and sent it to Agathocles in Africa. The Greeks, as has already been stated, were overjoyed at this token of their countrymen's deliverance, and Agathocles is said to have ridden with this trophy almost to the Carthaginian camp, and with a loud voice to have told the enemy of their disaster. Diodorus adds that when the Carthaginians saw their general's head they were filled with dismay, but mindful of the rank of the dead man, they did obeisance in their barbaric fashion[2].

This story does not sound like sober history. It is not likely that Hamilcar, an unusually generous foe, would have been made away with in so outrageous a way[3].

Syracusans found this out they made a vigorous sally and attacked the camp unexpectedly, and succeeded in making Hamilcar prisoner…and thus the dream was verified" (*trans.* Yonge).

This variant goes to prove what has already been said, namely that the downfall of Hamilcar seemed to need an explanation, especially to the enemies of Agathocles, and this myth was meant to supply it. Cicero's version confirms the disorder arising from a quarrel between the Greeks and Carthaginians. Otherwise his account is worth little. The story is also found in Val. Max. I. 7, *ext.* 8.

On the topography, cf. Lupus, *die Stadt Syr. im Altertum* 125 ff. Beloch believes that the Syracusans attacked Hamilcar higher up the Anapus-dale, before he drew near to the walls.

[1] D. xx. 30, 2.   [2] D. xx. 33, 1.

[3] Beloch 198 thinks that Hamilcar may have done some piece of harshness himself, which was now wreaked on his head. But there is no evidence of this.

Probably he was simply beheaded. It would have been a tiresome business to send the head to Africa, and such a savage act does not suit what is known of the Greek character. The head would have needed embalming, and it is hard to believe that so much trouble would have been taken to effect so little. It is possible that Agathocles was at some pains to let the Carthaginians hear of their misfortune in Sicily; but that he trusted himself within earshot of their camp is certainly false[1].

The shattered wreck of Hamilcar's host rallied on the morning after the disaster, but there was no longer a guiding spirit to restore order or make good defeat. Mistrustful of each other, the Greeks and Carthaginians parted their forces; the next in command to Hamilcar were raised by choice of the men to be leaders of the Carthaginians, while the Greeks elected Deinocrates for their general.

The siege of Syracuse was not altogether raised but merely lingered on.

5. THE ACRAGANTINE LEAGUE. 309—8.

The two leading powers in Sicily, Syracuse and the Carthaginians, were so stunned by the shock of this last encounter, that for the moment there was no likelihood of serious undertakings on the part of either. Now the lesser states in the island could once more raise their heads and carry out unchecked whatever plans the hour suggested. Of the old rivals of Syracuse only one had not tasted the

[1] The Romans after the fight on the Metaurus are said to have cut off Hasdrubal's head and thrown it before Hannibal's camp (Liv. xxvii. 51). But the Romans were much more savage then than were the Sicilian Greeks in the fourth century. Schubert 132–3 believes that all the details of Hamilcar's end were made up by Duris as a *pendant* to the story about the ships'-rams already given. This may be so.

vengeance of Agathocles. This was Acragas. She had
survived the fall of Messena and the punishment of Gela.
She owed her safety to Hamilcar and the Punic host; but
now that neither help nor hindrance could come from that
quarter, it was time for her to stand alone. It is good to
read that the democratic spirit was still alive and that
Acragas at such a time could rise to the understanding of
her call. The citizens resolved to shake off the control of
Syracuse, to drive out all Punic garrisons from Greek
Sicily, and to bind the cities together in a free and equal
alliance.

The hour was fair: the Punic army was helpless and no
fresh troops were likely to land from Africa; Deinocrates
and his party would be neutral, and the half-starved
guard of Syracuse had no taste for fighting in the open
field. Above all the Greeks hated the Carthaginian
supremacy and longed for independence[1].

The new movement was democratic, and Xenodicus of
Acragas, who was elected general by the Acragantine
assembly, became its chief promoter. A strong force was
put under his orders and he was soon invited by partisans
to free Gela, which seems to have had a Punic garrison.
The gates were opened by night and Xenodicus became
master of the place. The citizens welcomed him with
great enthusiasm and put the whole forces and treasure
of the state at his disposal. Of the garrison we hear no
more, perhaps they withdrew under a truce. The call to

[1] D. xx. 31, 2 ff. Cf. Freeman iv. 431 ff. The formation of the new
league led practically to a three-cornered warfare in Sicily. Agathocles
was at war with Carthage and with Acragas, and the two latter were also
at war with each other. Deinocrates seems to have been neutral: he
can hardly have joined the league, as Freeman suggests; for the new
movement was democratic, and his help would certainly have been
mentioned if it had been given. The weakness of the democrats in the
field is another sign of their isolation.

freedom was now raised throughout the island and taken up eagerly on all sides. The Sicel towns joined in the new movement and Henna[1] at once offered her alliance. Herbessus was guarded by the Carthaginians, but after a struggle in which the citizens joined, the garrison, having met with heavy loss, surrendered to the number of five hundred.

The next call came from the south-east. Camarina and Netum[2] had been harassed for some time by a Syracusan outpost at Echetla. The friends of Agathocles had kept a force there which wasted the lands of the two cities. Xenodicus now brought up his forces and stormed Echetla. The popular government was set up, and the Syracusans driven out. Thus Netum and Camarina were saved.

Xenodicus went to many other places in the island, and freed them from the Carthaginians. Among these seems to have been Heraclea[3]; but the old Phoenician posts were not touched.

One more event is given by Diodorus for this year[4]. The Syracusans were in sore straits through lack of food, and when they heard that some corn-ships were coming, they manned twenty ships and slipped past the blockading fleet into the open sea. They coasted along as far as

[1] D. *ibid.* Henna is now Castrogiovanni.

[2] D. xx. 32. The common reading of Leontini for Netum is mistaken, as Niese 454 points out. Netum had the site of Noto Vecchio, a place forsaken after an earthquake in the Middle Ages. The site of Camarina was being excavated in 1906 by Prof. Orsi, who found a small burial ground. The only ruin above ground is part of a temple wall now built into a barn. Echetla is south-east of Netum, and is sought at Occhiala six miles east of Caltagirone (Cluver, *Sicily*, 360). Other sites however are also suggested (cf. Schubring, *op. cit.* 112).

[3] This is implied by the fresh reduction of Heraclea by Agathocles (D. xx. 56). Thermae, as it appears from the same chapter, remained Punic.   [4] D. xx. 32, 3.

Megara Hyblaea, then a Syracusan post, where they
waited to convoy the corn-fleet. But the Carthaginians
had already found out what had happened, and sailed out
thirty strong to cut off the Greeks. The Greeks at first
thought of fighting, but soon lost heart, and beached their
ships, the crews swimming ashore to a shrine of Hera that
stood near. The enemy pressed on and dragged off ten
of the vessels with grappling irons. But a rescue party
from Megara saved the rest.

This small incident may be taken as a type of many
skirmishes that must have gone on between the Carthaginians and the defenders of Syracuse. It shows that the
Greeks had a certain number of warships at sea, and
that the blockade of the harbour was kept up, though
less closely than before. It is not stated that the corn-
fleet ever reached Syracuse, but this perhaps is implied,
for otherwise there is not much point in the story[1].

6. AGATHOCLES' THIRD CAMPAIGN. 308 (?).

The Carthaginians had now grown more used to the
sight of the Greeks, and by this time many of the runaways sheltering in Carthage must have been trained into
useful soldiers. The Senate therefore resolved on a more
active conduct of the war. A strong force took the field
and its first goal was to bring back the revolted Numidians
to the side of Carthage[2]. The army came among the

[1] For Megara Hyblaea, cf. Schubring, *Umwanderung des megar.
Meerbusens*, and on excavations there, Cavallari-Orsi, *Megara Hyblaea,
Storia Topografia*, etc., also Dr Evans' notes, Freeman IV. 439–40.
Megara had been used as a fort by Syracuse in the time of the Athenian
expedition (Thuc. VI. 75), and it afterwards belonged to Hiero II.
(D. XXIII. 4).

[2] D. XX. 38. Justin speaks in general terms of the revolt of the
Carthaginian allies (XXII. 7, 3).

Zuphonians, a tribe otherwise unknown, and most of these
declared for Carthage, while some who had joined
Agathocles returned to their allegiance[1].

The prince could not be blind to such doings; and he
set out with a picked body to meet the foe, leaving Archagathus to hold Tunis, with the main army. Agathocles
had 8000 foot, 800 horse, and 50 African chariots. With
these he hastened after the Carthaginians.

The latter had pitched on a high hill, at the foot of
which several deep streams flowed: of its position nothing
further is known. Agathocles came boldly up to the
attack, but he was sorely harassed by the light-armed
Numidians, and at last brought to a halt. Luckily there
was a detachment of slingers and bowmen in the Greek
army, and with these Agathocles cleared the way for the
advance of the foot. The Punic host was already in battle-
line in front of its camp, and chose the moment when
Agathocles was fording the stream to rush down upon
him in full charge.

A fierce struggle followed; the Carthaginians had the
better ground and outnumbered the Greeks, but the latter
were doughty fighters, and for a long time the balance
was even. The Numidian allies of both sides took no more
part in the fray, but waited to plunder the camp of whichever army should be put to flight. At length Agathocles
worsted the enemy in front of him, and forced the whole
Carthaginian infantry to draw back. A band of Greek
horse in Punic service under the leadership of Cleinon,
proved more stubborn, and would not give ground until
almost every man was cut down, a few only escaping.
Agathocles pressed forward and with a great effort drove

[1] Niese 456 thinks that one Sophon, mentioned in Alexander Poly-
histor, *ap.* Joseph. *Ant. Jud.* I. 241, may have belonged to this tribe,
and so taken his name.

the Carthaginians back to their camp. Meanwhile the Numidians, seeing both armies hotly engaged on the hilltop, swooped down on the Greek quarters. The campguard was cut to pieces, and nearly all the captives and booty carried off. Agathocles must have stormed the Carthaginian camp and driven the foe from the field, before he had time to march back to the rescue of his own baggage. He came too late to save more than a small part: the Numidians had made away with the rest, and the fall of night made it hopeless to pursue them. Agathocles however had taken much booty in the Punic camp, and this was given bodily to the troops, so that they did not feel the loss of their own belongings[1].

A trophy was set up in honour of the victory.

Among the captives were more than a thousand Greeks, including five hundred Syracusans, from the Carthaginian service. They were put under a guard, but in the night they broke away from their keepers and made off, fearing the anger of Agathocles. They were defeated by the guard, but at length withdrew in safety to a steep hill. Agathocles marched up with his army when he heard what had happened, and persuaded the men to come down from the hill under a truce. He then had them all slain[2]. It has been suggested as a ground for this harshness that among the runaways were the two hundred Greeks that had forsaken Agathocles after the mutiny of the year before. These perhaps, having no hope of mercy for

[1] Diodorus does not say that the Carthaginian camp fell, but there can be little doubt that it did; since (1) Agathocles would never have left the defeat of his foe incomplete for the sake of rescuing his baggage. (2) It would have been unsafe to march down the hill with an unbroken foe in the rear. (3) Agathocles would not have been able to dole out the booty to his men if he had not taken any. (Cf. Holm 248, and Schubert 142.)

[2] D. xx. 39, 6.

themselves, may have urged the rest to join them in trying to escape, and so have involved them in their own doom[1].

[1] This is Niese's reasonable suggestion. Schubert 142–3 is at some pains to prove that the account of this fight is drawn from Timaeus, and that the latter drew his knowledge from the Carthaginian side, and in fact from the survivors of Cleinon's band. His grounds are: (1) "The account favours the Carthaginians, and is unfriendly to Agathocles, who is made out to have dealt treacherously with his prisoners." (2) The feats, numbers, and fate of Cleinon's knights are given at length, while for the Punic army, as a whole, no such details are forthcoming, not even the general's name. (3) Generally the knowledge of Carthaginian customs which is found in Diodorus must have come, first of all, from some one who had lived in Carthage, and from a Greek, because such things struck him as remarkable. Against these it must be said: (1) Schubert's first point seems to be mistaken. Much is said of the bravery of Agathocles (D. xx. 39, 1). His treatment of the prisoners is not given as anything shameful, and his thoughtful act in doling out the booty is carefully noted. (2) The Greeks on the Syracusan side would know most about the enemy that fought best; just as the slingers at the Himeras and the Sacred Band in the fight before Tunis were most noticed. The fact that these hirelings were Greeks and most of them Syracusans, must have made them all the more noteworthy in the eyes of Agathocles' men, many of whom no doubt recognised their old friends. A Greek on the Punic side could not have failed to know who was in command of the whole army, but Agathocles' side may well not have known. (3) It has already been seen that the customs of the Carthaginians, their sacrifices and state-mourning, were a matter of common knowledge to the Greeks. It has also been noted that Timaeus was blamed by Polybius for his childish lack of knowledge of the country of Africa (cf. p. 17). This would hardly have been the case if Timaeus had had a Greek informant who knew the land himself.

7. THE MARCH OF OPHELLAS.   308 B.C. (?).

In spite of his victories in the field, Agathocles had begun to feel that his own forces were unequal to the hugeness of his undertaking. The news from Sicily was no longer good, and the party of Bomilcar gave no signs of overthrowing the government of Carthage and thus making peace easy. An ally was therefore needed by Agathocles, and he called in Ophellas of Cyrene.

Ophellas had been an officer in the army of Alexander on his eastward march, and afterwards took service under Ptolemy. When Thimbron was beleaguering Cyrene, Ophellas was sent by his chief to relieve the city, and quickly raised the siege. The whole land of the Five Cities became part of Ptolemy's kingdom, and Ophellas was left to rule it in his stead. This had happened in 322, and since then, save for a rising in 312, which was quickly crushed, the sway of Ophellas had been unquestioned, and so fully was he trusted by Ptolemy, that he seemed almost a prince in his own right; indeed Justin inexactly calls him the King of Cyrene[1].

Ophellas was a man of some ability and boundless ambition. He took every means of gaining influence in Greece, and he must long have thirsted for conquest in the West, where alone the barbarian seemed still to hold sway[2].

It was probably in the latter half of the year 309

[1] J. xxii. 7, 4. For the career of Ophellas and the history of Cyrene, see Grote xii. 578—583 ; Droysen, *Geschichte d. Hellenismus* ii. 2 ; 35, 64.

[2] The *Periplus* of Ophellas, spoken of by Strabo xvii. 3 (p. 826), is now thought to be spurious ; so Niese and Beloch. Grote and others accepted it. The attribution of such a work to Ophellas shows that he was credited with high ambitions. The spelling 'Οφέλας has better authority than 'Οφέλλας, but I have kept the traditional form.

that Agathocles' envoy, one Orthon of Syracuse, reached Cyrene with his master's proposals. The offer was fair and tempting. In return for help in the overthrow of Carthage, Ophellas was promised the whole kingdom of Libya[1]. Agathocles, said Orthon, wished for nothing but a stable rule over Sicily; if a wider field were needed, then Italy would be open to his valour. Africa was parted from Sicily by miles of stormy sea, and it was not lust of conquest, but necessity that had brought him to attack it.

To these words, which fell in with the dearest wishes of Ophellas, a favourable answer was forthwith given; the two princes joined in league, and Ophellas resolved to hasten at once to the help of his friend.

The winter and early spring were spent by Ophellas in making ready for the march. He sent his recruiting-agents to Greece, and men flocked to his standard. Long wars had wasted the land and drained her resources, while the iron rule of Macedonia left no opening for fame or adventure. Now a new field of glory and riches seemed to be opening up, and thousands came forward to share in the overthrow and plunder of Carthage.

At Athens Ophellas sought a formal alliance[2]. He was in high favour there as the husband of the noble and lovely Eurydice[3], the daughter of Miltiades[4]. This man

[1] D. xx. 40. J. *ibid.* seems to think of Ophellas as an ally of *Carthage.*

[2] D. *ibid.* 5 καὶ πρὸς μὲν Ἀθηναίους περὶ συμμαχίας διεπέμπετο.

[3] Also called Euthydice. After the death of Ophellas Demetrius wedded her; this shows that her family must have been very influential. Cf. Plut. *Demetr.* 14.

[4] Schubert 147 thinks that the stir at Athens was invented by Duris as a peg on which to hang some gossip about Eurydice. But as Timaeus was living in Athens at the time, he is more likely than anyone else to have known and stated what went on there. (On the colony in the Adriatic, cf. Niese I. 173.)

claimed to be of the race of Marathon's hero, and was probably the leader of the Athenian settlement sent to Hadria in 325–4.

Many Athenians joined the army of Ophellas, but no alliance seems to have been made. There is some reason for thinking that Carthage sent envoys to Athens to counteract the movements of Ophellas' party and by their means such a course may have been hindered[1].

Late in the spring of 308 the outroad began[2]. Ophellas had no warships, and Carthage was still strong at sea, so that the whole distance had to be crossed on foot. But no comrade of Alexander was afraid of a long march. The tale of the force was as follows: 10,000 foot, 600 horse, 100 chariots, with more than 300 drivers and champions[3]. Besides these there was a crowd of 10,000 unarmed followers, many of whom brought their wives and children and all their belongings, so that it seemed as if a whole people were wandering out in search of a new home.

Eighteen days' march brought them to Automala, the westernmost station of the Five Cities, and 325 miles from Cyrene. Thence they threaded a cleft between steep sheer rocks, at the foot of which was a huge cave thickly grown with ivy and bindweed. Here the wondering

[1] The inscription *I. G.* II. 235 (Hicks, *Manual of Gr. Hist. Inscr.* 142) proves that Carthage sought the friendship of Athens about this time. The inscription is a vote of thanks and hospitality to certain envoys from Carthage; but no details of their proposals remain in the small surviving fragment. The names of Synalus and Bodmoacas can be seen. The latter would seem to be the traitor Bomilcar; and thus the decree would date from a time when he was away from home, perhaps before 310, as Hicks suggests, or else between then and his revolt. In this case his removal on an honourable errand may have been a device of the Carthaginian government.

[2] D. xx. 41.

[3] Diodorus calls them ἡνιόχους καὶ παραβάτας. The latter means the men who fought beside the drivers in the cars—for this we have no exact word, "ἡνιόχους" would include outriders.

soldiers believed that they had found the home of the
Lamia, once a fair queen, as the tale ran, but long since
turned for her cruelty into a fearful she-dragon, the bug-
bear of Greek children[1].

The hardest part of the march was now to come. The
land round the Syrtes was bare and waterless, and the
men were like to die of hunger and thirst[2]. The waste
teemed with deadly snakes, and some of these were of the
same hue as the sand, so that many trod on them unawares
and were bitten: and the poison was so strong that the
help of the leech could not save them[3].

The host passed near the land of the Lotus-Eaters,
and for one or two days they ate the jujube fruit that grew
there, for they had no other food[4].

[1] Diodorus seems to have taken this account with the legend and the
couplet of Euripides from Duris. Cf. p. 19.

[2] D. xx. 42. The description here seems to be right in all its details,
and to have come from Callias; see above, p. 10.

[3] Cf. Cato's march, Lucan *Phars.* ix. 382:

> Vadimus in campos steriles, exustaque mundi,
> Qua nimius Titan, et rarae in fontibus undae,
> Siccaque letiferis squalent serpentibus arva,
> Durum iter.

and 715—6:

> Concolor exustis atque indiscretus arenis
> Ammodytes.

[4] The Lotus-Eaters lived in what is now the island of Djerba. The
jujube (*Rhamnus Lotus* or *Zizyphus Lotus*) grows there and on the
mainland near the Lesser Syrtis. Diodorus does not mention this
matter, which comes from Theophrastus, *Hist. Plant.* iv. 3 Ἐν Λιβύῃ
δ' ὁ λωτὸς πλεῖστος καὶ κάλλιστος…πολὺ δὲ τὸ δένδρον καὶ πολύκαρπον. Τὸ
γ' οὖν Ὀφέλλου στρατόπεδον ἡνίκα ἐβάδιζον εἰς Καρχήδονα καὶ τούτῳ φασὶ
τραφῆναι πλέους ἡμέρας ἐπιλιπόντων τῶν ἐπιτηδείων.

Cf. Pliny *N.H.* xiii. 17 (32) *Quin et exercitus pastos eo accipimus ultro
citroque commeantes per Africam.*

The jujube, which is now called *Sidra*, ripens in August, and is in
season for two months (Peysonel *ap.* Tissot *op. cit.* i. 320). This fixes
about the time of year when Ophellas passed the Syrtes.

At the end of two months the hardships of the way were over, and Ophellas pitched his camp near the position of Agathocles. Diodorus does not say where this was; but most likely the prince had marched down at least as far as Hadrumetum to meet his ally. The Carthaginians were much alarmed when they heard that this new force was marching against them[1].

What followed is thus told by Diodorus[2]: "Agathocles met the staff of Ophellas and kindly furnished them with all that they needed, advising them to rest their men after all their sufferings. He then waited a few days and watched everything that went on in the camp. Finally, when most of the army had gone out foraging, and Ophellas, as he saw, had no suspicion of the plan that had been formed, Agathocles called a meeting of his own troops, and charged Ophellas, who had come to be his ally, with plotting against his own life. In this way he roused his men, and at once bade them stand to arms, and led them to attack the Cyreneans. Ophellas was taken utterly by surprise; he tried to shield himself, but he had not enough troops left in his camp, and so died fighting."

Justin's account is as follows[3]: "When Ophellas came with a huge force to join Agathocles in the war, Agathocles met him with a winning address and flattering respect. The two princes dined together more than once; and Ophellas adopted the son of Agathocles. Thus Agathocles lulled all suspicion to rest, and so killed Ophellas."

---

[1] D. *ibid.*   [2] D. xx. 42, 3—4.

[3] J. xxii. 7, 5. The account in Orosius iv. 6 seems to be drawn from Justin: "...*etiam socii reges deficiebant; inter quos rex quoque Cyrenarum, Ophellas, pactus est cum Agathocle communionem belli, dum regnum Africae ardenter affectat. Sed postquam in unum exercitus et castra junxissent, per Agathoclem blandimentis et insidiis circumventus occisus est.*"

Polyaenus' version is to the effect that Agathocles
sent his son Heracleides to Ophellas as a hostage: and it
seems to imply that Agathocles stirred up the wrath of
his troops by pretending that Ophellas was ill-treating his
son[1].

From these three accounts certain facts are plain.
Agathocles welcomed Ophellas very friendly, dined with
him and very likely gave him his son to adopt[2]. The
adoption is probable for two reasons. It gave Ophellas a
hostage without implying that there was any need of
such precaution, and also, in case Ophellas should become
prince of Carthage, the adopted son would have kept the
succession for the house of Agathocles. That Agathocles
sent his son merely to disarm suspicion is of course the
meaning of Justin; but this is no more than an inference
and very likely a wrong one.

Thus far the course of events is clear; but there
remains the question: why did Agathocles suddenly turn
from friendship to enmity? Three answers are possible:
Agathocles may from the first have meant to murder
Ophellas: Ophellas may have meant to murder Agathocles
but have been forestalled: or both may have acted in good
faith, until some quarrel arose which led Agathocles to
get rid of his ally.

The first view seems to be that of Diodorus and Justin,
and has been followed by some modern writers[3]. Against

---

[1] Polyaenus v. 3, 4 Ἀγαθοκλῆς Ὀφέλλαν...πυθόμενος εἶναι φιλόπαιδα,
ὅμηρον αὐτῷ τὸν ἴδιον υἱὸν ἔπεμψεν Ἡρακλείδην, ὡραῖον ὄντα, ἐντολὴν
δοὺς τῷ παιδὶ ἀντισχεῖν τῇ πείρᾳ μέχρις ὀλίγων ἡμέρων. Ἧκεν ὁ παῖς.
Ὁ Κυρηναῖος τῆς ὥρας ἡττώμενος περιεῖπεν αὐτὸν καὶ περὶ τὴν θεραπείαν
αὐτοῦ μόνην ἠσχολεῖτο. Ἀγαθοκλῆς ἄφνω τοὺς Συρακοσίους ἐπαγαγών, τόν
τε Ὀφέλλαν ἀπέκτεινε...καὶ τὸν υἱὸν ἀπέλαβεν οὐχ ὑβρισθέντα.

[2] So Schubert 145 has suggested.

[3] e.g. Niese 459; but with some reserve. It is just possible that
Ptolemy, who was afterwards friendly with Agathocles, instigated the
crime, by which he regained Cyrene.

this it must be said that such a fiendish design was too
bad even for Agathocles, and that the adoption of his son
must have been meant to pave the way for a lasting
friendship.   The second view has found more favour and
its supporters argue thus[1]: Ophellas had everything to
gain by the murder of Agathocles, whose troops must
have come over: Ophellas as one of Alexander's captains
had no mind to follow the lead of Agathocles and preferred to plot his death: Agathocles' attack on the camp
of Ophellas was a desperate stroke with the Carthaginians
so near, and he would never have made it without the
utmost need.   These pleas seem rather inconclusive.   What
Ophellas would have gained by the murder of Agathocles
is by no means clear.   The Sicilian troops were not like
the fickle Macedonians, to whom one Successor was as
good as another, but they were personally attached to
Agathocles, and would undoubtedly have followed his
warlike sons to avenge his death.   Against their trained
valour the exhausted soldiers of Ophellas could have done
nothing.   The third plea, that the nearness of the Carthaginians made Agathocles' attempt desperate, is surely
absurd.   We have no evidence where any of these events
happened ; but it is clearly stated that the Carthaginians
were hindered by ignorance of what went on from taking
any advantage of the strife between the two princes.
Above all the fact that Ophellas' men were able to roam
in great numbers in search of fodder is proof positive that
the Carthaginians were nowhere near.   The remaining
plea that Ophellas gave offence to Agathocles, and that
they quarrelled, is likely enough, but this obviously does
not prove that Ophellas was plotting murder.

    Again, if we turn to the account friendly to Agathocles,

[1] So Schubert 148—9, Beloch III. 1, 201. The third plea is put forward
only by Beloch.

namely Polyaenus', we find no hint that Ophellas was plotting against Agathocles. No reason indeed is given for his death; for the offence there mentioned was trifling to the Greek mind, and Ophellas had not even tried to commit it[1]. Thus although the silence of Polyaenus naturally proves little, at any rate it does not acquit Agathocles. Furthermore, if Ophellas meant to murder Agathocles, he would certainly have done this when Agathocles was dining in his camp, and on no account would he have let his men stray far away; for a demonstration in force would have been needed to follow up the murder.

We are thus brought to take the third view, that both princes made their plans in good faith but fell out after their meeting. Agathocles perhaps was shocked when he saw the motley rabble of his ally. He had hoped for an active army, doubtless for a fleet also; he saw a whole townful of settlers, a mere hindrance in the field. Ophellas himself, as a comrade of Alexander, may have been overbearing; no doubt he had taken Agathocles at his word, and meant to be king of Libya, and no humble sheriff for the prince of Syracuse. This temper may have led Agathocles to put his rival out of the way without more ado.

After this hapless end to all Ophellas' hopes and plans, Agathocles called on the Cyrenean troops to pile their arms in token of yielding. The men bereft of their leader dared not do otherwise. Agathocles then sent a friendly message to them, and in the end the whole force entered

---

[1] Schubert, I think rightly, regards this *Buhlgeschichte* as a fiction of Duris. Meltzer and others believed it, and thought that the "adoption" of Agathocles' son was Justin's misunderstanding or mitigation of the same event. Droysen *l. c.* has chosen to follow Polyaenus without taking any account of Diodorus.

his service. The unwarlike fared worse. Agathocles put
them on board some freight-ships that were carrying his
plunder, and despatched them for Syracuse. But a storm
sprang up and wrecked most of the boats off the Pithecusae
islands near the Italian coast, and few of the prisoners ever
reached their haven.

Thus ended this melancholy episode, in which a splendid
and hopeful enterprise was brought by rashness and crime
to a miserable and disgraceful close.

8.   BOMILCAR'S RISING.   308.

Agathocles' forces were nearly doubled by the enrolling
of Ophellas' men; and thus strengthened he attacked a
large Carthaginian army, that had marched up, and routed
it utterly.   Unluckily a fresh mutiny arose in his camp,
and he was unable to follow up the blow at a moment
when a descent upon Carthage would have brought the
whole war to a triumphant end.

These events are given only by Justin, and most
historians have not recorded them[1]. But the truth of
the account cannot reasonably be doubted, especially as
it gives the only credible explanation of what next befell.

Bomilcar's long-planned revolt was at last to be tried[2].
He had returned to office early in 308, but in spite of
the chance afforded by the absence of many leading
citizens on the Nubian campaign, he had not had the

[1] J. xxii. 7, 6—7. Grote and Holm do not notice the passage,
Meltzer 527 and Niese 460 disbelieve it. Schubert 152 defends it. The
chief points are (1) The invention of such a serious event by Justin is
much less likely than its omission by Diodorus. (2) Some immediate
cause for Bomilcar's rising is needed. The actions of Agathocles are not
available as an explanation, because, as Diodorus expressly says, Bomilcar
knew nothing about them.

[2] D. xx. 43 ; J. ibid.

courage to make the bold stroke. Now he was still general[1] at the head of the home forces, but he could not get news of the movements of Agathocles nor send word of his own. The departure of the Carthaginian army, which was indeed too late to help Ophellas' men against Agathocles, and the tidings of its defeat at last roused Bomilcar to action. He must have expected that the victorious Sicilians would soon appear under the walls of Carthage, and then he would openly join his country's foes[2]. But the mutiny in the Greek camp, of which no news reached him, foredoomed his plans to failure.

Bomilcar held a review of the troops under his leadership in the suburb of Carthage called Neapolis. He then sent away all but his own followers, who amounted to 500 citizens, and perhaps 4000 hirelings[3]. To this force he declared himself tyrant, and was doubtless hailed with the name of king.

The army was divided into five companies, and ordered to force a way into the market-place, each company by a different road, killing any citizens that came in the way. Thus Carthage was filled with fear and uproar, for everyone thought that the enemy had been let in. But soon the truth was found out, and all those who could fight came together to withstand Bomilcar. The latter, after

[1] Inexactly called "*rex*" by Justin.

[2] J. *ibid.* *Hoc certaminis discrimine tanta desperatio illata Poenis est, ut nisi in exercitu Agathoclis orta seditio fuisset, transiturus ad eum Bomilcar, rex Poenorum, cùm exercitu fuisset.* This I take to be strictly true, and far preferable to the vague remarks of Diodorus xx. 43. It was not of course the *news* of the *seditio* that hampered Bomilcar; but the mutiny itself, of which he knew nothing, hindered Agathocles from marching on Carthage, especially as *he* did not know how far Bomilcar's plans had ripened. Those who, like Beloch 201, do not allow any collusion between the two generals, are left without the slightest clue to the meaning of these events.

[3] D. xx. 44. The number may be corrupt.

slaying many unarmed wretches, massed his forces in the
market-place. Meanwhile the loyal army had taken up
position in the surrounding houses, and climbing upon the
high roofs, began to shower darts upon the traitors. The
place thus became untenable, and Bomilcar was driven to
withdraw under a heavy fire to Neapolis, where he en-
trenched himself. By this time almost every burgess of
Carthage was up in arms, and an overwhelming force
encamped hard by the rebels. Then milder counsels won
the day; the elders of Carthage promised forgiveness to
all who would lay down arms, and the men of Bomilcar
gave up their hopeless undertaking. The promise of
mercy was faithfully kept: only Bomilcar himself, who
had perhaps been handed over by his followers as the
price of peace, was put to death. Diodorus says that he
was cruelly tortured, and Justin adds that he was crucified in the market-place[1]. This latter is no doubt true,
but the polished speech which the traitor is supposed to
have made as he hung on the cross, is certainly an
embellishment[2].

[1] Diodorus indeed says that the Carthaginians killed Bomilcar in
spite of their oaths; but the *perfidia plusquam Punica* is suspicious.
Bomilcar's treason was past forgiveness, and he must have known this
when he yielded. Crucifixion was the usual means of capital punishment
at Carthage, and the extra tortures may be doubted: *inhumana crudelitas*
was attributed to other Carthaginians besides Hannibal. The fate of
Hanno (J. xxi..4, 7) and that of Regulus seem likewise to have been
blackened with a gruesome ingenuity.

[2] Bomilcar's dying speech seems to be pure rhetoric, no doubt invented
by Trogus to suit the taste of his readers, with whom a *mors ambitiosa*
was a title to fame. The dying speeches of Seneca and Lucan will be
remembered as illustrating this very Roman idea.

Niese and Meltzer accept the substance of the speech, as Grote
(xii. 541 n.) seems also to do. Schubert treats it as unhistorical; I had
formed the same opinion before reading his book.

Orosius, *ibid.* tells of the rising in very much the same words as
Justin; but instead of the speech he merely says that Bomilcar " *crudele
spectaculum suis praebuit.*"

9. CONQUEST TO THE WEST OF CARTHAGE. 307.

The fate of Agathocles' undertaking was really settled
by the utter failure of Bomilcar's rising. The disloyal
party in Carthage would not dare to raise its head for
many years after such a blow, and the hands of the
Senate were strengthened for a more resolute conduct of
the war.

But for the moment the tide of the prince's success
flowed as strongly as ever, and he began an important
conquest on the western side of the land of Carthage[1].

His first object of attack was the coast town of Utica,
which according to Diodorus had formerly been on his
side[2]. So sudden was the onset that three hundred citizens
were made prisoners outside the walls. Agathocles hoped
that to ransom these men the government of Utica would
make peace, and he promised to overlook the offence of
revolt if the city would yield. But this the men of Utica
had no mind to do. Agathocles therefore bethought him
of a gruesome plan to make resistance impossible. He
built a large engine, and on this he hung his captives.
He also made his slingers, bowmen, and darters mount on
it, and so wheeled it up to the walls. At first the Uticans

[1] D. xx. 54. Diodorus mentions here that Agathocles took the name
of king, but this is too soon. The point will be discussed later.

[2] Diodorus says ἐπὶ μὲν Ἰτυκαίους ἐστράτευσεν ἀφεστηκότας. But
Polybius I. 82, 8 says that Utica remained faithful ; and therefore Grote
wished to read οὐκ ἀφεστηκότας. This, however, would leave the words
διδοὺς ἄφεσιν τῶν ἐγκλημάτων without meaning. Schubert thinks that
a counterpart of Bomilcar's revolt had occurred in Utica, and that its
failure made the place hostile to Agathocles. I rather think that Diodorus,
having put ἀφεστηκότας by mistake, altered a promise of fair treatment
into a promise of forgiveness. At any rate Utica had not been *taken*
before, and it was not likely that its Phoenician indwellers would have
willingly forsaken Carthage.

shrank from answering the enemy's fire, but as the attack
grew fiercer they could withhold their hand no longer, and
so the luckless captives were pierced by the arrows and
shafts of their own friends[1]. This shocking scene did not
tame the spirits of the besieged, and Agathocles had to
bring up his whole force to storm the town. At last he
found a weak spot in the walls; this was battered down,
and the Greeks poured into the breach. The Uticans
rushed to their homes or to the shrines for shelter, but in
vain: the men of Agathocles were enraged at the stubborn
defence, and a fearful slaughter was wrought. Some of
the Uticans were cut down in the fray, others taken
prisoners and afterwards hanged, and others were even
torn from the altars of the gods[2]. The booty was doled
out to the troops, and a guard left in the city[3].

The next point at which Agathocles aimed was the
city of Hippuacra or Mare's Hill, which held the site
where now is Bizerta[4]. The town stood very strongly,

[1] Dionysius I is said to have done the same (Philostrat. *Vit. Apoll.
Tyan.* vii. 3) but this is doubtful and goes against D. xiv. 112. Frederick
Barbarossa is said to have done likewise. Cf. Schubert 158 where both
instances are quoted. Diodorus enlarges on the horror of Agathocles'
act, perhaps following Timaeus.

[2] D. xx. 55.

[3] Utica is now more than a mile inland, and stands on the edge of
a mud-flat silted up by the Bagradas. It is still easy to trace the sea-
front of the old town. The Arabs call the place Henchir-bou-Chateur :
it is now the property of a French nobleman. There remain some traces
of Punic walls and harbour, but the ruins (of which a row of huge
store-tanks, now used as a stable, is the most striking) are chiefly
Roman. Small finds, Punic and Roman, are often made. (Cf. Tissot i.
675, and iii. Pll. 2—6.)

[4] There can, I think, be no doubt that Hippuacra and Hippo
Diarrhytus were the same, and held the site of the modern Bizerta.
(So Freeman, Schubert, and Beloch with others.) The name Diarrhytus
proves that the neck of land between the sea and the mere had been cut
through in antiquity, but whether Agathocles' shipyard was there or

protected by the sea and a wide deep mere. The citizens had a fleet, and Agathocles, who had by this time built warships, perhaps in the dockyard of Aspis or at Tunis, met and overcame them in a sea-fight. But whether they fought in the open or on the mere is uncertain. The town then yielded.

Agathocles, who saw its strong position and natural harbour, almost the only one on the whole coast, resolved to make of Hippo a fleet-station. He improved the anchorage, built docks and strengthened the walls and the keep. The time had come when sea-power was all-important, and this new arsenal on the western shore would be a valuable base for the final attack on the harbour of Carthage.

To guard the land-road from Hippo to Tunis, Agathocles built a tower near the point from which the Utica road branched off. There is still a small ruin near the coast road from Tunis to Bizerta, and in this the remains of Agathocles' tower are sought. The tower was about thirty furlongs from Utica[1].

The prince was now at the height of his power. All the chief coast towns were his and a large number of places inland had joined him, the open country was in his

in the smaller basin, now the Arab harbour, is uncertain. The cut had silted up, but has been lately cleared by the French for their naval station. The choice of such a place shows that Agathocles had a true general's eye. (Agathocles' works are not mentioned by Diodorus, but by Appian *Pun.* 110.) (Niese follows Appian in placing Hippo between Tunis and Utica; but probably Appian is mistaken.)

[1] The few remaining stones lie near a well to the south of the Bizerta-Tunis road, and east of the entrance to the pass leading up the Djebel-Menzel-el-Ghoul range. The position suits, but there is really nothing to prove that the stones belonged to the tower of Agathocles. No one at Utica or Tunis could tell me anything about such a ruin. (Cf. Appian, *Pun.* 14; Tissot I. 553—4.)

hands, but the Numidians still awaited the issue of the
whole war.   If only Carthage could be attacked from the
sea, she would hardly defy Agathocles any longer, and
in any case she might have been glad to make peace.
But in Sicily the cause of Agathocles had for some time

Ruins near Utica, supposed Tower of Agathocles.

been in a perilous state, and he resolved to sail back to
reassert his sway.   Gathering a fleet of open boats and
fifty-oared craft, which had been building at his orders,
he shipped 2000 of his men for Sicily, and thus started
from Africa, leaving Archagathus in command[1].

[1] D. xx. 55, 5 ; J. xxii. 8, 1.

10. THE OVERTHROW OF THE ACRAGANTINE
LEAGUE. 308—7.

Since the relief of Netum and Camarina in 308 nothing has been heard of the Acragantine movement; but there can be little doubt that it had been making great headway, for it is now stated that the Sicilians hoped that the whole island would soon be free[1].

About this time Xenodicus seems to have made up his mind to march on Syracuse, and advanced with more than 10,000 foot and about 1000 horse. To meet him, Leptines and Demophilus, who were leading the Agathoclean host, raised such troops as could be spared from garrison duty, and marshalled 8200 foot and 1200 horse. The allies had thus far more men, but their citizen levies seem to have been poorly trained and ill led. Xenodicus himself (like Aratus who inherited some of his ideals) had made his way by political means, or at most by small sieges and surprises: now he had to meet in fair fight a seasoned army under professional leaders. Still the blow at Syracuse had to be struck before freedom was assured, and perhaps the news of Agathocles' coming had reached Xenodicus and spurred him to make trial of battle[2].

At some nameless spot the armies met. The struggle was long and stubborn, but at length the allies were worsted. ◦Xenodicus himself fled straightway to Acragas, leaving fifteen hundred slain upon the field.

This untoward blow quite broke the spirit of the allies. The Acragantines gave up the active conduct of the war, and the smaller cities were left unsheltered to become the prey of the strongest party. In this way the whole movement fell to the ground; the historian may regret its fate,

---

[1] D. xx. 56.   [2] So Schubert, but this is quite doubtful.

but he cannot wonder at it. In an age of military powers
and trained soldiers a league of free cities could not hope
for a lasting success unless it had leaders of the highest
valour and ability. Acragas had preached freedom without counting the cost; and one defeat was the death-blow
of all her aspirations.

A short time after this fight Agathocles landed at
Selinus. He marched to Heraclea, which had been free
as a member of the Acragantine league. The city yielded.
Segesta may have been won about the same time[1]. Agathocles then marched over to Thermae, his own birthplace.
There he found a Punic guard, which seems to have agreed
to leave the city to be an ally of Agathocles[2].

Soon after this Agathocles must have been joined by
Leptines, no doubt with a large part of the Syracusan
army. An attack on the strong town of Cephaloedium[3]
was next undertaken: and this was carried by storm.
Leaving Leptines to hold the place, Agathocles marched
inland to Centuripa[4], where some partisans were ready to
open the gates. A surprise by night was tried, but the
alarm was given and the guard came up in time to save
the city. Agathocles was driven out with a loss of
500 men.

At Apollonia[5] there were also traitors at work, but
when the prince reached the gates these men had already
been found out and punished, perhaps with death, for

[1] So Niese. It is mentioned as Agathocles' ally in D. xx. 71, 1.

[2] Diodorus xx. 56, 3 says Θερμίτας μὲν προσαγαγόμενος ὑποσπόνδους
ἀφῆκε, τῶν Καρχηδονίων φρουρούντων ταύτην τὴν πόλιν. This is obscure;
Freeman and Schubert take it as above, but Holm thought that Thermae
was left to Carthage.

[3] Now Cefalu. The citadel there is perhaps the strongest point on
the north coast of Sicily.

[4] Now Centuripe.

[5] Now Pollina eight miles east of Cefalu on the north coast.

their evil designs.   There was nothing for it but to storm
Apollonia.   The first day's assault was beaten back, but
on the morrow, after a sore and bloody fray, the men of
Agathocles burst into the town.   Most of the citizens were
slaughtered and their goods plundered.   This no doubt
was a measure of vengeance for the punishment of the
prince's friends.

The headway made by the arms of Agathocles and the
ruthless manner in which his success had been used, now
thoroughly roused his enemies of all parties[1].   Deinocrates,
who had stood aloof from the Acragantine league, came
forward once more as the champion of freedom.   His
tried ability seemed to promise better things than the
feeble efforts of Xenodicus.   Men flocked to Deinocrates'
standard, and soon 20,000 foot and 1500 horse were in
the field: though they can hardly have been all old
soldiers, as Diodorus says[2].   Justin adds that a fresh
army from Carthage landed about this time[3]: and although the war in Africa must have swallowed up most
of the Punic forces, it is quite possible that a small
detachment may have been sent.   The fleet of Carthage
was still master at sea, and the wisdom of helping such a
movement as that headed by Deinocrates was undoubted.

Deinocrates camped in the open and offered battle to
Agathocles.   But the tyrant felt himself too weak to fight,
and withdrew step by step towards Syracuse[4].   Deinocrates

[1] D. xx. 57.   [2] Followed by Freeman.
[3] J. xxii. 8, 2.   Most writers have overlooked this passage or disbelieved it (cf. Niese 463, n. 4).   Schubert 163 argues strongly in favour
of it.   But Justin knows so little of Sicilian matters here, that it
would be rash to trust him.   There may have been a fresh force sent
from Carthage, but the oligarchic revival can be fully accounted for
without it.
[4] D. *ibid.* § 3 where φυγομαχοῦντος can only mean " refusing to fight "
not " skirmishing," as Freeman seems to think.

followed at his heels, and seemed to be winning a blood-less victory.

11. ARCHAGATHUS' WARFARE IN AFRICA. 306.

Archagathus had been left by his father as leader of the army in Africa. His wisest course would probably have been to stand his ground until his chief's return. But he seems to have longed to do some great deed on his own account, and thus engaged hotly in several rather useless undertakings.

His first act was to send Eumachus up land with a large part of the forces, in all about 8000 foot and 800 horse[1]. This outroad was aimed at the Numidians and other allies of Carthage; but chiefly perhaps it served to keep the men busy, and to win treasure and booty.

Eumachus was a good soldier, and his march proved an almost unbroken success. But from our lack of know-ledge we can scarcely trace his path through the dim wonderland of the southern waste.

He first took the large town of Tocae[2], which was perhaps the same as the modern Dougga, and thus no doubt was the key to the midlands[3]. The town may have been Phoenician, but the neighbouring country-folk, many of whom came over, were Numidians. Eumachus is next supposed to have stormed Phelline[4], a place now

[1] These numbers appear from D. xx. 60 below. By that time Eumachus had of course lost some men, but may have recruited others.

[2] D. xx. 57, 4.

[3] The geography of this campaign is very doubtful. The identifi-cation Tocae = Tucca—Terebinthina = Dougga was suggested by Grote and supported by Tissot I. 539. Davis put it at Machthar 40 miles further south.

[4] Phelline is supposed to be the same as Pallene, which is placed in the *Tabula Peutingeriana* between Zitha and Praesidium. Cf. Tissot I. 441.

sought on the sea-coast opposite the island of Djerba. If this is rightly placed, his march may have led him to the oasis of Capsa and thence along the line of road from Capsa to where Gabés now stands. This long march through partly hostile country was a great feat of generalship. The capture of Phelline was followed by the submission of the neighbouring tribe of the Asphodelians. These folk, who had a swarthy skin like the Aethiopians, may have lived in the basin of Nefzaoua, where a black race is still found[1].

The city of Meschela, said to have been founded by Greeks after the fall of Troy, was next taken. Diodorus does not seem to mean that this large town had any Greek elements left when Eumachus came up. Another city called Hippuacra and a free town named Acris were also stormed[2]. The latter was sacked and all the indwellers enslaved. Then Eumachus marched back to Archagathus, laden with plunder after a well-fought campaign.

The success of this venture led Archagathus to send Eumachus on another raid to the south[3]. Retracing his steps in the last march, Eumachus fell upon the town of Miltiane, the site of which is unknown. The citizens were taken by surprise, but after a fierce street fight Eumachus was driven out with heavy loss[4]. After this unexpected

[1] Tissot *ibid.*   [2] These places are unknown.

[3] D. xx. 58.

[4] Schubert 166 believes that the account of this march was related to Callias by the same authority that gave the story of the journey of Ophellas, i.e. one of Ophellas' men that afterwards joined Agathocles. Eumachus' army was later nearly cut to pieces, so that the survival of this narrator is as providential as that of Timaeus' informant mentioned above (p. 143).

There is of course no reason to doubt the substance of Diodorus' account. The geography of the second march is quite obscure.

11—2

failure the army marched through twenty miles of uplands which swarmed with wild cats, so that no bird could nest there. Then they reached a country full of apes, where there were three cities named after these brutes. The customs of the people astonished the Greeks not a little; for the apes were worshipped and lived in the houses, where they were allowed to steal whatever food they liked from the stores. The children too were named after apes, and to kill an ape was deemed something deathworthy. Eumachus took one of these cities, and the other two gave in. Then he heard that a Punic army was mustering to attack him, and thought it high time to withdraw to the coast.

So far Archagathus had had no trouble from the Carthaginians, but now the Senate resolved to carry on the war on a greater scale[1]. The crowds of runaways sheltering in the city had been trained to arms, and their absence would relieve the pressure and dearth at home; for by this time all the reserve supplies had run out. An attack on Carthage by Archagathus was not to be feared; the city was quite safe as long as the harbour was open, while the sight of a large army would strengthen the loyalty of the allies besides diverting the Greeks from Carthage.

The Punic forces were formed into three columns, one was sent down to the coast, another inland, and the third to the further south. In all thirty thousand men took the field, and thus those left behind in Carthage had ample supplies for their needs.

The threefold division of the Carthaginian troops made Archagathus' part a very hard one. His own fewer men could ill be separated, but if he kept them

[1] D. xx. 59.

in one place he was bound to lose the open country with
most of his allies.   He therefore made bold to split up his
own army, and to send divisions in pursuit of the enemy,
leaving only the guard of Tunis behind[1].   Eumachus had
not yet returned with his column, and of the remaining
troops Archagathus took half himself, and gave the rest
to another officer, named Aeschrion.   These huge undertakings were naturally watched with much eagerness
and dread by both sides.

Archagathus himself seems to have stayed near Tunis,
where he was confronted by Adherbal with one of the
Carthaginian divisions[2].   No battle however seems to
have been fought.

Hanno, who was in charge of the army in the midlands,
laid an ambush for Aeschrion, and took him unawares.
In this way 4000 foot, 200 horse, with Aeschrion himself,
were cut down.   The survivors—and probably there were
very few—fled straight back to Archagathus, who was
sixty miles away, no doubt near the coast.

Meanwhile the Carthaginian force under the orders
of Himilco had marched southwards to meet Eumachus,
who must have been returning from his second inroad, of
which the history has already been given[3].   The Greeks
were heavy-laden with the booty from the fallen cities,
and most likely had not heard of the new Carthaginian
plan of warfare.

[1] D. xx. 60.

[2] Adherbal is mentioned with Himilco in c. 61, as commanding a Punic
force, and it is no doubt implied that he had the coast army, the leader
of which is not explicitly named.

[3] Diodorus in xx. 60, 1 speaks of Archagathus' division of forces
without any mention of Eumachus : again in § 4 Eumachus is said to
have been encumbered with the booty ἐκ τῶν ἁλουσῶν πόλεων—which
would naturally refer to the cities of whose capture Diodorus had spoken
in c. 58.

Himilco quartered his army in a city on Eumachus' line of march[1]. He then sallied forth with a small detachment, leaving word to the rest to come into action when they saw the enemy in disorder. The Greeks were ready to fight, and seeing Himilco's advance party in front of their camp, they gave battle without further delay.

The Carthaginians drew back in face of the Greek onset, and the men of Eumachus followed them in headlong chase. All at once the city gate was thrown open, and the strong Punic reserve dashed out with a mighty cheer and fell upon the Greeks. The latter were in disorder, and this sudden attack utterly discomfited them. The Carthaginians had cut off their foe from their camp, and Eumachus was driven at last to take shelter on a waterless hill. But even there he was not safe: the enemy camped round about, and harassed him with ceaseless onslaughts, until at last, what with thirst and the unequal struggle, almost the whole Greek host was cut to pieces. Eumachus fell, and of 8000 foot and 800 horse only 30 footmen and 40 knights are said to have escaped: it is clear that the Carthaginians gave no quarter.

When the sad tidings reached Archagathus, he withdrew at once to Tunis, and gave up all hope of holding the open country[2]. Most of the outlying guards were called in, and an urgent message was sent to Agathocles to come back and save his friends. Nearly all the Numidian and other African allies forsook the losing side; and the Carthaginian armies closed around Tunis. Himilco camped twelve miles away on the south side, and Adherbal

[1] The "city" is nameless. Diodorus must have taken the phrase carelessly from his authority, overlooking the place where the name had been given. It cannot of course mean Carthage.

[2] D. xx. 61.

only five miles off to the east[1]. Thus Tunis was hemmed in on the land side, and the Punic fleet held the sea. Famine stared the Greeks in the face, and they waited in dismay for the coming of Agathocles, now their only hope.

12. THE END OF THE WAR IN AFRICA. 307.

Agathocles himself had been sitting helpless in Syracuse since his withdrawal before Deinocrates, and the Carthaginian fleet was still blockading the harbour. But, luckily for the prince, he had one ally remaining faithful, the Etruscans[2]. When or how the league had been formed is unknown: but no doubt the fear of Rome drove her neighbours to make friends wherever they could, and the good understanding between Rome and Carthage naturally threw them into the arms of Agathocles. Such a bond could be worth little to Etruria, for the war against Rome had to be fought out on land, and an inroad on Central Italy was hardly to be expected from their new ally. Beyond help in money, which Agathocles may have given or promised, the most that he was likely to do against Rome would have been a raid in Lucania. On the other hand the Etruscan sea power was useless at home, but some advantage might be gained by helping Agathocles against the fleet of a Roman ally.

For some such reason the Etruscans now sent eighteen warships to Syracuse; this squadron may have been found

---

[1] Diodorus, *ibid.*, who says that Atarbas (= Adherbal) camped on the opposite side to Himilco. But as Himilco had been fighting inland, and Adherbal had confronted Archagathus (who had remained near Tunis) it is natural to place them as above. Hanno had perhaps gone home to Carthage after his victory.

[2] D. xx. 61, 5 ff.

by Tarquinii, the chief harbour of free Etruria now that
Caere and Antium had fallen[1].

The Etruscan squadron slipped into the haven of Syracuse by night unseen of the Carthaginians.   Agathocles
himself could muster seventeen sail, so that the allied
fleet now outnumbered the thirty ships of their foe.   The
plan of battle was carefully laid, for great things hung on
the issue.

Agathocles rowed out of the harbour with his own
ships, leaving the Etruscans in hiding. The Carthaginians,
catching sight of him, began to chase him towards the
open sea, when the Etruscans in their turn sailed out
after the Carthaginians. No sooner did the Greeks see
their allies coming near, than they wheeled round and
faced the enemy in battle array. The latter were thus
caught between two hostile squadrons, and took to flight
in alarm. The Greeks and Etruscans followed, and cap-
tured five ships with all hands. So fierce was the struggle
that the Carthaginian sea-lord had slain himself for fear
of falling into the enemy's hands, although a gust of wind
afterwards carried the flagship beyond reach of pursuit.

This great success, far greater than anything that
Agathocles had hoped to achieve, broke up the blockade
of Syracuse, and threw open the way to Africa.   The
Syracusans, who had long been suffering from dearth
of food, now took in all kinds of stores, and again enjoyed great cheapness and plenty.

The great victory at sea was followed very soon by
a smaller win on land. Shortly before the Etruscan ships
sailed up, Agathocles sent Leptines for an inroad into the
land of Acragas[2]. Very likely Deinocrates' army was busy

[1] So Beloch 204 has shrewdly suggested.

[2] Diodorus first speaks of Leptines as commanding the land force
in xx. 61, 5, but the raid on Acragas comes in xx. 62, 2 and is thus

elsewhere, and Acragas, still too proud to take help from the oligarchs, lay open to the vengeance of Agathocles. Another reason for the attack lay in the political state of Acragas, where Xenodicus, though still general, was losing most of his following, and might be driven to risk a fight to retrieve his credit.

Leptines began by wasting the Acragantine fields, and at first Xenodicus watched him from the walls, knowing that the home forces were too weak to give battle. But soon his enemies taunted him with cowardice, and their challenge outweighed his better judgment. Xenodicus took the field with an army little less than that of Leptines, but made up of poorly trained men; for the burgesses of Acragas had always lived in the shady courts and alleys of the city, and were no match for his seasoned hirelings inured to every hardship.

The armies met, and after a short struggle the Acragantines were routed, and fled into the town, leaving about 500 foot and 50 horse dead on the field. Leptines did not press forward to attack the city; perhaps the news of the sea-fight had brought with it an order to send home his men to be shipped for Africa : or it may be that Deinocrates was hastening up with his overwhelming forces to save Acragas in spite of herself. Anyhow the campaign came to an end.

The Acragantines were very wroth with Xenodicus, to whose bad generalship they assigned both their defeats :

placed *after* the sea-fight. Although the land *battle* may have been later, it is likely that the inroad *began* before the Etruscans came, because (as Schubert 171 rightly notes) when once the sea was open, Agathocles was bound to hurry off to Africa with all available forces, and would not have waited to punish Acragas. In fact the sea and land operations were carried on about the same time, so that Agathocles had conquered on both elements in the course of a few days (D. xx. 63, 1).

and he was threatened with impeachment at the end of
his year of office. Not daring to stand his trial, Xenodicus
fled before his term of command was out, and took shelter
at Gela.

Xenodicus' history in Acragas is like the history of
Acragas in Sicily. Both had high aims, and both could
win success when no great barrier stood in the way. But
neither counted the cost of their undertaking, and defeat
was fatal to both alike. Xenodicus, who was nothing
more than a statesman, aspired to do a work that only
the soldier's arm could have carried through : eager and
energetic in prosperity, under ill luck he could as little
repair his country's lot as his own. Pathetic in his
weakness, he must none the less be honoured for his
single-hearted and honest aims : the movement for federal
freedom was not less noble because it was doomed from
the outset, and with the fall of Xenodicus his cause
perished.

It is uncertain whether Agathocles himself undertook
any more land-fighting about this time ; for the only hint
of such action is given by a trivial tale in Diodorus a
chapter or two after the record of the foregoing events.
The story reappears twice in Plutarch without any clue
to time or place[1]. " Once when Agathocles was attacking

[1] D. xx. 63, 5. Plut. *de cohib. Ira* 458 E, and *Reg. et Impp. Apophth.*
s.v. Agath. The complete account is in the last place only. Freeman
following Diodorus gives the imperfect version (IV. 451), but thereby
escapes the sad anticlimax of the ending. He puts the events before
the coming of the Etruscan ships, but not (I think) as his own order
would rather lead it to be supposed, after the flight of Agathocles before
Deinocrates, for then Agathocles had no means of besieging any city.
The only thing against Freeman's course is that he moves the event
a long way from the place where Diodorus puts it. But as the incident
may have happened anywhere, at any time, or, perhaps likeliest, not at
all, it is needless to say more about the matter.

a not unimportant city, men shouted at him from the walls, 'Man of the pot and chimney, when wilt thou pay thy soldiers?' and he answered, 'When I take this city.' Afterwards he stormed the town and sold all the indwellers into slavery, remarking, 'If ye mock me again, I shall have a word to say to your masters.'"

Diodorus, whose version of the story stops short of the end, gives this incident rather as an example of Agathocles' wit than as a fact of regular history. The whole account sounds untrustworthy, and all that can be said is that the event is as likely to have happened at this time as at any other.

Agathocles was now victorious on both elements, and he made ready to start for Africa. But before setting sail, he once more took upon himself to cleanse the city of all taint of disloyalty,—though after two massacres and two sweeping decrees of banishment there can have been left but the smallest remnant of the oligarchic party, enough however, he thought, to open the gates to Deinocrates.

As to the manner in which Agathocles found out and punished these suspected foes, only untrustworthy accounts have come down. Diodorus tells the following story[1]: "Agathocles, who had thus in a few days overcome his foes by sea and land, sacrificed to the gods and raised high the hopes of his friends. He laid aside in his cups all princely dignity, and mixed on a footing of greater equality with private persons whom he met. By this policy he not only hunted for popularity with the many, but by letting everyone speak boldly against him at their wine, he found out how each was minded, for the drink made the men speak the truth unguardedly."

[1] D. *ibid.* § 1.

Then follow some remarks as to the bearing of Agathocles: how he used to mimic his opponents in open assembly, thus setting the house laughing loudly, how he had no bodyguard, and so far from being ashamed of his earlier calling of potter, lost no chance of reminding his friends of his mean beginnings,—and so forth, until at last the main thread is taken up again. " Not but what, having found out which of his drunken boon-companions were opposed to his government, he invited them with other suspected Syracusans, in all about five hundred, to another banquet. Then he put the most active of his hired soldiers round them, and had them all slain."

Polyaenus' version is even sillier[1]: "Agathocles heard that the leading Syracusans were plotting revolt, after his victory over the Carthaginians : and on the occasion of his public thanksgiving he invited the suspects, to the number of five hundred, to the banquet. The feast was lordly, and when the guests were mellow, Agathocles came forward in a saffron robe draped with a Tarentine shawl; he piped, harped and danced until the delight of the onlookers voiced itself in general applause. In the moment of merriment, feigning weariness he slipped out of the banquet to change his dress. Then a strong body of soldiers beset the hall; and a thousand drew sword, two standing behind each guest, and so slew the whole party."

In all this mass of detail there is little real history. Agathocles no doubt suspected certain men, and followed the not uncommon plan of slaying them at a banquet. The number of five hundred victims may also be right. It is also possible that the rejoicing and revelry after the two victories may have given Agathocles, or rather his spies, the means of overhearing unwary remarks against the tyranny.

[1] Polyaenus v. 3, 3.

But the remaining statements are nonsensical. That
Agathocles by a modest bearing could have evoked in
a few days a number of treasonable sayings, or that he
played the harlequin before the assembly, or that he
boasted of a trade which he never plied, or that he
danced and sang like a stage-player before his guests,
is not for an instant to be believed[1].

Having thus freed Syracuse from foes without and
traitors within[2], Agathocles put his men on board ship
and sailed straight over to join his main body in their
quarters at Tunis. The number of his new troops is not
stated, but the total army now reached 8000 Greek foot,
and 8000, partly Celts, partly Etruscans, partly Samnites;
besides these there were 10,000 Libyans, an untrustworthy
arm likely to forsake the losing side; 1500 horse and some
chariots[3]. Now it has been mentioned that Eumachus'
army of 8000, which was cut to pieces, had been about
a third of the forces of Archagathus; nearly another
third fell under Aeschrion; thus Archagathus would
have saved rather more than 8000 foot, besides the garrisons left in Tunis; so that Agathocles' new troops were
probably less than 6000.

The prince found his men mutinous and down-hearted,
for Archagathus had been unable to pay them, and had
put them off with promises until his father's coming.

[1] For the tale about Agathocles' disuse of a body-guard see p. 59,
for his supposed calling of potter, p. 28. These remarks of Diodorus
are quite out of place here, and stamp the chapter as a string of
worthless anecdotes. Polyaenus' story is very much like Duris fr. 24,
where Polysperchon is likewise made to dance in a saffron robe: it is
therefore natural to suppose that the hand of Duris has been at work
in the present case also. In this same chapter of Diodorus is the tale of
the mockers on the city wall, which has already been discussed.

[2] D. xx. 63 fin.

[3] Diodorus says more than 6000, but this must be a false reading.

Agathocles called an assembly, and told the soldiers frankly that their only hope of pay lay in another victory over the Carthaginians[1].

He led out his troops and set them in array for battle, but the Carthaginians sat in their fenced camps and would not come forth, fearing to fight with such a handful of desperate men. They knew too that supplies, so plentiful in their own quarters, were running low behind the walls of Tunis, and hunger would bring the Greeks down more easily than the sword.

At length Agathocles could wait no longer, but was forced as a last hope to try to storm the Carthaginian entrenchments. It appears from Diodorus' account that the two camps, one five and the other twenty miles away from Tunis, had been given up, and the whole Punic army was massed together on a rising ground, in close and threatening nearness to the Greek lines[2].

When the Carthaginians saw the Greeks coming on to attack them they formed their array on the slope just below their camp, and there awaited the shock. The ground and superiority of numbers were in their favour, and though the Greeks fought stoutly for some time, the discomfiture of the hired troops soon compelled the whole army to retire. The enemy chased them hotly down the slope, and sparing the Libyans, who were likely to come

[1] J. xxii. 8, 4—5 where the account is quite circumstantial and cannot be doubted. Dr Evans (ap. Freeman iv. 441, n.) wishes to make this mutiny the same as that of 309 (D. xx. 34), but this must be a mistake. The form of the speech is of course rhetorical, and was probably embellished by the Roman historians. But the speech itself is confirmed by Diodorus: παρεκάλεσε τοὺς στρατιώτας εἰς τὸν κίνδυνον (xx. 64, 1). The remark of Justin interjectis diebus ad castra hostium exercitum duxit is also sound, and agrees with Diodorus.

[2] The exact site is not known; it might have been the hill now called the Belvedere, nearly three miles from the harbour of Tunis.

over in any case, they fell furiously upon the Greeks and
Italians, slaying 3000 (it is said) before Agathocles could
shelter inside Tunis[1].

That night the Carthaginians made a great thank-
offering to their gods, bringing them the fairest of the
prisoners to be burned in the sacred fire; and a mighty
blaze was kindled to consume the sacrifice[2]. Then all at
once a breeze sprang up and wafted the flames over the
tabernacle of the god which was near the altar. This
caught fire in an instant, and the general's tent which
was next to it; and then all the officers' quarters were
seized by the flames. Thus the whole camp was filled
with uproar and tumult. Some tried to quench the fire,
and others in striving to save their arms and belongings
were caught by the flames and perished. The tents were all
built of wattled reeds and grass, and the wind fanned the
fire so that the help of man could no longer cope with it.
Soon every part of the camp was alight, and many who
tried to escape through its narrow lanes were burned alive,
and so tasted the cruel doom which they had devised for
their captives[3].

Such as made their way out of the camp were met by
a new terror; for they saw by the flaring light a large
body of soldiers drawing near. It was a party of Agathocles' Libyans, 5000 strong, who had forsaken the
losing side, and were come to join the Carthaginians.
But the affrighted soldiers thought that the Greeks were
about to fall upon them; and in this new alarm all discipline and reason were forgotten. Even the officers did
not try to restore order, and the whole army fled in a
maddened rout towards Carthage, the men striking or
trampling down any that stood in their way. Five

---

[1] D. xx. 64.   [2] D. xx. 65, 1.
[3] *Ibid.* 2. This instance of heaven's *lex talionis*, αὐτῆς τῆς ἀσεβείας
ἴσην τὴν τιμωρίαν πορισαμένης, suggests the pious observation of Timaeus.

thousand met their death by fire or in the panic-stricken race. The shameful remnant threw themselves into Carthage, where the citizens naturally believed that the Greeks had won, and bade the runaways hasten through the gates, lest Agathocles' van should burst into the city in pursuit of them. Not till the morning was the truth made known[1].

The Greek army had not fared much better; for when the Libyans had seen the fire and heard the din, they dared not go forward, but shrank back towards the Greek lines. Agathocles' men saw them coming and thought that an attack by the Carthaginians was threatening. The tyrant bade stand to arms, and the host dashed out of the camp to meet the fancied enemy. Then they too caught sight of the flames and heard the shouting, and believed that the whole Carthaginian army was coming out against them. Terror set in and the Greeks made for their camp in headlong flight. Entangled with the Libyan detachment, the frightened soldiers struck out wildly at random, and a furious scuffle ensued. For hours the fighting raged, until four thousand of the Greeks had fallen on that awful night[2].

We have followed Diodorus in our account, and although his version is highly rhetorical, there is not much ground for doubting its truth. The numbers however must be overstated. Perhaps the total losses on each side, in the fight and afterwards, amounted to 4000 for the Greeks and 5000 for the Carthaginians[3]. A fire in an African camp was always a disaster, as the plan of Scipio

[1] D. xx. 66. [2] D. xx. 67.

[3] Justin xxii. 8, 7 says *ibi inconsultius proelium committendo majorem partem exercitus perdidit*. This must also be overstated.

The ingenuity of Schubert 177—8, in tracing the providential escape of another of Timaeus' Carthaginian informants, seems to be carried a little too far. Nor does it seem to me impossible that the Greeks and Libyans came to blows in the night, as Diodorus says.

Africanus proved later on, when he destroyed almost a whole army by setting light to their tents[1].

Agathocles' position in Africa was now quite hopeless[2]. The defeat was followed by the loss of his last African allies, and the temper of his own troops was threatening. They bitterly chid Agathocles for leading them to waste their strength against overwhelming odds, and clamoured once more for their arrears of pay. There was no means of making peace with the Carthaginians, for they were so elated with their victory, that they had resolved to punish the daring invaders in such a way as to deter for ever the boldest foe from doing as Agathocles had done. Thus the prince not unnaturally feared that his own surrender would be called for as an earnest of truce: and he knew that his discontented men would not shrink from paying such a price. There was nothing left but to give up the foothold on the African shore and to sail home to Sicily. Agathocles might perhaps have taken most of his men with him. For the fleet of Carthage had been unable to hinder his last landing with five or six thousand men, and in the weeks or days since the sea-fight little repair to the ships can have been done[3]. Still it would have been hard to take some of his soldiers home and to leave others behind, and perhaps the men were too downhearted to be trusted in

---

[1] Livy xxx. 5.   [2] D. xx. 68.

[3] Diodorus *ibid.* says that the Carthaginians were still lords at sea and that Agathocles had not enough troop-ships to take his men home. This view is followed by all modern historians. On the other hand Diodorus himself had said (xx. 62, 1) that the sea-fight off Syracuse had once more made Agathocles supreme on the water: and if he had had enough ships to land 6000 men, he could certainly have taken home the chief part of what remained after his defeat: unless of course we are prepared to believe that the Etruscans, after helping Agathocles against the Carthaginians, sailed home without waiting for further chances of giving aid.

T.   12

another sea-fight. But most likely Agathocles had no time for these calculations: the soldiers were ready to hand him over to the foe at any moment, and instant flight afforded the only chance of safety.

Of the details of Agathocles' escape two versions have come down. Justin's is as follows[1]: "When Agathocles saw that the men were angry with him for his rash attack, and fearing too that the old trouble about arrears of pay would arise, he slipped away at dead of night with no one but Archagathus, his son....The soldiers tried to run after him, but they were met by the Numidians and driven back into the camp; they did however seize Archagathus, who had missed his way and lost his father in the darkness. Agathocles sailed back to Syracuse with the same fleet that had brought him from Sicily, the guards on board going with him....Meanwhile in Africa the soldiers made a truce with Carthage after Agathocles' flight, and after slaying his sons, surrendered themselves."

Diodorus thus[2]: "Agathocles resolved to slip away with a few followers, and was for taking his younger son Heracleides with him. Archagathus however he wished to leave, fearing that he might intrigue with his step-mother, and with his reckless temper plot against his father. But Archagathus suspected the plan and was prepared to reveal it to the troops....Therefore when Agathocles and his followers were ready to set out, he betrayed them to some of the officers. The latter assembled, and not only hindered their general's design, but informed the soldiers of his treachery. Enraged at this, the men took Agathocles and threw him into chains. Then there was uproar and din and tumult in the camp, and when night fell the alarm of a Carthaginian attack

[1] J. xxii. 8, 8—14.   [2] D. xx. 68, 3—69, 3.

was given. A panic ensued, and each man armed and
rushed out without waiting for orders. Meanwhile the
keepers of Agathocles, who were as alarmed as the rest,
and thought that someone had called them, led the prince
forward loaded with chains: and when the crowd saw the
sight they were moved to pity, and shouted for him to be
set free. As soon as Agathocles was released, he ran to
the landing-place with a few followers, and sailed away
unseen in the stormy weather, about the setting of the
Pleiads."

It does not seem at all likely that Agathocles really
meant to leave his eldest son behind[1]. So far the best
understanding had ruled between them, and it is hard
to believe that the troops would have slain Archagathus
if he had served their cause by the betrayal of his father;
thirdly Agathocles was at great pains later on to avenge
the death of both his sons on the kinsfolk of the African
army; and lastly the gossip about Alcia and her stepson

[1] So Polyb. vii. 2, and the account of Archagathus' death in J. xxii.
8, 14 prove. The Alcia story has already been mentioned in D. xx. 33,
where it is not much more in place than here. Archagathus had not
seen Alcia for four years, and although Agathocles might have met her at
Syracuse, and she in some way have compromised herself, this does not
seem explanation enough. A Greek prince would have got rid of a
faithless wife much more readily than he would have forsaken a warlike
son. Perhaps Diodorus is here following Duris, and so made two
accidents—the leaving of Archagathus and the betrayal of the plan
of flight—into deliberate plots: a tendency of "Duris" that has been
noticed before. (I agree with Schubert 180—1 in preferring Justin's
account to Diodorus' here. Most writers have taken the other view;
cf. Freeman iv. 454.) The suggestion of De Sanctis 316 that Agathocles
left both his sons with their own consent, meaning to return shortly
with a fresh army, is unlikely; for in that case he would never have
waited to go to Segesta and punish the burgesses, but would have sailed
back to Tunis with whatever forces he had raised. De Sanctis lays too
much stress on Justin's failure to mention the fate of Heracleides: it is
merely a careless omission.

Archagathus is worth little in any case, and is much too
far-fetched here to be taken seriously.

From these two accounts it may be gathered that
Agathocles really meant to take both his sons with him.
Before he could start, his plan was betrayed, perhaps by
one of the officers.   The men heard of this and put
Agathocles under a guard; but when the alarm of a
Carthaginian attack was given, Agathocles either man-
aged to slip away, or else was set free by his men, who
wanted their leader in the hour of need.   Then Agathocles
fled, but his sons both missed their way or came too late,
and so fell into the hands of the soldiers.

The army was enraged at the news of Agathocles'
flight, and at once had his sons put to death.   Archagathus was slain by one Arcesilaus, who had formerly
been a friend of the prince, and when Archagathus asked
him, " What thinkest thou that Agathocles will do to thy
children, who now slayest his son ? " he answered, " It is
enough if my children outlive the children of Agathocles[1]."

The troops then chose leaders of their own, who at once
began to treat with Carthage.   The terms were thus fixed :
the Greeks were to give up all Carthaginian towns still in
their hands; and for these they were to be paid three
hundred talents; as many as wished could enlist on the
Carthaginian side at their old scale of pay, and the rest
were to be settled at Solus in Punic Sicily, where the arm
of Agathocles could never reach them[2].

Nearly all the Greeks came over on these terms; but
a few of the outlying garrisons still hoped that Agathocles
was coming to relieve them, and held out.   These places

[1] J. xxii. 8, 14.

[2] D. xx. 69, 3; J. xxii. 8, 13 : *Interim in Africa post fugam regis
milites cum hoste pactione facta, interfectis Agathoclis liberis, Cartha-
giniensibus se tradidere.*   This last phrase is a little careless.

however were soon stormed by the Carthaginians: the leaders were crucified, and the men were put in fetters, and forced to till again the lands that they had wasted in the war.

Thus Carthage, after four years' fighting at her own doors, was at last freed from the fear of Agathocles[1].

THE AFRICAN WAR AS A WHOLE.

The end of the struggle was failure for Agathocles: the whole fruits of the war seemed to have been lost by the last disasters, and his position in Sicily had to be won back at the point of the sword[2]. Carthage had come out uppermost in the fray; but of her spent state and sufferings during the slow years of recovery nothing is told us. It was unlucky for Agathocles, who had staked everything on the chance, that the moment for making an easy peace seemed always at hand, but never came. The effect of his first victory over the Carthaginians was nullified by the burning of his fleet. The death of Hamilcar was outweighed by the mutiny in the prince's camp. The fall of Ophellas did him less good than the harm caused by the failure of Bomilcar. At the height of his good fortune, after the taking of Utica and Hippo, Agathocles was recalled to help his friends at home; and the sea-victory over the Carthaginians was more than counterbalanced by the ruin of his African army. Thus in a

[1] D. *ibid.* 4, 5.

[2] The account in Val. Max. VII. 4, ext. 1 is quite mistaken: *Repentino ejus (=Agathoclis) adventu perculsi, Poeni, libenter incolumitatem suam salute hostium redemerunt, pactique sunt ut eodem tempore et Africa Siculis et Sicilia Punicis armis liberaretur...Quo aequiore animo regnum deseruit eo tutius recepit.*

This confusion between the flight of Agathocles and his return to power, and between his hopes and his achievements is remarkable.

sense Agathocles was unlucky, but it may be that a greater man would have triumphed in spite of all. It will be clear to all readers of his story that Agathocles was dauntless as an adventurer, and heroic in face of the enemy; with other gifts of a true leader he was less highly endowed. We hear several times of mutinies in his camp, and one ground of discontent seems to have been that he favoured his own sons to the slighting of other, perhaps abler, officers. Agathocles in fact suffered constantly in Africa from the lack of a good second in command;—whenever his back was turned, something went wrong.

Even Eumachus, the best of the officers, wasted his strength on useless raids into unknown lands, and gained nothing better than plunder. Such good leaders as Agathocles had he seems to have been unwilling to trust. He quarrelled, as we shall see, with Pasiphilus; and Leptines and Demophilus were not allowed to carry on their wise defensive policy against the Acragantine league. In such an act as Agathocles' hurried crossing to Sicily, when of all times he was most needed in Africa, there are signs of a fickle and hasty temper naturally fatal to a great undertaking. Archagathus, as far as can be seen, was an ineffective commander, who had not the sense to stand his ground until his father returned; by his rash ambition the Sicilian cause was ruined.

Another trouble of Agathocles lay in the temper of his men. Of their mutinous spirit we have already spoken; it was needful at all times to keep them busy, but never to strain their endurance too far, and to satisfy them with plunder without allowing ease to spoil them for the field. An army of this kind might be disorganised by a single reverse.

The Carthaginians also made mistakes, but they seem to have grown wiser by trial. The hasty levy and offer

of battle in face of the invaders is naturally comparable
to the earliest acts of the Romans in withstanding Hannibal in Italy. It needed two or three defeats to teach
the home power that patience alone could mend the
shattered fortunes of the state. Then the policy of in-
action came in, and the army of Agathocles was allowed
to waste its strength until the time arrived for striking
back. The recall of Hamilcar's men from Sicily was
strategically wrong, though it is excused if the Carthaginians were in danger of starving unless their roads were
kept open. But later we hear that the Punic government,
for all the stress in Africa, still spared a force to keep the
oligarchic cause alive in Sicily. A more serious mistake
of the Carthaginians seems to have been their failure to
garrison the chief towns outside the capital: for proper
guards in Hippo, Utica, Neapolis and Hadrumetum would
have helped greatly to bar the progress of Agathocles.
But we know so little of the government of these places
at the time, that there may have been some hindrance
to the acceptance of Carthaginian help of which we are
unaware.

But all these matters are of little weight beside the
main and obvious cause of Agathocles'failure,—his lack of a
strong fleet. It was the fate of almost all Syracusan rulers
to discover too late that sea-power was essential to their
greatness. The reason seems to have been that Syracuse
was bound to become a Sicilian power first and a world-
power afterwards. Now in Sicily her empire was on the
land, so that all her energies had to be centred in her
army, and the fleet inevitably took second place. This
can easily be seen in the history of Agathocles. On land
he has an almost unbroken run of victories up to the
defeat of the Himeras (itself due to his over-confidence in
his own land-forces). On the water his ships are surprised

by the Carthaginians, or at best keep out of their way; he
raises just enough ships to carry his men over to the firm
land of Africa, and then sets his fleet on fire as an en-
cumbrance. His one victory at sea was gained by the help
of the Etruscans.

There is no point in the war at which Agathocles'
having a strong fleet would not have changed the whole
face of affairs. The Carthaginian invasion of Sicily might
have been stopped, or if the fleet were too late for this,
at least the harbour of Syracuse might have been kept
open. The attack on the Punic dominion, instead of being
a series of inroads and small sieges, could have been
driven home by a descent on the haven of Carthage itself;
and such an attack would have been irresistible. Later
too when Africa was lost, an unconquered Syracusan
fleet might have carried the army safely home to
Sicily.

Agathocles himself became aware of his need. He
founded dockyards at Aspis and Hippo, and he allied
himself with the Etruscan coast-towns. It is not unlikely
that he hoped for a fleet with Ophellas. At the end of
his life, when Agathocles planned another Punic war, his
first act was to set building a fleet of two hundred ships.
But again he had learnt his lesson too late.

Although the inroad of Agathocles was a failure in
itself, it was a great event in the history of Europe. It
showed men the possibility of attacking Carthage at her
own doors, and there were not wanting bold spirits to try
the same venture. To Pyrrhus an invasion of Africa
was a dream[1]: its fulfilment was fatal to Regulus: but it

---

[1] Plut. *Pyrrh.* 14 Τίς γὰρ ἂν ἀπόσχοιτο Λιβύης καὶ Καρχηδόνος ἐν ἐφικτῷ
γενομένης, ἣν Ἀγαθοκλῆς ἀποδρὰς ἐκ Συρακούσων κρύφα, καὶ περάσας ναυσὶν
ὀλίγαις λαβεῖν παρ᾽ οὐδὲν ἦλθεν;

was in store for the Scipios to march to victory in the footsteps of Agathocles[1].

DATES FOR THE AFRICAN WAR.

It has already been seen that events placed by Diodorus in 310 would seem rather to belong to 309 (p. 125 above).

The end of the war is dated by Diodorus, xx. 69, 3 ff., where it is said that Agathocles fled about the setting of the Pleiads, and that the war lasted four years. Thus apparently the year of its end would be 307, and the day Oct. 12 (according to modern calculations)[2]. This would make the war last only three years and two months. Holm and others however have put Agathocles' flight in 306 owing to the number of events before it, which seemed too great for the year 307. This would make the war last from Aug. 310 to Nov. 306 = over four years; and the words of Diodorus would rather imply that the war stopped short of the end of the fourth year.

It is safer perhaps not to deviate from Diodorus here, and thus we have the following order, although this arrangement is not without difficulty:

310. Landing and first operations (from Aug. 15 onwards), fight before Tunis, capture of Hadrumetum, and 200 towns. Hamilcar fails at Syracuse; at end of campaign he sends home 5000 troops. First relief of Tunis.

309. Second relief of Tunis.
Death of Hamilcar.
Mutiny in Agathocles' camp.   Orthon sent to Ophellas.
The Acragantine movement.   Sea-fight off Megara.

---

[1] Cf. Scipio's speech, Livy XXVIII. 43 *cur ergo, quoniam Graecas fabulas enarrare vacat, non Agathoclem potius Syracusanum regem, cum diu Sicilia Punico bello ureretur, trangressum in hanc eandem Africam avertisse eo bellum, unde venerat, refers?*

[2] Cf. Meltzer in *Neue Jahrb. f. Phil.* CXI. 753.

308.   Battle among the Zuphonians. Ophellas starts (about
       May); his march and death (about the end of Aug.)[1].
       Defeat of the Carthaginians: failure of Bomilcar.
       Success of the Acragantine League.

307.   (Early Spring.) Capture of Utica and Hippo.
       First raid of Eumachus (almost the same time).
       Defeat of the Acragantines.
       Agathocles sails to Sicily.
       (Summer.) Second raid of Eumachus. Defeat of Aeschrion
           and Eumachus by the Carthaginians.
       Victory of Agathocles and the Etruscans at sea. Xenodicus
           beaten before Acragas.
       (Sept.) Return and defeat of Agathocles.
       (Oct. 12.) His flight. (Later.) Punishment of Segesta[2].

306.   War in Sicily. (Latter half.) Agathocles' treaty with
       Carthage.

305.   Battle of Gorgium. Pacification of Sicily.

Beloch (III. 2, 204) wishes to put the death of Ophellas in 309
instead of 308 (Niese, 468 n. 2, rather leans to this view). His
arguments are: (1) There are in Diodorus too many events for 307;
by putting back Ophellas' death we can move the capture of Utica,
Agathocles' crossing to Sicily, and the first raid of Eumachus to
308, and thus simplify matters. (2) In Suidas s.v. Demetrius it is
said that Ptolemy held the Isthmian games (= spring 308) and then
went over to Africa when he took Cyrene; therefore, Beloch thinks,
Ophellas must have fallen in 309, otherwise the news would not
have reached him before the late autumn of 308, and he would not
have had time to start that year. But this hardly proves the
point: for Ptolemy need not have waited for the news of Ophellas'
death, but may have set sail when he heard that Cyrene was vacant.
Again, if Ophellas fell at the end of August the news might have
reached Ptolemy in a fortnight, and he could, I think, have started
in time. (3) The Parian Marble has 'Οφέλας [ε]ἰ[ς Κα]ρ[χηδόνα

---

[1] Diodorus says that Ophellas was killed on the same day of the same
month as that on which the sons of Agathocles afterwards died. But
this is probably a pious fable and not to be taken seriously.

[2] *V.* next chapter.

μεταβὰς ἀνῃρέθη] in the archonship of Demetrius 309—8. This entry, apart from the uncertainty of the reading, is in itself indecisive and might be applied to either date.

Thus although there is a good deal to be said for Beloch's view, we have not really the means of settling the matter either way.

Beloch puts the final pacification of Sicily in 304 on the strength of D. xx. 90, where it is said that the war against the Sicilian Greeks had lasted two years. But there can be no objection to reckoning 306 as a year of this war, as both sides were up in arms : and in 304 Agathocles was so far at leisure that he could sail to the Lipari Islands, which would hardly have been possible, if the war had been only just over.

CHAPTER V.

1. ACTS AT SEGESTA AND SYRACUSE.

AGATHOCLES reached Sicily with a small band of followers, and found Deinocrates at the height of his power. The prince resolved to show men that, though he had left Africa like a runaway, he had come back to Sicily as her master.

Where Agathocles landed is uncertain; perhaps he put ashore at Selinus, and waited there for his ships to bring him troops from Syracuse; at any rate his small forces could never have marched overland with the oligarchs in the field, and no more is heard of the fleet of Carthage. When part of his army had come, he marched to Segesta, a city of his own alliance[1]. There he lacked for funds, and prepared to wring money out of the Segestans to fill his war-chest. The citizens numbered ten thousand men, and when Agathocles called on

---

[1] D. xx. 71 where it is said that Agathocles sent for part of his troops, and J. xxII. 8, 11 where it is said that he went to Syracuse with the ships and their guards; very likely Justin is slightly mistaken, and the fleet may have gone to Syracuse without Agathocles, and then sailed back with the troops on board.

the rich to pay over a large share of their belongings, the public discontent voiced itself in an indignant assembly. The prince could not brook such a slight on his will; fear and disaster had made him ruthless, and anger drove him to the most gruesome deed that ever Greek wrought on the heads of his countrymen.

On a trumped up charge of treason Agathocles had the poorer citizens driven out of the city and slaughtered in cold blood on the banks of the Scamander. The wealthy were sent to the rack, that they might be forced to tell how much they owned. Some were broken on the wheel, some shot from spring-guns, others beaten with loaded whips until they died in shocking torment[1]. Agathocles even improved on the bull of Phalaris; he made a brazen bed to fit the shape of the body, and on this the victims were clamped down, and a slow fire lighted beneath. Thus while Phalaris could only hear the shrieks of the sufferers, Agathocles glutted his cruel eyes with their tortured looks. Even the women were not spared if their wealth was coveted; but the historian shrinks from the hideous tale of their agonies[2]. So great was the fear of Agathocles that some men hung themselves to forestall his harshness, and others fired their houses over their own heads, and perished with all their home-folk in the blaze. It was as if the whole people of Segesta had been cut off in one day. The boys and maidens were shipped over to Italy, and there sold to the Bruttians. Even the name of Segesta was changed in mockery to Dicaeopolis— Justitia, and the city was given to be the home of run-

---

[1] D. *ibid.* 2. Freeman renders Diodorus' words τοὺς δ' εἰς τοὺς κατα-πέλτας ἐνδεσμεύων κατετόξευεν as above. Schubert takes it that the men were bound to the beams of the engines, and then shot from below.

[2] The details may be found in D. *ibid.* and in Schubert 185, in German.

190 AGATHOCLES' LAST WAR AGAINST THE SICILIANS

aways[1]. But the newcomers soon forgot that Agathocles had been their founder, and deemed themselves heirs of old Segesta and her nobler past[2].

After Agathocles had worked his will at Segesta the tidings reached him of his two sons' death at the hands of the African army. This so enraged him that he sent a few of his friends to Antander at Syracuse, bidding him slay all kinsfolk of the guilty soldiers. Antander carried out this fell command forthwith, and the city was once more filled with fear and bloodshed. Hitherto the victims had at least been grown men with some means of defending themselves, but now old men, women and babes were dragged down to the shore for wholesale destruction. The uncertainty of the doomed wretches as to their own fate made greater the misery of the hour; and to the Greek mind, the worst horror was the lack of proper burial: for the dead bodies were thrown out on the

[1] D. *ibid.* 5. The most has certainly been made of Agathocles' cruelty, and in any case he must have spared his own trustiest partisans. The rich men who suffered most probably belonged to the oligarchic side, but there is no ground for believing (as Beloch 206 does) that these men were really plotting against him. The change of name must mean that the city needed repeopling, which proves that the slaughter must have been frightful. (Cf. De Sanctis 317.)

[2] Cf. Freeman IV. 458—9. The name Dicaeopolis is not read on any coin and cannot have been long in use. The view often put forward that the unfinished state of the temple at Segesta was due to the interruption of the work by Agathocles' act, is quite impossible; as Dr Evans (note to Freeman IV. 458) has proved (in contradiction to Holm, Freeman himself, Niese, and Meltzer, *N. Jahrb. f. Phil.* CXI. 753). Evans notes that (i) the Segestans were so impoverished by the war against Selinus and Syracuse that in the fourth century they would never have begun to build so huge a work in the Agathoclean age ; (ii) the style of the building is Doric of the fifth century, which proves that the work must have stopped long before this time: probably the war with Selinus was the cause. In the temple, as now seen, the columns are unfluted, and it appears that the cella was never built.

beach, and none of their kinsfolk dared do the last rites, lest their act should bring suspicion on themselves. Thus the sea swallowed up the victims, and its waves were dyed red with Syracusan blood[1].

2.   AGATHOCLES' TREATY WITH CARTHAGE.   306.

Agathocles had not furthered his own prospects of victory by these ruthless deeds[2]; he lived in fear of losing such hold on Sicily as he still kept, but he could do nothing in the field against Deinocrates. Indeed after he had strengthened the guards in his few cities in western and northern Sicily, and raised what funds he could, there was nothing left but to stand his ground and to wait for a turn of the tide. Meanwhile Agathocles' oldest general, Pasiphilus, hearing the news of the disaster in Africa and the death of the prince's sons, made up his mind to forsake a lost cause, and to join Deinocrates before it was too late. He induced his men to go over with him, and so betrayed a few posts that he held for Agathocles. In this way he earned a welcome to the oligarchic side.

This loss drove Agathocles to despair, and he sent envoys to Deinocrates to make peace. He offered to give up Syracuse to the oligarchs and to lay down his own power, if only the two towns of Thermae and Cephaloedium might be left in his hands. Deinocrates would not hear of such a thing, but called on Agathocles to withdraw from Sicily altogether[3]. The prince repeated his prayer, but Deinocrates was unyielding, and insisted

[1] D. xx. 72. This passage again is very rhetorical. Agathocles, as has been seen (p. 90), had taken his soldiers from as many households as possible: this partly accounts for the number of victims here.

[2] D. xx. 77.   [3] D. xx. 79, 4.

at least that the children of Agathocles should be handed over as pledges of his good faith. No agreement therefore was reached.

Diodorus beholds with some astonishment the proud and ready-witted Agathocles driven at last to seek for safety on hard terms, and contrasts his poor spirit with the greater courage of the elder Dionysius. On the other hand Diodorus has no doubt as to the motives of Deinocrates in rejecting the prince's offer[1]. " Deinocrates coveted supreme power for himself and was no friend of the popular cause at Syracuse: he was on the contrary very well pleased with his post of general at the moment. At the head of more than 20,000 foot and 3000 horse, with many great cities in his hands, he was called indeed the leader of the exiles, but in reality his power was kingly and his sway despotic. If however he went home to Syracuse, he must have become once more a private man, and one of the many—for freedom means equality—and he might have been overborne by the mob-orator of the hour; since the commons always oppose the boldness of anyone that speaks his mind plainly. Thus it would not be too much to say, that Agathocles had given up his power, but that Deinocrates was the cause of his regaining it."

Although some modern admirers of Agathocles have done their best to find noble and unselfish motives for his acts in the present case[2], it seems most likely that the

[1] D. xx. 79, 2—4.

[2] Beloch 206 says that Agathocles might have made peace with Carthage at any moment, but that he thought more of what Beloch calls " *das nationale Interesse* " than of his own advantage. But in the light of Agathocles' later action it is clear that the " *nationales Interesse* " was far less important in the prince's estimation than his own power. If Agathocles cared so dearly for the cause of Greek Sicily, he might have preferred to leave the country for a few years rather than undo all the

crafty prince, finding himself outnumbered, wished to buy peace with a great show of concession, while keeping a foothold in Sicily, from which he could soon renew his intrigues and plans. That Agathocles meant to throw an apple of discord between Deinocrates and the oligarchs is also quite possible, but it is not at all likely that he succeeded. Diodorus at any rate is quite wrong in blaming Deinocrates for not taking Agathocles' profferred terms. It would have been utter folly after so long a war to have left the work half done by failing to drive Agathocles out of Sicily: and Deinocrates must have believed that a little firmness in treating would soon bring the prince to see reason[1].

In so doing Deinocrates made two mistakes: firstly he acted in a way displeasing to his own followers; and also he gave Agathocles a breathing-space of which he made very good use. Firstly, then, it is quite clear that the so-called exiles in Deinocrates' army were no longer in reality outcasts from their homes[2]. All the chief cities of the island, as Diodorus implies, were in the hands of Deinocrates, and this is another way of saying that the oligarchs had come into their own again, and only kept

work of the last war by calling in Carthaginian help. De Sanctis 318 has been ingenious enough to discover that Agathocles' wish to keep Thermae implied an *ipso facto* declaration of war with Carthage: and he infers that Agathocles meant to force the oligarchs to continue this war in alliance with himself. This I think is too astute even for Agathocles.

[1] Grote 604, Holm 259, Freeman 463, and Niese 470 accept Diodorus' view of the motives of Deinocrates; but Schubert has taken more or less the opinion in the text. Beloch 206 remarks that Deinocrates was suffering from " *Doktrinarismus*," and that he would not take less than the "*Absolut Wünschenswerth*." If by all this he means that Deinocrates' refusal was due entirely to his adherence to certain abstract principles apart from questions of policy, I think his view is very unlikely.

[2] Cf. also Agathocles' proclamation after the battle of Gorgium. D. xx. 89, 3.

the field from hatred of Agathocles. They cannot in any case have loathed him as bitterly as did the Syracusan exiles, to whom their city was still closed. To the more part of Deinocrates' followers the hope of a speedy end of the war was very dear, and when the proposals came to nothing, men began to read double-dealing into his acts.

That Deinocrates, as Diodorus says, really dreaded going home to Syracuse as a private man, cannot easily be believed; for after all the exiles were oligarchs, and if they won the upper hand, the likelihood of Deinocrates' being out-faced in the assembly by a mob-leader was not very great. Moreover if Deinocrates wished to set up as a prince on his own account, it would have been foolish to intrigue with Agathocles, who could never have granted him more than a second place. Further the idea that Deinocrates simply wished the war to drag on so as to lengthen his own spell of leadership, is not sound; for Agathocles would have been ruined by delay as surely as by action, while, if he retrieved his fortunes, Deinocrates would once more have defeated his own ends. At this stage, therefore, it is found that Deinocrates acted with perfect good faith.

Thus the first mistake of Deinocrates was diplomatic; the other was an error in generalship: with his overwhelming forces he ought to have fallen upon Agathocles and driven him out of Sicily. The prince could not have withstood such an attack, especially as the loyalty of his allies was wavering: and the war might soon have been ended. But Deinocrates hoped to win full submission by patience, and, in so doing, he really gave Agathocles the means of regaining his power. For the latter, when he found that Deinocrates was firm, bethought him of a forlorn hope in seeking to patch up an agreement with

Carthage.   Diodorus gives the following account[1]: "Agathocles, on learning the temper of Deinocrates, sent to
the exiles and charged him with standing in the way
of their freedom.   He also sent envoys to the Carthaginians, and made peace on condition of giving back all
the cities in Sicily that they had formerly held.   For this
he got a sum of money in gold worth 300 talents of silver,
or, as Timaeus says, 150 talents, and 200,000 bushels of
wheat[2]."

It was quite natural that Agathocles should try to stir
up ill-feeling against Deinocrates among the oligarchs;
but this was a trifling matter beside the remarkable
success of his reconciliation with Carthage.   Some strong
motive must have driven the Punic government to this
sudden change of front, but there is some uncertainty as
to the real reason.   Many have said that Carthage now
began to fear Deinocrates more than Agathocles : but this
view after all is unlikely.   For Carthage had trusted and
befriended the oligarchs for many years and can scarcely
have forgotten that her worst enemies had always been
tyrants.   She must also have known that the success of
the oligarchs rested chiefly on her own alliance and that
her change of side would mean the return of Agathocles
to power.   It would thus be a mistake to say that Car-

[1] D. xx. 79, 5.

[2] The two accounts of the sum of money are thus explained (cf.
Hultsch, *Metrologie* 428).   The Carthaginians undertook to pay in gold a
sum worth 300 talents of silver.   The legal relation of gold to silver was
ten to one; but as in commerce the value of silver was depreciated, the
Carthaginians would in the end have parted with rather less than 30
talents of gold.   Again (*ibid.* 429) the Carthaginian talent was only half
the value of the Greek, so that Timaeus had taken the trouble to turn the
sum into Greek money while the other authorities left it in Carthaginian.
Thus all alike intended to denote the same amount.

(Schubert 189 connects this with Timaeus' Carthaginian informant,
but for no very strong reason.)

thage meant to wear out both sides by helping the weaker[1]. Another theory is that a change of party had taken place in the Carthaginian government, and that the side to which Hamilcar and Bomilcar had belonged, having regained the upper hand, was returning to its old policy of friendship with Agathocles[2]. This is quite possible, but rests on no evidence whatever. On the whole it seems best to believe that Carthage snatched at the chance of pushing forward her bounds in Sicily at small cost, and trusted to the weariness following a long war to keep Agathocles from reconquering what he was then giving up. The sum of money was a trifle, and the corn, now peace reigned in Africa, was easily raised, and for this Carthage won back the old march of the Halycus, as we must believe; and Selinus, Segesta, Heraclea, and Thermae were all to pass into her hands. This was far more than the oligarchs would have granted, for Heraclea, at any rate, was actually theirs. On these terms peace was made; and the outcome proved that Carthage was not altogether wrong. Agathocles stood by the terms, and not till the very end of his life did he think of wresting from his new allies the cities that he now gave up to them.

The withdrawal of Carthaginian help was ruinous to the hopes of the oligarchs. It is uncertain, indeed, whether any land army had been fighting on their side up to that time; but the new conditions meant that no more such aid would be forthcoming, and that the fleet of Carthage would not blockade the Syracusan harbour again. In other words Deinocrates had no longer the means of dealing a telling blow at Agathocles. The

[1] This view is Meltzer's. Most historians have left the matter open.
[2] So Schubert; but party changes at Carthage may be rather a *deus ex machina* to some writers.

spirits of his army sank, and many men began to fall away or to buy their safety by secret promises to the enemy.

3. The Campaign of Gorgium. 305.

The winter seems to have passed in these negotiations, and in the next year Agathocles took the field. He is said to have had no more than 5000 foot and 800 horse, while Deinocrates had 25,000 foot and 3000 horse. But many of the oligarchs were waverers, and not a few had already pledged themselves to come over to Agathocles[1].

The armies camped at a place called Gorgium[2]; the site is unknown. Soon the fight began, for which the more vigorous oligarchs were naturally eager. For a long time the struggle went on without advantage to

[1] D. xx. 89. Plass 290 even says "...alles vorher durch Verrath vorbereitet war."

[2] The mss. of Diodorus have Γοργόνιον; of this Cluver made Torgium which is mentioned by Hesychius, Τόργιον· Ὄρος ἐν Σικελίᾳ ὅπου νεοττεύουσιν αἱ γῦπες, ἀφ' οὗ καὶ αὐταὶ Τόργοι. Coscia, Delle ant. Città di Sic. di ignota Sit. cited by Holm II. 479, identified Torgium with Caltavuturo, which is above the pass over which the road from Termini to Leonforte now runs. Whether Caltavuturo (= Vultures' Rock) is really an ancient name or merely a popular form of the Arab name Kalat-Abi-Thaur, may be uncertain, but there can be no doubt that such a mountain region would be the last place where a Greek battle would have been fought. Nor is its nearness to Thermae and Cephaloedium, the two places sought by Agathocles, anything in its favour. Agathocles was much more likely to have rallied his forces at Syracuse, his natural headquarters. I believe therefore that this identification must be given up. I would suggest that Gorgium is the better reading, and that this may have been a village near Leontini, and that Gorgias, the famous Leontine rhetorician, took his name from that place. That Sicilians sometimes took their names from towns is well known (cf. Gelo from Gela, Thermon from Thermae, and inversely Phintias from the prince of that name). The neighbourhood of Leontini is flat ground, suited for a pitched battle, and no unlikely place to fight, as Syracuse was the real object at stake.

either side. Then more than 2000 of Deinocrates' men
passed over to Agathocles. This act turned the scale.
The oligarchs, fancying that the desertion was more wide-
spread than it had really been, were seized with fright,
and soon gave way before the fierce onset of the Agatho-
cleans. Then a headlong flight set in. But the prince
soon stayed the chase, and sent to offer fair terms to the
worsted side. They must see, he said, that after such
a defeat by his own smaller army it was vain to go on
fighting. Let them lay down arms and return freely to
their own homes.

The horsemen, who had fled in safety to a hill called
Ambices[1], and such of the foot as had got clean away,
lent no ear to these fair words. But the more part of the
infantry, who had sheltered on a hill near the battle-field,
were ready enough to listen. They now despaired of
victory, and longed to see their homes and kinsfolk once
more. A truce was made, and the men came down from
the hill. Agathocles bade them pile arms, and then had
the whole body surrounded and shot down. In this
way 4000, or, as Timaeus said, 7000, victims met their
death. The smaller number is doubtless nearer the
truth; but what led Agathocles to break faith with his
prisoners is uncertain. Diodorus speaks of his act
as one more example of that faithless cruelty, which
ever preyed upon the defenceless[2]. But this explains
nothing. Agathocles was bringing the war to an end,
and it would have been impolitic to have broken faith
with any Greeks that were ready for peace. It has been
suggested that the prisoners had themselves been the first
to break the truce, and so brought down the vengeance of

[1] The spot is unknown.

[2] This sounds as if Diodorus had borrowed some of Timaeus' invective
as well as his figures.

Agathocles[1]. But to have taken such revenge for what
can only have been a technical breach of the terms of
surrender would have been just as impolitic as a slaughter
for its own sake: and Agathocles would have had too
much sense to embitter the Sicilians at the very moment
when he was trying to win them over by his declaration
of forgiveness. The truth must be that the victims
belonged to a different class of men from the rest of the
army. We know that the latter were not really exiles,
since Agathocles could bid them return to their own
cities. On the other hand it is said that the surrendered
Greeks had yielded chiefly because they longed for their
homecoming. Now the real outcasts were the Syracusan
nobles, and it is likely that the vengeance of Agathocles
fell designedly upon them, his oldest and bitterest foes.
Perhaps Deinocrates led his followers to trust the promises
of Agathocles, knowing himself what lay beneath them,
and thus bought back the favour of the prince.

This view explains the act of Agathocles, and also
accounts for his treatment of Deinocrates. So far from
punishing his rival, the tyrant at once forgave him and
set him over part of his army: and it was noted that
Agathocles, so faithless towards most men, ever treated
Deinocrates with unswerving truth and goodwill. No
doubt the prince could respect and value as a helper the
man whose gifts of leadership and shifty dealing were so
little inferior to his own.

Deinocrates and Agathocles then set themselves to the

---

[1] This is Schubert's view (192); it is backed by no evidence. Niese
supposed (471) that the slaughtered men were hirelings who had been
faithless to both sides, and of whom the two leaders agreed to be rid.
But in this case the homesickness of the captives would be quite pointless;
since to a hired soldier return could only mean loss of employment. The
view taken agrees in the main with Freeman and Grote.

final reduction of Sicily. Pasiphilus who was holding
Gela for the oligarchs was seized and slain. But whether
he was betrayed by Deinocrates, of whose change of side
he may have been uninformed, or merely surprised in
a sudden attack, is uncertain[1]. From the smaller towns
no further resistance was met; their surrender seems to
have been quick and abject. How far Agathocles fulfilled
the hopes raised by· his promise of forgiveness, and
how far his old harshness still made itself felt is another
doubtful point. At Leontini, indeed, stern measures seem
to have been taken; although the tale of Polyaenus is
rather fanciful[2].

"When Agathocles had conquered the Leontines, he
sent his general Deinocrates to the city, to say that
Agathocles was trying to rival the fame of Dionysius, and
wished to spare them, as Dionysius had spared the Italian
Greeks who were defeated at the Helleporus. The Leontines believed this and gave their oaths. Then Agathocles
came into the city, and bade them come to the assembly
unarmed. The general put the question, 'Those who
agree with the proposal of Agathocles hold up their
hands.' Agathocles said: 'My proposal is: to slay everyone here.' There were ten thousand sitting; and forthwith the soldiers surrounded and slew all that were in the
assembly[3]."

---

[1] Diodorus (xx. 90, 2) says ὁ δὲ Δεινοκράτης προδοὺς τοὺς συμμάχους, τὸν
μὲν Πασίφιλον ἐν τῇ Γέλᾳ συναρπάσας ἀπέκτεινε; the exact force of συναρπάσας may be doubted. Schubert 193 takes the former view, Freeman
(iv. 468—9) seemingly the latter.

[2] Polyaenus v. 3, 2.

[3] The point of the story is not that absolute powers were voted to
Agathocles: the chairman's (στρατηγός) question really was, " Those who
agree to the peace with Agathocles, hold up their hands " (ὅτῳ δοκεῖ ὅπερ
καὶ Ἀγαθοκλεῖ).

But Agathocles punned on the sense of δοκεῖ—" Δοκεῖ μοι πάντας

From this story it may be gathered that Leontini yielded at discretion, and that Agathocles punished a great number of the citizens. The rest of the tale is hardly historical.

The subjection of Sicily was accomplished in two years' time. Nothing is said of the fate of Acragas, the one still powerful enemy of Agathocles. But it is most likely that Agathocles left her in peace. Her power was narrowed down to her own lands, and she could not hope to vie with Syracuse again, while with his own wearied troops a long siege would have been an unwise undertaking. No treaty is recorded, but one may well have been made; or perhaps the freedom of Acragas was in the terms of Agathocles' agreement with Carthage. For, although nothing of the kind is mentioned, it is quite possible that the Punic government may have done this last service to a former ally[1]. Outside Acragas the sway of Agathocles reached to the marches of the Punic dominions.

ἀνελεῖν." The mistake of Freeman IV. 521, in referring this trick to Agathocles' capture of Leontini c. 319, has already been noticed. Schubert rightly places it here. A summary of the war is given in J. XXIII. 1, 1.

[1] That Acragas remained free is stated positively by Beloch 208. Freeman is doubtful on the point, and indeed there is not much evidence either way.

CHAPTER VI.

AGATHOCLES AS KING.

1. HIS GOVERNMENT.

THE true kingly power of Agathocles dates from the pacification of Sicily after the campaign of Gorgium; but it is uncertain when he took the name of king. Diodorus dates this after the fall of Ophellas in 307[1]. Antigonus certainly took the title in that year after his victory over Ptolemy[2]. But when Diodorus implies that the other Successors followed his lead forthwith, he is undoubtedly mistaken. Ptolemy reckoned his years of kingly rule from November 305[3]. Ptolemy's example was followed by Seleucus and Lysimachus and Cassander. Last of all Agathocles, who felt himself in no way inferior to these rulers, added the royal title to his own name[4]. It is therefore not likely that he called himself king before 304, when the Sicilian war was over; but it is even possible that his assumption of the name falls still later[5].

In Syracuse Agathocles seems to have ruled and behaved very much as he had done since the beginning of

[1] D. xx. 54, 1.

[2] Demetrius likewise. D. xx. 52, 53 and *I.G.* II. 238, where Demetrius is called king: date Dec. 307. Schubert, I believe, was the first to explain clearly the error in D.

[3] Cf. Droysen, *Gesch. d. Hell.* II. 2, 140, n. 1.

[4] D. xx. 54, 1.

[5] Schubert 157 would bring down the date to the time of the occupation of Corcyra c. 301. But the earlier date seems more likely.

his tyranny. His bearing was still genial and popular. He wore no diadem, but often put on a myrtle wreath, to which a priesthood entitled him, but which, as his enemies were unkind enough to say, was meant to hide his unsightly baldness[1]. He put his name on the coins of Syracuse, but not, as far as is known, his head. Thus it happens that no true likeness of Agathocles has reached modern students.

Of the nature of his rule outside Syracuse very little is known. There seems to have been an end of slaughter and plunder, and so far the new order must have furthered the welfare of the island. To these later years of Agathocles the oft-quoted words of Polybius would best apply. "What writer has failed to record that Agathocles, the tyrant of Sicily, who in his first undertakings and in the establishment of his power seemed to be the harshest of men, afterwards, when his sway was firmly grounded, is thought to have become of all men the gentlest and mildest[2]?" Before the battle of Gorgium it would have been a mockery to use such words of Agathocles, but to the years of his unchallenged rule they may not be ill fitted. This period was the most glorious and noteworthy of his life; but as the history of Diodorus is here known to us only from fragments, we are very ill-informed on the course of events.

2. AGATHOCLES' ACTS ON THE LIPAREAN ISLANDS. 304.

In the year 304 Agathocles seems to have wished to assert his sway over the Lipari islands. He sailed down upon them in peace time, and called for the payment of

[1] D. xx. 54, 1, and even more extravagantly in Aelian, *V. H.* xi. 4.

[2] Polyb. ix. 23. The words are usually applied to the time from B.C. 317 onwards.

fifty talents of silver[1]. The islanders had no means of withstanding the tyrant, and at once placed in his hands such sums as could be raised. They asked Agathocles to wait for the payment of the balance that they might not be forced to draw upon temple hoards. To this plea Agathocles refused to listen; and obliged the Lipareans to give up some costly objects which stood in their town-hall; for all that some of these treasures were labelled as offered to Hephaestus and others to Aeolus. With this plunder Agathocles' set sail. But heaven wreaked this godless act on the tyrant's head. For Aeolus the god of the winds, raised a mighty storm on the open sea, and the treasure-laden ships, eleven all told, were sent to the bottom. The god of fire nursed his wrath for long years; but his vengeance overtook Agathocles in the end: for when the king lay speechless in his last illness, he was placed still living on a burning pyre, and thus fearfully paid his debt to Hephaestus.

In this account of Diodorus the moral of the tale rather overshadows the facts. It was of course a common belief in old times that heaven took upon itself to punish impiety, and often chose to suit the vengeance to the crime, so that all men could see for themselves that the wicked man had incurred a merited fate. Examples of such ways of the gods have already been remarked in Agathoclean history, and whether or not these pious fancies were always the work of Timaeus, it is at least possible that the story may have been a little embellished to point the moral. That Agathocles wrung a sum of money out of the islanders is clearly historical. But the other details are far from certain. The sacred treasures

[1] D. xx. 101. Agathocles' descent on the islands may have been meant to counteract the influence of Rome; for she seems to have had friendly dealings with them at an early date. D. xiv. 93, 4.

are not taken from a shrine as would have been natural, but merely from the town-hall; and this suggests that the plea of sparing votive offerings may have been nothing but the Lipareans' excuse for their short payment. At the same time Agathocles was not the man to shrink from sacrilege if he wanted money; in this he was only following Dionysius. It is also possible that the shipwreck was a fable and that the king came safely home with his spoils[1].

3. THE ADVENTURES OF CLEONYMUS. 304—303.

After his sorry exploit in the Liparean islands, Agathocles lived for some time in peace. As far as Sicily is concerned, the next few years are a blank, but it will be worth while to look further abroad and to trace the causes that led Agathocles to step out from his island-realm into the wider field of Hellenistic politics.

In 305 the Samnites had made peace with the Romans; but the Lucanians, Rome's allies, whose freedom the new treaty safeguarded, went on with their war against Tarentum. The Greek republic, unwilling as usual to sacrifice comfort to the demands of a great undertaking, bethought herself once more of seeking a champion from Sparta. An opening for western adventure was still alluring to needy princes, and the call of Tarentum was at once taken up by Cleonymus, the son of Cleomenes. Cleonymus was the brother of Acrotatus, who had failed to save Sicily from Agathocles, and when Acrotatus died before his father, Areus his son was chosen to be king instead of Cleony-

---

[1] This story of Agathocles is like the account of Pyrrhus' robbery of the temple of Persephone (Appian, *Samn.* 12). There too a storm is supposed to wreck the ships that bear the plunder. The story is as suspicious there as here. Cf. Schubert 194.

mus. Thus Cleonymus, having lost his hope of kingship at Sparta, was glad to seek his fortune elsewhere[1].

The Tarentines sent a fleet to fetch Cleonymus, and handed him a sum of money, with which he hired 5000 troops on the recruiting-ground of Taenarum. Then he sailed to Tarentum and hired other 5000. He also enrolled the home force to the number of 20,000 foot and 5000 horse. The Messapians and most of the Italian Greeks threw in their lot with the new deliverer. Cleonymus survived an attempt on his life made by two Peucetians; and boldly took the field. His mighty array so frightened the Lucanians, that before a blow had been struck, they made peace with Tarentum[2]. This peace led to a treaty with Rome: for when once the Samnites were quiet, Rome cared little what went on in the south of Italy, and she had no wish to fight with Cleonymus unless he became troublesome. At this time must probably be placed the famous agreement that forbade the Romans to send warships round the Lacinian headland[3].

Cleonymus was now at the height of his power, and the object of his coming being thus easily attained, he found himself out of employment. He was unjust enough to use his position to the ruin of a Greek city. Metapontum had been almost alone among the Italiot states in standing aloof from Cleonymus' undertaking, and he now persuaded the Lucanians to march into the Metapontine lands. Soon afterwards he drew near himself, and the city yielded at discretion. Cleonymus entered Metapontum, " as a friend," and wrung from the citizens no less than six hundred talents. He also carried off two

[1] On Cleonymus, see D. xx. 104 f.; Paus. iii. 6, 2; Livy x. 2, and Rospatt in *Philologus* xxiii. 72 ff.; Droysen ii. 2, 188 ff.; Mommsen, *Rom. Hist.* i. 482; Lenormant, *La Grande Grèce* i. 42, 43, 130.
[2] D. *ibid.*   [3] Appian, *Samn.* 7.

hundred of the fairest and noblest maidens as hostages[1]. This wanton and outrageous act showed how far Cleonymus had sunk from the Spartan ideal. He had left off his Spartan dress, and lived in luxury, tyrannising over his friends and letting his forces lie idle. At last ambition roused him from his stupor, and he formed the bold plan of crossing to Sicily, and freeing the country from Agathocles. But for some reason the carrying out of this design was put off[2].

Cleonymus seems instead to have gone on a plundering raid in Italy; of his adventure a much confused account is given by Livy[3]. Cleonymus first took an unknown town called Thuriae[4] in the land of the Sallentini; this was perhaps the place called Thyraeum by the Greeks, which lay between Tarentum and Brundusium. From this point he was apparently driven out by the Romans, although the reports varied. One story was that the consul Aemilius met and routed Cleonymus, and left Thuriae in freedom. Another related that the dictator Junius Bubulcus marched into the Sallentine land, and that Cleonymus fled to his ships without even facing the enemy. All this sounds suspicious.

It was perhaps after this failure that Cleonymus planned a greater undertaking. He sailed to Corcyra, which had been free since 312, took the city and wrung a sum of money from the citizens. He then guarded the place strongly, and resolved to use it as a base from which

---

[1] D. *ibid.*; cf. Athenaeus XIII. 605 D, where Duris is mentioned as the author of the tale. The account must none the less be accepted. Metapontum was ruined by the payment of so large a sum of money; and her coinage stopped. Cf. Evans, Freeman IV. 475, n. 1.

[2] D. *ibid.*   [3] Livy x. 2.

[4] This place cannot be the same as Thurii, with which some have confused it. The Sallentini were in Calabria. Rospatt *l.c.* thinks it may be the Θυραῖον of Strabo VI. 3 (or Uria) between Tarentum and Brundusium.

he could watch the course of Greek politics. So formidable did he seem on this point of vantage that Cassander and Demetrius the Besieger (then installed as the deliverer of Greece) both sought his alliance. But Cleonymus listened to neither[1].

Soon he heard that his Italian and Tarentine allies were wavering, and hastened back to punish them. It is uncertain to what this defection really amounted; some have thought that the treaty between Rome and Tarentum had only just been made, and that Cleonymus felt this to be against his own interests[2]. Anyhow Cleonymus left a guard in Corcyra, and sailed back to Italy. He took a nameless place which the " barbarians," as Diodorus says, were guarding, enslaved the indwellers and harried the land.

Then Cleonymus, finding perhaps that the loyalty of Tarentum had been unduly suspected, sailed for a roving cruise up the Adriatic. The western shore was almost harbourless, and the Dalmatian creeks swarmed with pirates, so that Cleonymus found an easier prey in the land of the Veneti[3]. He sailed into the river Meduacus[4], and leaving at last his bigger boats as the water grew shallow, he took his men up stream in skiffs. Soon they came to three hamlets of the Patavians that stood on the river's bank about forty miles from its mouth. These were taken, sacked and burned. When the news reached Patavium itself, the men, whom the nearness of the Gauls obliged to be ever active in arms, at once made ready to withstand the raiders. Half marched down stream to attack the boats in the naval camp fourteen miles from the town, and the rest fell upon the plunderers. Both

[1] D. *ibid.*   [2] So Droysen *ibid.* has thought.   [3] Livy *l.c.*
[4] Now the Brenta; it would seem that Cleonymus entered the mouth near which Venice now stands, as Patavium was forty miles from there.

strokes succeeded. The land army of Cleonymus was routed and the boats were driven to shelter on the further bank of the river. Thus the flight of the Greeks was cut off, and an onset of the Veneti from the east barred the way to the main fleet. A great number of captives were taken, and from these it was found out that Cleonymus and the fleet were only three miles down stream. Thereupon the Patavians manned flat-bottomed boats and gave chase. Many of the Greek ships ran aground in the shoals and were set on fire; others were surrounded and taken, and not more than a fifth of the fleet escaped with Cleonymus after a desperate pursuit right down to the river's mouth.

The ships' beaks were taken to Patavium and set up in the temple of Juno, where they had been seen by many in Livy's own day; and a solemn feast with a boat race or sham fight on the river kept up the memory of the city's deliverance.

This reasonable account of Livy is undoubtedly sound; but it is uncertain whether Diodorus' narrative relates to the same or to another mishap of Cleonymus. It is said that he took a place called Triopium (of which nothing is known elsewhere) and a thousand captives. He was then set upon at night by the barbarians, and lost 4000 killed and 1000 taken. At the same time his fleet, moored near the camp, suffered from a storm and lost 20 ships[1]. It is certainly tempting to believe that Triopium might have been the general name for the three hamlets on the Meduacus, and that Diodorus, who used a Greek source friendly to Cleonymus, understated the number of casualties. But the whole matter is very uncertain[2].

[1] D. xx. 105, 2—3.

[2] Droysen seems to identify the two raids. (He also puts here the attack on Thuriae.) Freeman makes them separate and places the

Whatever the exact nature of Cleonymus' disasters had been, he had no longer any foothold in Italy, and hastened back to Corcyra.

4. AGATHOCLES' WARS IN CORCYRA AND ITALY.
c. 300.

The next events are wrapped in mystery. No more is heard of Cleonymus in the west[1]; but it is said that Demetrius had been in Corcyra before his return to Athens in 303—2.   Whether Demetrius had seized the island while Cleonymus was up the Adriatic, and so obliged Cleonymus to sail home to Sparta without landing, or the Corcyreans had themselves driven him out and welcomed Demetrius as a friend, without his interfering in the government, is uncertain[2]. For the moment at any rate Corcyra was a free state.

But before long new troubles arose. When Demetrius was busy on the campaign of Ipsus, or perhaps soon after his defeat, Cassander saw his chance of bringing the island once more under the Macedonian sway. He swooped down upon Corcyra with his fleet; his troops landed and beleaguered the city. The place was on the brink of capture,

Venetian disaster before the capture of Corcyra. This seems less likely: for after such a blow Cleonymus would not have been ready for a fresh conquest.   Freeman thinks that the attack on Thuriae was Livy's version of Cleonymus' first fighting in Italy, drawn from *laudationes* and quite fictitious.   Rospatt insists that " Triopium " must be the place in Caria: but this naturally brings him no nearer to a solution of the difficulty.

The chronology is doubtful. Diodorus relates the whole episode under 303: but this would seem to apply only to the later events, and Cleonymus probably came in 304.   (Cf. Droysen II. 2, 188—9; Freeman IV. 477 and 526 ff.)

[1] For Cleonymus' later life cf. Rospatt *ibid.* 78—80.

[2] That Demetrius had been in Corcyra is proved by Demochares fr. 4 in Müller *F. H. G.*; cf. Droysen 190.

when Agathocles came to save it. Perhaps the Corcyreans had themselves called him in, fearing a Sicilian lord less than the hated Macedonian. At any rate Agathocles and his ships brought a quick deliverance. He fell upon Cassander's fleet and a furious struggle set in. The Sicilians thirsted to show that their valour, already dreaded by Phoenician and Italian, was more than a match for the prowess of the Macedonians, the conquerors of Asia. And so the outcome proved, for the fleet of Cassander was thoroughly worsted, and every ship set on fire. This blow brought on such a panic among the land troops on Corcyra that Agathocles might, it is said, have landed his army and cut the whole force to pieces, but, not knowing his own chance, he did no more than set up a trophy on the shore[1]. But it would probably be nearer the truth that Agathocles, seeing Corcyra and its besiegers in his power, refrained from useless bloodshed, and rightly claimed a complete victory. Cassander must have been allowed to withdraw under terms, and the island was left in the power of Agathocles.

How far the Corcyreans were content with him as a master is uncertain, the only information on the matter being a tale in Plutarch. It is said that the Corcyreans asked Agathocles why he wasted their land. "Why," said Agathocles, "because your fathers gave shelter to Odysseus." And further when the men of Ithaca complained that the Sicilian soldiers had been stealing their sheep, he answered, "Well, when your king came to

---

[1] D. *ibid.* The platitude at the end of the last section, that in war ignorance and deception often effect more than force of arms, suggests that D. is summing up some kind of "stratagem" or anecdote, now lost. For such reflexions cf. xx. 30, 1; 67, 4.

There is obviously a gap between all three sections of this fragment.

Sicily, he did worse than that; he blinded the shepherd[1]."
If Agathocles thus jestingly posed as the avenger of Poly-
phemus, it is not to be believed that he really behaved as
an enemy to Corcyra[2]. His sallies were only meant to
excuse the unbridled greed of his hired soldiers, and his
own inability to check it. Corcyra was far too valuable
an outpost for Agathocles to trifle wantonly with the
feelings of the indwellers.

It may have been about this time that Ptolemy sought
the friendship of Agathocles by offering him the hand of
his step-daughter Theoxena, who seems to have been the
daughter of Berenice by her first husband. Agathocles
accepted the offer, and he may have wedded the princess,
his third wife, a year or two later[3]. This step of Ptolemy
is a sign of his crafty policy: Cassander was his friend,
but Cassander's power seemed to be growing too great:
therefore Ptolemy joined hands with Cassander's foeman.

Agathocles was soon recalled from Corcyra by news of
a rising among his Ligurian and Etruscan troops in Sicily.
The men had been left under the command of Agathocles'
grandson Archagathus, or perhaps of his son Agathocles[4],
and were clamouring for their pay. The king himself set
upon the mutineers with his other soldiers, and slew them
to the number of 2000. This act, according to Diodorus,
angered the Bruttians; and the reason may have been

[1] Plut. *de Sera Numinis Vindicta*, 557 c, and *Reg. et Imp. Apophth.*
s.v. Agathocles.

[2] As Droysen 242 has supposed.

[3] Since the two children of Theoxena were still *parvuli* (J. xxiii. 2, 6)
about 290, when Agathocles sent them home to Egypt. (In spite of
Beloch iii. 2, 208 n. I prefer the common form.)

[4] D. xxi. 3, 1—2. Diodorus says τὸν υἱὸν 'Αρχάγαθον, which cannot be
right as Agathocles' *son* Archagathus had been killed in 307. But whether
Archagathus is right, = Agathocles' grandson (reading υἱωνόν), or υἱόν is
right, = his son Agathocles, is doubtful. Agathocles himself was about 60,
and his grandson would have been rather young to command an army.
This young Agathocles was probably the son of Alcia (cf. Beloch iii. 2, 208).

that the discontented Italian troops had made common cause with the enemies of Agathocles beyond the strait[1]. There is no ground for believing that Agathocles had been in league with the Bruttians against the Greek cities[2]. He now declared war on the Bruttians, and laid siege to a town called Ethae[3]. But while he lay before it, the barbarians raised a strong force, and fell upon him by night, so that Agathocles lost 4000 men and had to withdraw to Syracuse.

After this rebuff Agathocles seems to have sat peaceably in Syracuse for some time; but his diplomacy was busily at work, and presently he gained another powerful ally. About 297 Pyrrhus was sent home from Egypt by Ptolemy with men and money to claim the throne of Epirus. There he set himself up as joint ruler with Neoptolemus[4]. At the same time mention is made of the betrothal of Agathocles' daughter, Lanassa, to Pyrrhus. It is therefore quite likely that Ptolemy brought about this union, hoping at once to have a trustworthy agent in Epirus, and to draw closer the bonds of his friendship with Agathocles.

Before the wedding was held, Agathocles made a surprise attack on Croton. The event is thus narrated[5]. Agathocles got together his naval forces and crossed to Italy, meaning to descend upon Croton. He sent a messenger to Menedemus, the prince of that place, who was his friend, telling him that the Crotoniates need not fear. In reality Agathocles meant to besiege Croton, but he pretended that he was sending his daughter, Lanassa, in

[1] So Schubert 196.

[2] As Freeman iv. 480, and seemingly Niese 482 have thought.

[3] The site is unknown.

[4] Cf. Droysen ii. 2, 256. Lanassa's mother may have been Alcia (Beloch, *l.c.*).

[5] D. xxi. 4. As the consulship of Fabius = 296 is in fr. 6, and the fragments seem to be in order, we have a lower limit for these events.

royal array to her wedding. In this way he took Croton quite unprepared. Then he laid siege to the place, building lines round it from sea to sea; and with artillery and mines he overthrew the strongest of the defence works. The Crotoniates were so alarmed at the sight that they opened the gates and let in Agathocles with his army. The town was given up to plunder and slaughter.

If Menedemus, as has been thought, was the same as the Crotonian democrat who may have been acting with Agathocles in his Italian campaign, and who helped to defeat the Crotonian oligarchs about 317 B.C.[1], then his friendship with Agathocles would have been of very long standing, and some strong reason must have led Agathocles to turn against so useful an ally. What plans were brewing in the tyrant's mind can only be guessed. It may be that he began to feel that Corcyra was too far off to be a useful outpost for Syracuse, and this may have led him to undertake the foundation of a south-Italian empire, of which Greek and Italian were alike to be subject.

It has been objected that the means taken by Agathocles to cajole Menedemus were childish and that Diodorus' statement of the unpreparedness of the town is disproved by the stubborn resistance that was offered[2]. But it seems most likely that Agathocles really tried to lull the suspicion of the Crotoniates to rest, but only succeeded so far that his onset was unexpected: it had to be followed up by a regular siege. A town so open to attack as Croton can never have been in a state of utter unreadiness; and without treason within the walls a complete surprise would have been hopeless.

After the fall of Croton Agathocles widened his influence in Italy by a league with the Iapygians and

[1] D. xix. 10, 3—4, v. p. 44 above.

[2] So Schubert, who regards the plot as a fiction of Duris.

Peucetians.   These people had an ill name for roving, and Diodorus says that the prince lent them ships for their evil trade, and took himself a share of the booty. From this statement there is every reason to believe that a regular alliance was formed, and that a desultory war of plunder and raids was carried out by the joint forces on the Italian coast.   Agathocles must have aimed at something more vigorous than robbery on the high seas[1]. Indeed he seems to have visited the Peucetians' land himself, which proves that their friendship was a matter of some weight to him[2].   It is possible that these Apulian tribes were really calling in the help of Agathocles against the Romans, who for the moment were too busy with the Etruscans and Samnites to take any action in southern Italy.   The settling of Venusia a few years later with a strong body of Latin colonists shows that the Romans were anxious to strengthen their hold on these lands[3].

[1] D. *ibid.* Schubert 198—9 thinks that Agathocles may *once* have shared in an act of piracy with the Peucetians, and that this has been magnified into a regular practice.   I think the account in the text more likely.

[2] This is proved by the following story in [Arist.] *Mirab. Aus.* 110: " Among the Peucetians they say there is a shrine of Artemis; and in it a brazen necklace, very famous in that neighbourhood, was said to have been offered bearing the title ' Diomede to Artemis.'   The legend is that he put the necklace round a stag's neck, and that the skin of the stag grew over it, and they say that in this way it was found, and was afterwards offered by Agathocles, king of the Sicilians, in the temple of Zeus." Into the curious details of the tale there is no need to enter.   The point of it seems to be that the necklace was already a curiosity among the Peucetians, and that Agathocles, as a mark of honour, was allowed to dedicate it.   That he found the necklace himself does not seem to be meant.

[3] In 291, 20,000 settlers were planted there.   Venusia was perhaps meant first of all to bar the road between Tarentum and the Samnites, but no doubt also, as Beloch 212 has noted, to check Agathocles and his Apulian allies.   That Agathocles took serious account of the Romans is proved by the digression about them in Callias' history (frg. 5).   Duris' life of Agathocles may also have dealt with them.   Cf. D. xxi. 6.   The part taken by Tarentum about this time is doubtful.   Niese 483 thinks that she too was at war with Agathocles, but there is no evidence.

Soon after these events the wedding of Pyrrhus and
Lanassa was actually held; and Corcyra was handed over
as Lanassa's dowry[1]. Thus Agathocles hoped to have
placed his dependency in safe keeping.

But the union was brief and unhappy[2]. Lanassa indeed
bore Pyrrhus a son named Alexander, but presently she
grew sick of her husband, who, like other Hellenistic
princes, was ready to marry any number of wives, Greek
or foreign, for political reasons. The princess withdrew
to Corcyra, and sent a message to Demetrius with flattering
proposals, knowing, as Plutarch says, that of all rulers he
had most taste for such adventures. Demetrius at that
time was fairly set upon the throne of Macedonia, and
the chance of winning a bride and the precious island at
the same time was most alluring. It will be seen that
Pyrrhus in allowing Lanassa to retire to her own dower-
land virtually accepted the severance of their wedlock,
for in Greek law a man could be rid of his wife if he
repaid her marriage-portion. Demetrius sailed to Corcyra
with an army, wedded Lanassa, and after leaving a guard
in the chief city once more departed.

5. AGATHOCLES' LAST ITALIAN WAR.

After his success at Croton Agathocles may have spent
some time in raising forces to carry out an undertaking on
a greater scale. He seems to have planned nothing less
than the conquest of Bruttium. This is proved firstly

[1] Plut. *Pyrrh.* 9 (his wives)...καὶ Λάνασσαν τὴν Ἀγαθοκλέους τοῦ Συρα-
κοσίου προῖκα προσφερομένην αὐτῷ τὴν Κερκυραίων πόλιν ἡλωκυῖαν ὑπὸ
Ἀγαθοκλέους.

[2] *ibid.* 10 ἡ γὰρ Λάνασσα μεμψαμένη τὸν Πύρρον, ὡς μᾶλλον προσέχοντα
ταῖς βαρβάραις γυναιξὶν εἰς Κέρκυραν ἀπεχώρησε; and 9 Γυναῖκας δὲ πραγμά-
των ἕνεκα καὶ δυνάμεως πλείονας ἔγημε.

The date of these events is uncertain, perhaps a year or two before
Agathocles' death.

by the large muster of troops, and again by the long
digression of Trogus on the nature and ways of the
Bruttians, of which a bald summary has come down in
Justin[1]. Such an account must have been meant to lead
up to the story of a great campaign, and no mere plundering inroad. The occasion of the outbreak was an appeal
from Tarentum to Agathocles[2]. It was to no unselfish
mission that he was called; so valuable a base as Tarentum
would be a great help in the war; and if the Tarentines
had little ground for trusting Agathocles, the prospect of
his treason or harshness was less dreadful than the fear of
utter destruction at the hands of the Bruttians.

Agathocles raised 30,000 foot, 3000 horse, and a strong
fleet[3]. This ready-making frightened the Bruttians, who
sent envoys to him with an offer of friendship. The king
dined the envoys, at Messena apparently, and promised
to give them his answer on the morrow. But while the
banquet went on, the army was quickly ferried over the
strait, and before the next day dawned, Agathocles himself had slipped away on shipboard.

The Syracusan fleet was put under Stilpo, and perhaps
with the help of the Apulian allies, began to raid the
Bruttian shore. But before much had been done, a storm
sprang up in which Stilpo lost most of his ships[4].

---

[1] Trog. *Epit.* xxiii.; J. xxiii. 1, 6—9.

[2] J. *ibid.* 17 *ad postremum imploratus Agathocles spe ampliandi regni a
Sicilia in Italiam trajecit.*

Justin only speaks of *Graecae civitates* as calling in Agathocles, *as
they had called in Alexander of " Epirus."* This proves that Tarentum is
really meant here. Cf. Strabo vi. 3, 4 (p. 280). There Agathocles is mentioned after Cleonymus as a deliverer of Tarentum. There is certainly no
occasion other than this last war, undertaken at the call of Tarentum, to
which the passage of Strabo and D. xxi. 8 could refer. The Peucetian
alliance was no bar to friendship with Tarentum: the real enemies of all
three were Rome in the north, and the Bruttians nearer home.

[3] D. xxi. 8.   [4] D. *ibid.*

Agathocles himself marched against Hipponium, from which movement it seems likely that he was using Tarentum as his base. The walls were breached by his siege engines, resistless as usual, and the city fell. The Bruttians were alarmed at this loss, and sent to Agathocles begging for peace. The king might not have been willing to grant their prayer, had he not been already sickening for his last illness[1]. As it was Agathocles took 600 hostages and left them with a guard in Hipponium. Then he sailed home to Syracuse. But soon the Bruttians forgot their fright, and mustering in full force, fell upon the Sicilian army, which was cut to pieces. The hostages were set free, and Bruttium shook off the yoke of Agathocles[2]. It is likely, however, that Hipponium itself was not lost to his sway; for Strabo speaks of a dockyard there, built by order of Agathocles, and this work must have needed some months to carry out[3]. Clearly the king dreaded the fickleness of his Tarentine friends and wished to have a harbour of his own on the Italian coast. Another reason was that Bruttium, the land of forests, was the best possible place for ship-building. Croton no doubt also remained in his hands, so that the toil of the war had not been thrown away[4].

6. AGATHOCLES' LAST ACTS AND HIS DEATH. 290—289.

The union of Lanassa and Demetrius, whatever Agathocles may have thought of it, was a deed done, about which it was useless to grumble. Agathocles therefore

---

[1] J. xxiii. 2, 3.   [2] D. *ibid.*

[3] Strabo vi. 1, 5 (p. 256) Ἱππώνιον...ἔχει δὲ ἐπίνειον, ὃ κατεσκεύασέ ποτε Ἀγαθοκλῆς ὁ τύραννος τῶν Σικελιωτῶν κρατήσας τῆς πόλεως.

[4] Beloch 213 says that Agathocles kept not only Hipponium, but all the land south of it. For this I can find no evidence.

resolved to seek the friendship of Demetrius. He sent his
son, who bore his own name, to the Macedonian court
with offers of a regular alliance. The days were passed
when Demetrius, or his flatterers, had mocked Agathocles
as the lord of one poor island[1]. He caught eagerly at
the Syracusan king's offer, which seemed to open a grand
prospect of western extension. He welcomed the young
Agathocles with every mark of honour, put a kingly robe
on him, and loaded him with gifts. When it was time
for Agathocles to fare homewards, Demetrius sent his
own adviser and friend Oxythemis with him, to take
from king Agathocles his formal consent to the league,
although, says Diodorus, what Demetrius really wished
was to spy out the state of Sicily[2]. Agathocles had a
further end in view, when he sent his son to Demetrius.
He wished to mark out Agathocles as his heir, and in
this solemn recognition and investiture by Demetrius the
rights of the younger Agathocles were clearly established.
It has even been thought that the old king appealed to
Demetrius to make safe the succession for his son, and
that Oxythemis came for this very purpose. But the
avowed motive of Demetrius in sending Oxythemis to
secure confirmation of the alliance was probably his real
or at least his chief reason.

It has already been said that Agathocles had two
young children by his Egyptian wife, of whom one at

[1] Plut. Πολιτικὰ Παραγγέλματα xxxi. (823 D) (cf. *Demetr.* 25) οἱ μὲν γὰρ
Δημητρίου κόλακες οὐκ ἠξίουν βασιλεῖς τοὺς ἄλλους προσαγορεύειν, ἀλλὰ τὸν
μὲν Σέλευκον ἐλεφαντάρχην, τὸν δὲ Λυσίμαχον γαζοφύλακα, τὸν δὲ Πτολε-
μαῖον ναύαρχον ἐκάλουν, τὸν δὲ Ἀγαθοκλέα νησιάρχην. Cf. Sejanus'
comparison of himself with Tiberius, Dio C. LVIII. 5.

[2] D. xxi. 15. Droysen seems to have thought that Oxythemis was
sent to plot the overthrow of Agathocles; this, as Schubert 202—3 points
out, is quite unlikely. For Oxythemis cf. *I. G.* [= *C. I. A.*] II. 243; Hicks,
Man. of Gr. Hist. Inscr. no. 143.

least must have been a son[1]. He now sent both Theoxena and her children home to Ptolemy. The reason for this course is thus explained by Justin. Agathocles' grandson Archagathus was a man of violent temper; and the old king feared that he would slay Theoxena and her children to win the kingdom for himself[2]. Others have thought that Agathocles, wishing his own son of that name to be the next ruler, got rid of the young children to clear the way for the succession; or else that in befriending Demetrius Agathocles was defying Ptolemy, and followed this up by sending away his Egyptian wife so as to leave Ptolemy no opening for interference in Sicily[3]. But, as Justin notes that Theoxena was sent away with her royal array, retinue, and treasure—or in other words, with every mark of honour—the last view is not very likely. So remote a power as Sicily might have kept on good terms both with Demetrius and with Ptolemy.

The parting scene was mournful; for Theoxena was losing her queenly state, and seemed to be leaving Agathocles at the mercy of his quarrelsome heirs. But the account in Justin of Theoxena's tears and protestations is such a mixture of false sentiment and tasteless rhetoric, as must surely have been made up by one of the Roman historians[4].

[1] Justin speaks of *parvulos*: masculine. Below § 12 they are called *filios*, so doubtless both were sons.

[2] J. XXIII. 2. Justin puts the departure of Theoxena *after* the death of Agathocles the younger. But this is unlikely, for Agathocles, when he had disinherited Archagathus, might rather have wished for the *parvuli* back again to supply him with an heir. Justin's order is influenced by his desire to lead up to a rhetorical climax.

[3] So Droysen 287 and Dr Evans have thought; but as Niese 485 points out, this does not really follow.

[4] J. XXIII. 2, 7—9. Such descriptions were a favourite topic among

About this time Agathocles planned a fresh war against Carthage, and as his weakness in his earlier years had been lack of a proper fleet, he now resolved to make a bid for sea-power, to sweep the Punic corn-ships off the water, and to land another army in Africa. It is also possible that Carthage too was making ready for another war, and that the armament which invaded Sicily not long after Agathocles' death, was already mustering. Agathocles had a fleet of two hundred ships nearly equipped, some triremes, some even of huger build. But when the forces were ready, a fresh attack of sickness put a stop to the king's undertaking[1].

The last days of Agathocles' life were embittered by a feud between his son Agathocles and his grandson Archagathus. The father of the younger man was that Archagathus who fell in Africa, and the son though still very young was remarkable for bravery and fierceness[2]. Most of the military command seems to have been in his hands, and he was at that time in charge of an army at Aetna, which had perhaps been raised for the African war.

The king sent for his own son, and proclaimed him at Syracuse as his heir. Then he sent him with a letter to

the Romans; compare the parting of Ovid from his wife: *Tristia* I. 3, 17:

> Uxor amans flentem flens acrius ipsa tenebat,
>   imbre per indignas usque cadente genas.

and 79:

> Tum vero conjux humeris abeuntis inhaerens
>   miscuit haec lacrimis tristia dicta meis.
> Non potes avelli: simul hinc simul ibimus ambo;
>   te sequar, et conjux exulis exul ero.

Even these pompous lines have more sincerity about them than the passage of Justin.

[1] D. xxi. 16, and 18. Agathocles must have had this war in his mind for some time.

[2] D. xxi. 16, 7.

Archagathus, who was to hand over the command of the army to his uncle. Seeing himself thus slighted Archagathus was driven into a murderous plot. He happened to be going to offer a sacrifice on an island off the coast near Aetna; before starting, he sent a ship with an invitation to his uncle to come to the sacred feast with him. Agathocles came, and they sat down to the banquet together. Late in the evening, when Agathocles was drunk, Archagathus rose up and slew him. His body was cast into the sea; but those that found it knew it again, and sent it to Syracuse.

At the same time it is said that Archagathus plotted the death of his own grandfather. Diodorus relates that the king had a courtier, one Meno, who had survived the fall of his home, Segesta, and for his good looks had been taken into the king's service as a page. But the wrongs of Segesta rankled in his heart, and he awaited the day for wreaking them on his master. To him Archagathus now sent word to carry off Agathocles by poison. It is said that the king used to clean his teeth after supper with a feather, and Meno dipped this in a biting poison, so that when Agathocles put the feather into his mouth it smarted; but instead of getting rid of the venom, he plied the feather all the more vigorously. From this his gums broke out into abscesses, and he suffered horribly with ever-growing pain[1].

This story is for two reasons improbable: it is evident from Justin that Agathocles was seriously ill when he came home from Bruttium, and the symptoms mentioned suggest a case of cancer. There was thus little to be

[1] D. *ibid.* For a medical account of Agathocles' illness *v.* Schubert 205. He entirely rejects the story of the poisoning: which Droysen and others accepted. Agathocles might have had cancer and been poisoned as well; though in that case his end would have been rather more sudden.

gained by hurrying on a death which could not have been delayed more than a few weeks. It seems most likely that, as the illness was somewhat rare, Meno was popularly accused of murder, and his later crime in killing Archagathus lent colour to the charge.

When Agathocles saw his dead son and heard how his end had been brought about, he called a last assembly of the people. There he denounced the outrageous deed of Archagathus, calling upon the people to punish the murderer. With his last public utterance Agathocles named no heir to his power, but proclaimed the renewal of the democracy[1].

After this the old king sank fast, and soon lay speechless and unable to move. At the last Oxythemis had his body laid on a pyre, and some said that Agathocles still breathed when the fire consumed him. This was believed to be the judgment of Hephaestus for the godless act of Agathocles on the Lipari Islands[2].

Agathocles died seventy-two years old[3]. Soon after his death the Syracusan people escheated his property and tore down all his statues. Meno, the reputed murderer, fled from Syracuse and took shelter in the camp with Archagathus. But the presence of his fellow-plotter made Meno feel unsafe, and in no long time he murdered the young prince and took command of the army himself.

---

[1] D. *ib.* § 4. The constitutional point is discussed by Freeman IV. 485, who seems to forget that Agathocles was βασιλεύς and not merely στρατηγός.

[2] Cf. p. 204. There is no reason whatever for believing the pious fable.

[3] D. XXI. 16, 5 where Timaeus, Callias, and Antander are all given as authorities. The statement of [Lucian] *Macrob.* 10 must therefore be a mistake. Ἀγαθοκλῆς δὲ ὁ Σικελίας τύραννος ἐτῶν ἐννενήκοντα πέντε τελευτᾷ, καθάπερ Δημοχάρης καὶ Τίμαιος ἱστοροῦσιν.

Thus the whole house of Agathocles was involved in ruin[1].

7. AGATHOCLES' CHARACTER AND MONUMENTS.

Agathocles was above everything else a man of action and a soldier[2]. Through all his restless life he was never at peace for more than a few years together. Yet none of his wars can be called purposeless or merely adventurous; there was a well-laid plan underlying his wildest undertakings, and through all his acts his ambition centred in himself. There is something splendid in Agathocles' resolute advance to the highest place, his dauntless valour, his championship of a discredited party, his stern destruction of all that stood in his way. But whether for

[1] D. xxi. 16, 6. Diodorus clearly implies that the confiscation (p. 225) was one of the first acts of the restored democracy. But Schubert *ad fin.* believes that it did not really happen until after the return of Meno and the oligarchs. It is however quite possible that the people had begun to hate Agathocles without feeling any more friendly towards Meno and his side. On the whole it is safer to follow Diodorus, but in dealing with fragments it is not easy to be quite certain. The confiscation did not go very far, for Pyrrhus found enough of Agathocles' creatures enjoying their wealth to make it worth his while to rob them. Dionys. Hal. xx. 8. Πύρρος...τάς τε γὰρ οὐσίας τῶν Ἀγαθοκλέους οἰκείων ἢ φίλων ἀφαιρούμενος τοὺς παρ᾽ ἐκείνου λαβόντας τοῖς ἑαυτοῦ φίλοις ἐχαρίσατο.

[2] It need hardly be said that the most various views have been taken of Agathocles' character. The opposite views of Callias and Timaeus have already been contrasted; beyond these, few general estimates of Agathocles occur in antiquity. The opinion of the emperor Julian (*Conviv. Caes.* 332 c *fin.*) may be mentioned; he speaks of Agathocles as a worse tyrant than Dionysius. Among modern writers the same disagreement prevails. Thus Plass 271 calls him, "One of the worst military despots or rather a great robber chief." This view is also given by a reviewer of Schubert's book in the *Litterarisches Centralblatt* (1888) xxv. 845.

On the other hand De Sanctis and especially Beloch 215—217 wish to regard Agathocles as a noble and heroic character, generous to his foes, and harsh only in the pursuit of high ideals.

Between these extreme views all shades of opinion are held.

this shocking record of bloodshed he had the supreme excuse of having ruled Sicily for her own good, is unhappily a matter on which there is little evidence. Polybius' testimony that Agathocles, when his rule was safe, became the mildest of all tyrants, will not help us here. For any monster might become humane when there were no enemies left to punish. Not that Agathocles ever forgave the Syracusan nobles; for it needed another Carthaginian invasion to secure their homecoming after his death. Even his good treatment of Deinocrates was noticed as something unwonted; and there, as has been seen, the tyrant's motives were by no means disinterested.

That Sicily fell into confusion when Agathocles was no more, is a proof that no one else was strong enough to keep order. But it is also a sign that his rule, resting purely on force, or at most on the unnatural alliance between tyranny and democracy, had no sure foundations. It is also clear that the treacherous grandson who upset all the king's plans, had copied too well the nature of Agathocles himself. There have been few men as great as Agathocles whose work has fallen so utterly to the ground in so short a time. Gelo and Dionysius not only founded but handed on their power. Agathocles declared that his kingship must die with him; and the first act of the new republic was to throw down all memorials of their popular tyrant. It may be true that in such hard times no fixed government could maintain itself in Sicily: but it is also true that such a course of slaughter and injustice as Agathocles had, could never secure a stable throne nor endear the ruling house to the hearts of the subjects. It was the tragedy of Agathocles' life that he saw on his death-bed the downfall of his own work, and that the recipients of his highest favours had become his worst enemies. There was an element of divine justice in such a fate.

As a general Agathocles was at his greatest. In battle by land or sea he was skilful in his dispositions, quick in action, and dauntless in bravery[1]. It has been seen that in the fight on the Himeras he was misled by over-confidence. In his later engagements, as far as can be judged from scanty accounts, he seems to have adopted the most scientific tactics of his age. In the rout of Bomilcar and Hanno Agathocles clearly followed the Macedonian plan by falling upon the Sacred Band with his own division, and letting the weaker parts of the line stay out of action. Only the cavalry charges of Alexander are wanting in this case. In sieges Agathocles seems to have been almost irresistible: a very great number of strong places such as Utica, Croton and Hipponium were breached by his artillery. Here again we see the work of a worthy contemporary of Alexander the overthrower of Tyre, and Demetrius the besieger. When Agathocles met Cassander in battle, his signal victory proved that he was indeed a match for the best tacticians of the Greek east. His success was all the more praiseworthy for being won with unruly hired troops and unwilling levies of Syracusans.

In public life Agathocles was a vigorous speaker, quick to rouse the feelings of the army or assembly. His manner seems to have been direct and fiery, sometimes theatrical. As ruler of Syracuse his bearing was jovial and popular; as has already been seen he put on no kingly airs, was easy of access, and did not scorn to amuse the mob by a jest.

[1] D. xxi. 17. Cf. Scipio's famous saying, Polyb. xv. 35, 6. Scipio was asked what men in his opinion showed the greatest power of action and the highest courage combined with judgment; he answered, the Siceliots, the followers of Agathocles and Dionysius.

Apart from his great stroke of diplomacy, the peace with Carthage in 306, Agathocles gave little sign of any high order of statesmanship. He failed to manage Ophellas, and had to kill him instead; his defiance of Rome led to nothing; and in his eastern relations he seems to have been ready to join hands with any prince who would treat him regally. The sending away of Theoxena and her children amounted to a confession of failure to regulate matters in Sicily; and the embroilment of Agathocles' heirs makes the same thing only too clear. In short Agathocles was a great general, but as a king he was only moderately successful: with far greater military gifts than Dionysius he effected very much less.

Of Agathocles' private life little is known. Neither the slander of Timaeus recorded in Suidas and Justin, nor yet such a sentimental affair as the farewell of Theoxena can be taken at all seriously. It can only be said that we often hear of Agathocles at his wine, and he seems to have been a merry boon-companion. If any truth underlies the stories of his early trade as a potter, it may be this, that he scorned all show of luxury and refinement, and, as Plutarch suggests, liked best to drink from earthenware.

For art and letters Agathocles seems to have cared nothing. The greatest Sicilian writers of the age, such as Timaeus, Dicaearchus, and Euhemerus, lived and thought away from their troubled home in the milder air of Greece itself[1]. Callias alone and Antander worked under the eye of Agathocles, that men might know of his deeds in after years. In this neglect of men of letters Agathocles made a break in the tradition of Sicilian princes, which had been so splendidly established by

[1] On these writers cf. Holm ii. 267—276.

Hiero, carried on by Dionysius, the Elder and the Younger, and which was afterwards revived by Hiero II. One comic poet, called Hermippus or Boeotus, was allowed to write his poor verses to amuse the Syracusans; until he too was banished by Agathocles[1].

As a builder Agathocles was more noteworthy. Besides restoring the walls and outworks of Syracuse, where this was needed, he set up a huge building on Ortygia, which is thus described: "There was in Syracuse the so-called House of the Hundred Beds on the Island: this surpassed in size and workmanship all other buildings in Sicily. Agathocles the tyrant set it up. Owing to the size of the erection, it overtopped the temples of the gods, and received a mark of the divine displeasure in being struck by lightning. There were also the towers by the Little Harbour with inscriptions in mosaic, giving the name of the builder who was Agathocles[2]."

The towers were naturally meant for the defence of the harbour, and the other building must have been Agathocles' own dwelling. Of these works nothing now remains, for the ruin called the House of Agathocles has not the slightest claim to the title. It is also possible that Dionysius' castle at the entrance to Ortygia was rebuilt by Agathocles[3].

But the king was a destroyer as well as a builder. It is said that he wrecked the monument of Gelo. This stood without the city, and was girt with nine towers.

[1] This poet is mentioned in an epigram of Alexander of Aetolia quoted by Athenaeus xv. 699 c :

Ὡς Ἀγαθοκλῆος λάσιαι φρένες ἤλασαν ἔξω πατρίδος· κ.τ.λ.

[2] D. xvi. 83, 2. The story of the house being struck is suspicious because there was an older legend of another Agathocles, whose house suffered in the same way for the same reason. D. viii. 9; cf. Lupus, *Die Stadt Syrakus im Altertum* 92, 204, 208.

[3] Lupus *ibid.*

The grave itself had been overthrown by the Carthaginians; and Diodorus states that Agathocles through envy of Gelo had all the towers pulled down[1].

One other monument of Agathocles is mentioned. This was a picture set up in the temple of Athena in Ortygia, where it stayed until the time of Verres. Cicero speaks of it thus[2]: "There was a cavalry fight of king Agathocles painted on panels; with these panels the walls of the temple were covered. There was nothing more famous than this picture, and no sight at Syracuse reckoned worthier to be viewed." This painting had survived the sack of Syracuse under Marcellus, but it was carried off by the godless greed of Verres. This picture must have been painted on wooden panels, and most likely it was done in the lifetime of Agathocles and spared by his enemies as a work of art.

CONCLUSION.

In spite of the outward splendour and military glory of Agathocles' reign, the whole period was really a time of decadence for Greek Sicily. The prince ruled by the help of his hired soldiers and by pandering to the tastes of the mob. He was ready to fight on any side, for his countrymen or against them, as his own interests demanded. Thus his success brought temporary peace and wealth to the island, but for this the Greeks paid dearly with the decline of their national spirit. How low they had sunk is shown by their utter confusion and helplessness after Agathocles' death. Evidently they had lost all power of acting together or even of thinking for themselves. Agathocles' Italian troops, that only his strong

[1] D. xi. 38. [2] Cic. *Verr.* iv. c. 55.

hand could keep in order, soon became the scourge and terror of the Greek cities; and brought Sicily to a pitiable state of unlaw. The prey of petty tyrants, the Greeks next called in Pyrrhus, but were too weak to help or hinder him. Henceforward they became a prize to be fought for, and suffered terribly at the hands of Rome for the equally hated cause of Carthage. The ruin of Gela and Messena wrought by the Italian soldiers of Agathocles, and thus the direct outcome of his policy, led on to the more awful fate of Acragas, the most hapless sufferer in the first Punic war. Syracuse herself was saved for a while by the cautious policy of Hiero, the last ruler of free Sicilians. But her fate was not long delayed, and with her fall, the Greece of the west was finally lost in the Roman empire.

INDEX

For EU product safety concerns, contact us at Calle de José Abascal, 56–1°,
28003 Madrid, Spain or eugpsr@cambridge.org.

www.ingramcontent.com/pod-product-compliance
Ingram Content Group UK Ltd.
Pitfield, Milton Keynes, MK11 3LW, UK
UKHW012328130625
459647UK00009B/142